The Social Imagination of the Romantic Wife in Literature

The emergence of social change in the daily lives of English society appeared most noticeably through the Romantic-era response of human emotions to a period of reason that has defined the era of Enlightenment, scientifically and philosophically. Remarkably, the dramatic political shift that occurred in 1789 from a French monarchy to a constitutional democracy foreshadowed social changes to the family unit that were more slowly evolving throughout England during the eighteenth century. An intellectual movement to educate all members of society strengthened efforts to loosen ecclesiastical control, allowing more secular definitions of social roles to emerge. The nature of marriage during this period in England is central to understanding how the marriage covenant became a widely accepted civil contract. Examining the sentiments of passion and virtue, the dynamics of traditional marriage emerge through newly established perspectives. The role of the wife as a Romantic-era concept tells the story of two women through their married lives and literary identities. The social imagination provides a new perspective on domestic concerns to illuminate a feminine aspect of the literary market through an understanding of the ordinary wife among female writers. Moreover, a specific focus on marriage, virtue, and friendship as seen through two relationships examines individuals who define both a traditional and a non-conforming approach to their domestic lives. Two husbands who were political and religious activists with wives who were atypical domestics were chosen to exemplify the effects of social change on their particular lives and marital roles in an expanding literary world.

Linda L. Reesman is a professor of English at Queensborough Community College, City University of New York. She also teaches as an adjunct associate professor at Hofstra University. Her articles appear in the Coleridge Bulletin, most recently in 2018. Her reviews appear in the Eighteenth-Century Current Bibliography (ECCB) and other publications. Her current essay on Coleridge appears in the 2021 edition of *1650–1850: Ideas, Aesthetics, and Inquiries in the Early Modern Era*.

Routledge Studies in Romanticism

Robert Pollok's The Course of Time and Literary Theodicy in the Romantic Age
The Rise and Fall of a Christian Epic
Deryl Davis

Romantic Futures
Legacy, Prophecy, Temporality
Edited by Evy Varsamopoulou

Dante and Polish Writers
From Romanticism to the Present
Edited by Andrea Ceccherelli

William Blake's Divine Love
Visions of Oothoon
Joshua Schouten de Jel

Wordsworth's Trauma and Poetry
1793–1803
Richard E. Matlak

Reading Keats's Poetry
Alternative Subject Positions and Subject-Object Relations
Merve Günday

The Social Imagination of the Romantic Wife in Literature
Marriage, Virtue, and Friendship
Linda L. Reesman

For more information about this series, please visit:
https://www.routledge.com/Routledge-Studies-in-Romanticism/book-series/SE0699

The Social Imagination of the Romantic Wife in Literature
Marriage, Virtue, and Friendship

Linda L. Reesman

NEW YORK AND LONDON

First published 2025
by Routledge
605 Third Avenue, New York, NY 10158

and by Routledge
4 Park Square, Milton Park, Abingdon, Oxon, OX14 4RN

Routledge is an imprint of the Taylor & Francis Group, an informa business

© 2025 Linda L. Reesman

The right of Linda L. Reesman to be identified as author of this work has been asserted in accordance with sections 77 and 78 of the Copyright, Designs and Patents Act 1988.

All rights reserved. No part of this book may be reprinted or reproduced or utilised in any form or by any electronic, mechanical, or other means, now known or hereafter invented, including photocopying and recording, or in any information storage or retrieval system, without permission in writing from the publishers.

Trademark notice: Product or corporate names may be trademarks or registered trademarks, and are used only for identification and explanation without intent to infringe.

ISBN: 9781032817408 (hbk)
ISBN: 9781032823843 (pbk)
ISBN: 9781003504238 (ebk)

DOI: 10.4324/9781003504238

Typeset in Sabon
by Newgen Publishing UK

To my mom and my aunt, two sisters who shared their love of literature with our family, I dedicate this manuscript to
                      Lila Reich Breiter and Claire Reich Samkoff

Contents

List of Figures	*viii*
Acknowledgments	*ix*
Chart of Significant Events and Lives	*x*
Introduction	*xii*

1	Marriage, Passion, and Justice in English Society	1
2	Reason and Passion in the Education of Virtue	22
3	Portrait of an Intellectual Wife: Mary Wollstonecraft Godwin	41
4	Portrait of a Lake Poet's Wife: Sara Fricker Coleridge	66
5	Idyllic Marriage, Motherhood, and Literary Genius	86
6	Circle of Friends and Family	109
7	National and Domestic Identities	126
8	Marriage Law and the Rights of Woman: Sacred to Secular	143

Conclusion: "Love in Fairy-land"—*Sara Coleridge Coleridge and Mary Godwin Shelley*	*160*
Index	*178*

Figures

3.1 *Mary Wollstonecraft,* James Heath after John Opie, 1797   42
Courtesy of *Wikimedia Commons*, Public Domain
3.2 *William Godwin*, From *Illustrations of Phrenology*
by Sir George Steuart Mackenzie, 1820   61
Courtesy of *Wikimedia Commons*, Public Domain
4.1 *Sara Fricker Coleridge,* by Mary Matilda Bentham, 1809   68
Courtesy of *Wikimedia Commons*, Public Domain
4.2 *Samuel Taylor Coleridge,* Project Gutenberg   74
Courtesy of *Wikimedia Commons*, Public Domain

Acknowledgments

For the opportunity to research the social and historical resources about marriage in the eighteenth century, I am most grateful to Queensborough Community College at City University of New York, for two fellowships and several grants awarded throughout my academic career. With the assistance of librarians at the British Library in London, the Harry Ransom Center at the University of Texas in Austin, the E. J. Pratt Library of Victoria University in the University of Toronto, the Carl H. Pforzheimer Collection at the New York Public Library, the J. Pierpont Morgan Library in New York, and the Axinn Library at Hofstra University in New York, I am grateful for their resources and original materials including personal letters of the Coleridge and Godwin families that breathe life into their stories. The Friends of Coleridge has supported my scholarly work along with the South-Central Society for Eighteenth-Century Studies to afford me opportunities to present my scholarly research and to publish articles and reviews in their publications. I would like to mention just a few of the scholars with whom I exchanged ideas and was privileged to be among such as Tim Fulford, Nicholas Roe, Joanna Taylor, Felicity James, Timothy Whelan, Jeffrey Barbeau, Graham Davidson, Gloria Eive, John Scanlan, Iska S. Alter, and David Shimkin. With my most affectionate appreciation, I could not have accomplished this manuscript without the loving support of my children, Meredith Owens and Joshua Reesman, whose inspiration and moral encouragement led to the accomplishment of this manuscript.

Chart of Significant Events and Lives

Name	Birth	Death	Marriage	Event(s)
William Godwin	3 March 1756	7 April 1836	29 March 1797 m. MW, St. Pancras Church, London	Birth of daughter Mary 30 August 1797
Mary Wollstonecraft	27 April 1759	10 September 1797	29 March 1797 m. WG, St. Pancras Church, London	Birth of daughter Fanny Imlay in May 1794; Birth of daughter Mary 30 August 1797
Samuel Taylor Coleridge	21 October 1772	25 July 1834	4 October 1795 m. SF, St. Mary Redcliffe, Bristol	Births: Hartley 19 September 1796, Berkeley 1798 to February 1799, Derwent 14 September 1800, and Sara 23 December 1802
Sara Fricker Coleridge	10 September 1770 (born Sarah)	24 September 1845	4 October 1795 m. STC, St. Mary Redcliffe, Bristol	Births: Hartley 19 September 1796, Berkeley 1798 to February. 1799, Derwent 14 September 1800, and Sara 23 December 1802

Name	Birth	Death	Marriage	Event(s)
French Revolution				6 October 1789
Lord Hardwicke's Marriage Act (Clandestine)				England 1753
Civil Marriage Act				England 1836

Introduction

The emergence of social change in the daily lives of all class levels of English society appeared most noticeably through the Romantic response of human emotions to a period of reason that defined the era of Enlightenment, scientifically and philosophically. Remarkably, the dramatic political shift that occurred in 1789 from a French monarchy to a constitutional democracy foreshadowed social changes to the family unit that were more slowly evolving throughout England during the eighteenth century. An intellectual movement to educate all members of society strengthened efforts to loosen ecclesiastical control allowing more secular definitions of social roles to emerge among all members of society. This study attempts to trace these social changes during the height of the Romantic period from the 1790s to the early 1800s just prior to the next significant shift in social roles with the Victorian Era beginning in 1830. Moreover, this study specifically focuses on marriage, virtue, and friendship as seen through two marriage relationships, and an examination of the individuals who define both traditional and non-conforming approaches to their domestic lives. Husbands who were both political and religious activists exemplify the effects of social change in their own literary lives, and wives who were atypical domestics challenge their roles as ordinary wives in an expanding literary world.

The domestic and professional roles of women have become a contemporary focus of how women as the traditional "fair sex" have risen in our culture to the fore front of social relationships. Changes in religious beliefs and advancements in scientific theories have readily contributed to the evolution of these roles both in enlarging the professionalism of women and in the manner in which domesticity is realized in the social unit of the married couple and the family. Tradition and its defining features of socially constructed gender roles were naturally challenged by changing religious, political, and scientific beliefs about society and its values, both philosophically and psychologically. Many aspects of this study will demonstrate these social changes through the particular lives of two selected couples, chosen as illustrations of how traditional values were challenged through the advancement of social reform to marriage and the moral perceptions of virtue and justice.

William Godwin—political activist, philosopher, and literary writer—and Samuel Taylor Coleridge—poet, essayist, and preacher—epitomize two generations of contradictory religious beliefs yet share mutually compatible perspectives on social and political issues. As the revolutionary period gave rise to a transforming society in both England and France, the political ambitions of these two philosophical writers spurned domestic change as well. The confluence of political and literary thought can be readily illustrated in the poetic imagination of other writers such as Robert Southey, brother-in-law to Coleridge, whose writing sparked historical and literary thought for both Godwin and Coleridge. As Southey writes to Grosvenor Charles Bedford on 14 July 1793, "I cannot see so many children of both sexes wasting away their youth or abusing it in learning every vice without experiencing some sensations too Rousseauish to be practicable and I almost fear, too good to be general."[1] Southey acknowledges the importance of learning virtuous behavior in the midst of wartime, recognizing Enlightenment philosopher Jean-Jacques Rousseau's influence among men and women. Southey exalts the higher values of virtue above the brutishness of war as he composes his poem *Joan of Arc*. He explains to Bedford,

> The blank verse flows easily from the pen—as for machinery there was no ready made to assist me—so I een [even] people the airy vast with unembodied sprites and allot the Genius of Liberty to defend the French from Ambition—Hatred—Slaughter and England.[2]

The collaboration of writers during this period is further evidenced in the intellectual interest in advancing female education. Mary Wollstonecraft—political activist, essayist, and novelist—and Sara[3] Fricker Coleridge—literary wife, mother, and linguist—are contrasted in this study as their roles will illustrate how the Romantic imagination redefines the feminine tradition of women in eighteenth-century English society. To establish the premise of this study, my use of the terms "imagination," as applied to the literary period of Romanticism and social conditions, and "virtue," as an underlying philosophy of what comprises the moral excellence of human behavior, requires further definition. Beginning with Samuel Taylor Coleridge's explanations and refinement of the imagination into two categories of primary and secondary imagination, I understand the social imagination as inclusive of both secular interests and divine inspiration. Relying on his readings of several German philosophers, Coleridge writes,

The IMAGINATION then I consider either as primary, or secondary. The **primary** IMAGINATION I hold to be the living Power and prime Agent of all human Perception, and as a repetition in the finite mind of the eternal act of creation in the infinite I AM. The **secondary** I consider as an echo of the former, co-existing with the conscious will, yet still as identical with the primary in the *kind* of its agency, and differing only in *degree*, and in the *mode* of its operation. It dissolves, diffuses, dissipates, in order to re-create; or where this process is rendered impossible, yet still at all events it struggles to idealize and to unify. It is essentially *vital*, even as all objects (as objects) are essentially fixed and dead.[4]

The rhetorical liberty expressed by Coleridge expands this all-encompassing definition of the imagination into a social realm. It allows for the freedom to express secular interests inspired by divine influence, affording the reader of this study a better understanding of the domestic shift in values. How these domestic values reposition women as writers and as wives within this Romantic context is the focus of this study on the social imagination of the wife.

Additionally, locating the historical origins for the term "virtue" builds a foundation for the social imagination that creates a consistency and credibility to the literary interpretations of the lives and thinking of the women and men highlighted in these pages. From early antiquity the virtues of human behavior have primarily defined and shaped the ethics of human experience and also established the moral excellence of human action. Beginning with the earliest work of Plato's *The Republic*, circa 357 BCE, the four cardinal virtues of prudence, fortitude, temperance, and justice have served as fundamental values to achieve happiness and well-being. As Benjamin Jowett acknowledges in his translation of *The Republic*, "In English philosophy too, many affinities may be traced, not only in the works of the Cambridge Platonists, but in great original writers like Berkeley or Coleridge, to Plato and his ideas."[5]

Along with Coleridge's philosophical and religious interests in the psychological nature of these cardinal virtues as moral qualities,[6] William Godwin and Mary Wollstonecraft contributed to the significance of these virtues as necessary to the human experience as evidenced in their writings, Godwin relying on reason and Wollstonecraft advocating for natural origins. According to biographer Ford K. Brown, Godwin's treatise on *Political Justice*, first published in 1793 with a second edition in 1796, was his attempt "to define the status of man in society." As Brown notes, "he had come to regard politics as the 'most important vehicle of a liberal morality'." Godwin himself explains how his treatise relies on the cardinal virtues when he describes *Political Justice* as "an advantageous vehicle of moral improvement," which he further asserts, states Brown, "and a work 'from the perusal of which no man should rise, without being strengthened in habits of sincerity, fortitude and justice'."[7]

Wollstonecraft, on the other hand, in her treatise *A Vindication of the Rights of Woman*, published in 1792, asserts,

> But I still insist, that not only the virtue, but the *knowledge* of the two sexes should be the same in nature, if not in degree, and that women, considered not only as moral, but rational creatures, ought to endeavour to acquire human virtues (or perfections) by the *same* means as men.[8]

Both writers are clearly attentive to educating the social classes on the moral necessity of the cardinal virtues. Their distinctive viewpoints on these principles, however, provide the purpose of this study which is to elevate the relationships of these individuals who together were determined to improve the social and political status of the English society. Through exchanges in their writings coupled with their interconnected personal lives, this study examines the philosophical and social ramifications between and among four individuals from the Romantic period, William Godwin and his wife Mary Wollstonecraft, Samuel Taylor Coleridge and his wife Sara Fricker Coleridge.

Furthermore, the period during which the Romantic wife emerges is an era fraught with political strife and one dismantled by changing social convention. As representative of a newly forged independence, the Romantic wife redefines the role of women for whom virtue and social propriety previously meant the dependency of women on men instead of the emancipation of women's rights. With shifting values of political conservatism and unorthodox social fashions, the power of the rising bourgeois class threatened traditional religious beliefs as society, particularly women, became educated readers and thinkers. Through the literature of the Romantic poets and writers, a new poetic vision invoked a creative spirit giving authority to the imagination while subordinating reason. A developing sense of the eighteenth century social imagination, as I am using the term, unites the poetic and private imagination with a public and social discourse about wives.

While many other significant changes occurred during this period politically, socially, and economically, the transformation of women marked a historical moment in the progress of the female gender. The emergence of the wife as an intellectual partner and social equal altered the fabric of eighteenth-century society and re-envisioned a new foundation for marriage and family. Within pre- and post-revolutionary times from 1780 to 1830 in England and France, the propriety of women was questioned, challenged, and resisted within British society. This book does not attempt to retell an array of historical details which have been told more adeptly by political historians nor to try and simplify the complexities of this age into a broad spectrum of social change; however, the focus within these pages is to confine the reader to an examination of the lives and literary influences of two women who have been maligned and persecuted by the constraints of these times and who stand as emblems of the feminine transformation of Romantic values of the wife within this cultural setting.

As the emergence of the wife as independent in the marriage began to distinguish the eighteenth-century woman as a free thinker, women found their roles as wives and mothers in conflict with a developing personal self. Gary Kelly remarks that this "culture of subjectivity" disrupted the ordinary lives of married women in their traditional roles. In *Bluestocking Feminism: Writings of the Bluestocking Circle, 1738–1785*, he explains, "Domesticity would include the idea that the quotidian, local, and particular were 'real' life, in contrast to the courtly and cosmopolitan, represented as artificial, fantastic, a mystification of 'reality', a figment of ideology as false consciousness."[9] The real life of married women in the domestic sphere was challenged by the "mystification of reality" often seen as the dangers of educating wives as individuals in literary, political, historical, and economic matters. The model wife and good mother were more apt to be identified by the sewing needle than the written word.

> Middle-class ideology articulated women's domestic roles as vital, not only to the strength of the family as it was constructed by the increasingly powerful middle-class and Evangelical culture, but to the moral, economic, and political strength of a nation that anxiously posited itself as morally superior to dissolute, anarchical, godless France,[10]

as Carol Shiner Wilson explains.

Moreover, the conflict for married women to engage in creative and intellectual activities can be better understood as the ideology of virtue is examined in the particular lives of women like Mary Wollstonecraft and Sara Coleridge who struggled to manage their love for their husbands and families with a yearning for creative self-expression. As Sylvia Myers suggests, Englishwomen experienced discomfort in the mid-eighteenth century "about being known as learned ladies" in her article "Learning, Virtue, and the Term 'Bluestocking'." Along with breaking the cultural convention of domestic activities as more virtuous than learning came the breaking of a longstanding taboo which Myers explains was "against learning for women which had been imposed intermittently since classical times."[11]

Other writers such as Susan M. Yadlon, Nancy Armstrong, and Mary Poovey have established their claim that the feminine ideal of this period exemplified a woman who embodied qualities of "modesty, chastity, passivity and frugalness" on a normative definition of femininity that implies the passivity of virtue as an intrinsic female characteristic.[12] In effect, this approach would bind a woman's potential for individual accomplishment and justify an ongoing conflict between virtue and intellect in women. Rather than accepting the passivity of this normative role, eighteenth-century wives such as Mary Wollstonecraft and Sara Coleridge exemplify active reasoning, passionate creativity, and liberating virtue in their roles of authorship, both as private and public writers, as well as in their social and domestic spheres, thereby challenging the traditional role and limited view of domestic passivity.

While women writers have been the foreground in recent scholarship, an analysis of their roles as literary agents has ignored their roles as wives even though their maternal roles have been thoughtfully examined as in Susan C. Greenfield's and Carol Barash's 2015 book *Inventing Maternity: Politics, Science, and Literature, 1650–1865* and in Julie Kipp's 2003 book *Romanticism, Maternity, and the Body Politic*. Whether this is due to the elusiveness of the role of the wife or because the wife has traditionally been a secondary figure to the role of the husband as a public image, this study undertakes the importance of advancing the "ordinary wife" and reframing her position to lead with the authority of her role rather than submit to the passive view of domestic life. To accomplish this task requires a view more intimately linked to the two wives central to this study through their personal letters written to lovers, husbands, children, and friends. Treating the intimacies of these letters with an acknowledgment of their literary as well as personal value suggests that both women deserve credible recognition intellectually and socially.

During this age of sensibility, individual feelings became elevated to a status that outweighed reason on many social and political issues as the writings of Jean-Jacques Rousseau popularized the overt expression of the emotions. Heavily influenced by Rousseau's exposition on the education of boys and girls in his book *Emile*, Mary Wollstonecraft began to explore her own unique ideas on the education of women which were to change the way women perceived themselves in relationship to men's perceptions of them. Like Sara Fricker, Wollstonecraft struggled against the restraints of her sex, the limitations of wife and mother, by an unpopular dismissal of public opinion. Yet, from what was often the depths of despair for loved ones grew Wollstonecraft's emanations for her vision of the independent woman, a vision that materialized for her as the wife of political activist William Godwin and as mother of Gothic novelist Mary Shelley. Wollstonecraft's life as a writer, but even more meaningfully here in this study, as a wife, both literally and figuratively, reveals itself through her novels, essays, and letters.

Contrasting the literary career of Wollstonecraft with the domestic yet intellectual expression of an ordinary woman, the life of Sara Fricker Coleridge as the wife of a poetic genius illustrates a confluence of the ordinary and extraordinary virtues of the eighteenth-century woman. Sara demonstrated a determination and courage that withstood public criticism of her intellectual abilities as inferior and helped her to surpass her role as the victimized wife. She kept a consistent communication with Thomas Poole, friend and neighbor of the Coleridges from Nether Stowey, as evidenced in a volume of her letters aptly titled *Minnow among Tritons*. From these letters written between 1799 and 1834, a portrait emerges that withstands the scrutiny of female weakness and elevates her important contributions to the social imagination of the Romantic wife. In addition, Sara maintained a regular correspondence with her husband even through years of separation, a correspondence that Robert Southey desired but was not able to achieve with his wife, Edith Fricker, Sara's sister. She offered caring and nurturing support for her children's physical well-being while she also never missed an opportunity to nurture their literary interests and education. To say that she expressed the sacrifices of a loving mother would be an accurate depiction but her sacrifices went beyond the ordinary role of a mother and wife. Through her devoted love for her children—Hartley, Berkeley (who did not survive infancy), Derwent, and Sara—she became a stronger parent who sacrificed her own individual development and public recognition to become the wife of an enigmatic and poetic genius. Sara created an inventive language, her *lingo grande*, to communicate with her brother-in-law, Robert Southey, her children, and anyone else in her immediate household in this "jabberwocky" style of affectionate names and epithets that would mystify even Alice in Wonderland. As Molly Lefebure notes,

> Sara had deep-seated needs for inventing a private language—needs never analysed but only felt: release from the tensions of constant suppressed anxiety; the necessity to have something of her very own that could not be taken from her as everything else was taken; the need for privacy in a world which gossiped freely about her as the deserted wife of Samuel Taylor Coleridge.[13]

The range of her emotional expression was more deeply illustrated in the sonnets she wrote during Berkeley's illness. These varying facets of Sara's self-expression and rhetorical style will be exposed in the following chapters as her life reveals its literary potential and commitment to poetic language.

The lives of Mary Wollstonecraft and Sara Coleridge may appear as separate and diametrically opposed as any young women during the late eighteenth century—Wollstonecraft—a radical young woman determined to reform women's self-conception of the dependent wife, and Coleridge—an abandoned young wife of a literary genius committed to raise and support her family. While Wollstonecraft made her way in the world through her literary ability and revolutionary fervor in the 1790s, Coleridge embarked upon stormy marital seas and found her way through friendships and family members. The unlikely pairing of these two women provides an introspective view into the subject of the education of women during the late eighteenth and early nineteenth centuries. Many scholars have unearthed and brought to light the plight of women writers, both married and single, who forged a path for other women, those unable to voice their ideas in a public arena, and have given utterance to the individual nature of women redefining their domestic roles and their gender limitations. It is my contention that Mary Wollstonecraft, the voice for independent women in England, also gave strength to the silent women like Sara Coleridge who followed a more moderate lifestyle and whose individual voice was unheard except through her status as the wife of a famous poet, essayist, and literary giant. This inclusive study of two Romantic women asserts their influence on the literature of the period but also, and even more importantly, on the significance of the Romantic wife as a reinvention of the cultural norm. A marriage of the ordinary with the ideal wife is the contention of this examination of the social imagination during the eighteenth century.

Notes

1 Kenneth Curry, ed., *New Letters of Robert Southey, Volume One: 1792–1810* (New York: Columbia University Press, 1965), 27.
2 Curry, ed., *New Letters*, 28.
3 The birth spelling for Sara Fricker was Sarah, but I will use the spelling of her name without the "h" as was designated by her husband Samuel Taylor Coleridge.
4 Bold terms are my own emphasis. Samuel Taylor Coleridge, *The Collected Works of Samuel Taylor Coleridge*, vol. 7: Biographia Literaria or Biographical Sketches of My Literary Life and Opinions, see vol. I: Chapter 13, eds. James Engell and Walter Jackson Bate (Princeton: Princeton University Press, 1983), 304. The historical origins of Coleridge's definition of the imagination are explained more fully in the Editors' introduction to *Biographia Literaria* where they state:

> But in Chapter 4 Coleridge also mentions that German, as a "homogeneous" language, maintains a distinctness of terms. And in a number of German thinkers Coleridge encountered a wealth of distinctions between imagination and fancy, relatively recent and relatively consistent with each other, and all giving imagination the more creative role and fancy the important

xx *Introduction*

> but basically inferior power of selecting and connecting images without actually creating new ones. These German distinctions aided Coleridge to make his own.
>
> (*Biographia Literaria*, Introduction xcix)

5 Plato's *The Republic*, trans. Benjamin Jowett (Oxford: Clarendon Press, 1888, 1925), The Project Gutenberg eBook of *The Republic*, September 11, 2021.
6 "Virtue" is defined in the *Oxford English Dictionary* as "I.1.a. A moral quality regarded (esp. in religious contexts) as good or desirable in a person, such as patience, kindness, etc.; a particular form of moral excellence." Further reference can be found to the four cardinal virtues as the definition continues,

> I.1.b. Each of a specified number of morally good qualities regarded (esp. in religious contexts) as of particular worth or importance, such as the four cardinal virtues (see CARDINAL *adj.* 2), the three theological virtues (see THEOLOGICAL, *adj.* 1), or these seven virtues collectively as opposed to the seven deadly sins.

7 Ford K. Brown, *The Life of William Godwin* (London and Toronto: J. M. Dent & Sons, 1926), 44.
8 Mary Wollstonecraft, *A Vindication of the Rights of Woman*, ed. Carol H. Poston (New York: W. W. Norton, Second Edition, 1988), 39.
9 Gary Kelly, ed., *Bluestocking Feminism: Writings of the Bluestocking Circle 1738–1785*, 6 vols. (London: Pickering & Chatto, 1999), xxii.
10 Carol Shiner Wilson and Joel Haefner, eds., *Re-visioning Romanticism: British Women Writers, 1776–1837* (Philadelphia: University of Pennsylvania Press, 1994), 168.
11 Sylvia Myers (Harcstark), *The Bluestocking Circle: Women, Friendship, and the Life of the Mind in Eighteenth-Century England* (Oxford: Clarendon Press, 1992), 279.
12 For a more detailed description of a normative definition of femininity during the eighteenth century, see Janet Doubler Ward, ed., *Communication and Women's Friendships: Parallels and Intersections in Literature and Life* (Bowling Green: Popular, 1993).
13 Molly Lefebure, *The Bondage of Love: A Life of Mrs. Samuel Taylor Coleridge* (London: Victor Gollancz, 1986), 222.

References

Brown, Ford K. *The Life of William Godwin*. London and Toronto: J. M. Dent & Sons, 1926.
Coleridge, Samuel Taylor. *The Collected Works of Samuel Taylor Coleridge*: vol. 7, Biographia Literaria or Biographical Sketches of My Literary Life and Opinions, eds. James Engell and Walter Jackson Bate. Princeton: Princeton University Press, 1983.
Curry, Kenneth, ed. *New Letters of Robert Southey, Volume One: 1792–1810*. New York: Columbia University Press, 1965.

Kelly, Gary, ed. *Bluestocking Feminism: Writings of the Bluestocking Circle 1738–1785*, 6 vols. London: Pickering & Chatto, 1999.

Lefebure, Molly. *The Bondage of Love: A Life of Mrs. Samuel Taylor Coleridge.* London: Victor Gollancz Ltd., 1986.

Myers, Sylvia (Harcstark). *The Bluestocking Circle: Women, Friendship, and the Life of the Mind in Eighteenth-Century England.* Oxford: Clarendon Press, 1992.

Plato's *The Republic*, trans. Benjamin Jowett. The Project Gutenberg eBook of *The Republic*, September 11, 2021. Oxford: Clarendon Press, 1888, 1925.

Ward, Janet Doubler, ed. *Communication and Women's Friendships: Parallels and Intersections in Literature and Life.* Bowling Green: Popular, 1993.

Wilson, Carol Shiner, and Joel Haefner, eds. *Re-Visioning Romanticism: British Women Writers, 1776–1837.* Philadelphia: University of Pennsylvania Press, 1994.

Wollstonecraft, Mary. *A Vindication of the Rights of Woman*, ed. Carol H. Poston. New York: W.W. Norton, Second Edition, 1988.

1 Marriage, Passion, and Justice in English Society

> *Of all the systems… which human nature in its moments of intoxication has produced; that which men have contrived with a view to forming the minds, and regulating the conduct of women,* [marriage] *is perhaps the most completely absurd.*[1]
>
> (Mary Hays)

The baroness Germaine de Staël voices her interpretation of love in her essay "On the Influence of the Passions" published in the October 1813 issue of the ladies' magazine *La Belle Assemblée*. She elaborates on how the intensity of "love" intoxicates our emotions, as she says,

> Glory, ambition, fanaticism, and enthusiasm, have their intervals: in this sentiment alone, every instant is intoxication, nothing interrupts the influence of love; no fatigue is felt in this inexhaustible source of ideas and of happy emotions. As long as we continue to see, to feel only in another, all nature to us is under different forms, the spring, the prospect, and the climate, which we have enjoyed with the beloved object.[2]

The intoxicating nature of the passions as de Staël describes "love" resonates with the eighteenth-century discovery of the term sensibility as passion, and furthermore, the influence of the French to define this excessive emotion as morally acceptable. To distinguish the passions as sensibility is a profound deviation from the term "sentimental" as used in Laurence Sterne's 1768 novel *A Sentimental Journey*. Sterne describes passion as the effusive expression of emotion, but instead of an unregulated effusion, this one is shaped by social conditions that define moral behavior from an orthodox Christian view. In an age where sentimentalism was on the defensive, according to Janet Todd, it is no wonder that the social reformer and feminist writer Mary Wollstonecraft defined the virtues of men and women as natural affections of the passions in her counterattack against

DOI: 10.4324/9781003504238-1

the norm. Her perspective on the sentimental followed the broader view of the Dissenters, a view that favored virtue as natural through a greater reliance on the intellectual interpretation of proper moral conduct.

As Wollstonecraft's advocate for feminine reformation, Mary Hays describes these liberal passions in her novel *The Victim of Prejudice*. In the narrative Mr. Raymond responds to Mary's confession of her deep love for William Pelham, glorifying her passions as moral excellence. Mary receives his remarks as thoughtful approbation of her expression of love, and as Mr. Raymond exclaims,

> "You have fulfilled, my dearest child", said he, in his reply to my appeal, "my most sanguine expectation". Continue to act up to the dictates of your own admirable judgement: if I had not assisted you in forming principles of rectitude, and in acquiring courage to put them in practice, I should not now dare to add, to the crime of negligence, the tyranny of control.

Furthermore, he continues to praise Mary's affections as virtuous passion when he tells her,

> Your affection for William Pelham, not more natural than laudable, has hitherto produced upon your character the happiest effects: *virtuous tenderness* [italics mine] purifies the heart, carries forward the understanding, refines the passions, dignifies the feelings, and raises human nature to its sublimest standard of excellence.[3]

Happiness as an expression of passion is described as "virtuous tenderness," an eighteenth-century reformation of female virtue promulgated by Wollstonecraft and Hays in England and de Staël in France. Passion was aligned with a purer emotion of human happiness, one that Wollstonecraft sought after in her life and writing. Rather than devalue the feminine passions to frivolous coquetry in relationships of friendship and love, Wollstonecraft magnified the expression of these passions like Hays in her fictional stories while, paradoxically, struggling with these same passions in her personal relationships.

These passions express a delicacy of emotion that Wollstonecraft both honored as virtuous but also feared as weakness. During her courtship with William Godwin, Wollstonecraft describes an erotic encounter of their first kiss. In her letter of 22 August 1796, she recounts, "Our breaths intertwined and, at last, *at long last*, his lips pressed mine. He kissed softly, clinging, unwilling to release me from his embrace. I raised his hand in mine and drew it to my breast."[4] Wollstonecraft, clearly the pursuer, continues to describe this tender intimacy with Godwin's hand on her breast.

She notes the erotic placement of the chairs drawn to the fireside, and comments, "[he] prodded one of them, a bit furtively, with his toe, till they touched."[5] Enthused by the passion of the moment, Wollstonecraft applauds these feelings and honors their power in her remarks to Mary Hays the following day. During her visit with Wollstonecraft, Mary Hays was reading a fictional account of her character Mr. Francis, a wise counselor whose character was modeled after Godwin. When Godwin entered the room, Wollstonecraft recalls:

> It put me into an ironic mood to have lifted from listening to letters from the fictional Mr. Francis to face the actual model, whom Reason had so totally abandoned the night before in the necessities of love—for we are all of us children... when it comes to these urgencies where Aphrodite, if we observe not her dominion, wreaks powerful vengeance.[6]

This power of love motivated Wollstonecraft to foster individual change both in consciousness as well as in the marital relationship, shifting the balance of power from male dominance to intellectual equality where the roles of men and women were no longer solely defined by patriarchal privilege. From the philosophies of Rousseau and Shaftesbury, this shift from moral to natural virtue reinforced the innate goodness Wollstonecraft honored in her passions. The natural sensibility that Jean-Jacques Rousseau brought to bear on sentimental thought during the eighteenth century led Wollstonecraft to choose the power of the passions over moral restraint; however, she also "feared the anarchic stress on overwhelming feeling and the linking of sex and sensibility," as Todd explains.[7] As a result, society began to shift the moral ground of goodness or virtue from a religious sentiment to one of benevolence, a view favored by the second Earl of Shaftesbury who understood that the sentimental expresses "a hope in human goodness and perfectibility."[8]

However, this radical view of virtue as passionate feeling was not without controversy. The marriage contract was an ambiguous form of commitment between a man and a woman where irregular marriages, those ceremonies performed outside the Church, often challenged the legality of Church sanctioned marriages. Separation of marital relationships occurred through less costly and unencumbered means than divorce. Couples frequently agreed to separate by social rather than legal approval when one or the other found a more compatible partner. Since individual choice initially determined these affectionate relationships with little interference from institutional authority, individuals could also claim their liberty without institutional approval. As Roderick Phillips explains, "It is likely that in early modern society the great mass of the population distrusted the law, its institutions, and its personnel, be they the police, lawyers, or judges."[9] Alternatives to divorce included informal separation, desertion, wife sale, customary divorce, bigamy, *lettres de cachet*, spouse murder, suicide, and prayer.[10] Later in this chapter, the legal conditions of marriage are treated in more detail with respect to the rise in companionate marriages.

For Wollstonecraft, personal freedom was an essential component to the romantic relationship but one that would cause her much suffering. Her suicidal attempts point to the internal anguish she experienced because of her non-conformist behavior and unrequited affection. Her advocacy for natural virtue above moral virtue led Wollstonecraft to display publicly her behavior as an unmarried woman with a child, leading to her social condemnation. Her reputation as an aggressive spokesperson against feminine weaknesses of beauty and ignorance encouraged by masculine domination diminished her effectiveness as a social reformer during her lifetime. Yet, Wollstonecraft was undaunted in her efforts for female reform. In her treatise *Vindication of the Rights of Woman* she insists, "Taught from their infancy that beauty is woman's sceptre, the mind shapes itself to the body, and, roaming round its gilt cage, only seeks to adorn its prison."[11] Her actions may not have achieved their full impact for institutional reform, but her powerful rhetoric awakened skepticism in the promotion of marriage laws that unjustly served men over women. She attacked Edmund Burke's adherence to traditions of property inheritance and emphasized inconsistencies in other aspects of the law that produced injustices for women and the common person. Asserting the freedom of independent thinking, Wollstonecraft avows,

> The preponderance of inconsistencies, when weighed with precedents, should lessen the most bigoted veneration for antiquity, and force men of the eighteenth century to acknowledge, that our *canonized forefathers'* were unable, or afraid, to revert to reason, without resting on the crutch of authority; and should not be brought as proof that their children are never to be allowed to walk alone.[12]

Nature and reason outweigh tradition and authority according to Wollstonecraft and lead both men and women into an improvement of marital relationships that build more secure families. As she claims, "The only security of property that nature authorizes and reason sanctions is, the right a man has to enjoy the acquisitions which his talents and industry have acquired; and to bequeath them to whom he chooses."[13] After her non-conforming relationships with Henry Fuseli and Gilbert Imlay failed to satisfy her passions, Wollstonecraft succumbed to social pressure and married William Godwin when she was five months pregnant with his child. Her novel writing reveals similar injustices experienced by women in oppressive relationships under inadequate marriage laws.

As she pursued an intellectually and emotionally stimulating relationship with the French artist, Henry Fuseli, Wollstonecraft found herself an object of rejection, a pariah both personally and socially. While she entertained the idea that living with Fuseli and his wife would enhance her emotions, Fuseli's wife vehemently refused the concept of co-habitation. Meanwhile, Wollstonecraft persisted in a relationship that inspired equality of intellect and an aesthetic sensibility but one plagued by a powerful emotional attachment. Her strong feelings for Fuseli pushed Wollstonecraft to suggest her plan to join his wife and himself as part of their family, a plan that met with a staunch refusal from both. As Todd explains, "… with Fuseli, she was aiming for the nurturing friendship experienced with Johnson [her publisher and friend]."[14] Refuting Rousseau's argument that sexuality determines superiority by nature, Wollstonecraft continued her plea to Fuseli that her "strength of feeling [was] unalloyed by passion."[15] Wollstonecraft's passion for Fuseli grew from her admiration of his artistic sensibilities that inspired her own writing.

In June of 1792 Wollstonecraft describes her plans for "a summer excursion to Paris" where she can enjoy a morally freer atmosphere for her life and writings.[16] The height of her moral idealism for the freedom to think, feel, and act independently of convention meets with a social realism that dampens her spirit. On 24 December 1792 she wrote to her sister Everina from Paris explaining her predicament: "Authorship is a heavy weight for female shoulders, especially in the sunshine of prosperity."[17] Furthermore, she insisted that women were denied "[t]he power of generalizing ideas, of drawing comprehensive conclusions from individual observations…" that would enhance the immortality of their insights. As a result, women writers struggled to elevate their intellectual individuality beyond the social attention to their physical bodies where female passions were seen to debase strong feelings.[18] The female body was not to be an obstacle to the pursuit of higher aspirations. Wollstonecraft joins passion to the individual expression of the arts to locate virtue as a source of happiness.

For the next three years, Wollstonecraft remained in Paris surrounded by friends, both men and women, from England, America, Germany, Switzerland, Ireland, and France, all of whom were sympathetic to the Revolutionary activities in France:

> They included Thomas Christie, founder of *The Analytical Review*; Thomas Cooper of Manchester; Thomas Paine; Helen Maria Williams and her lover John Hurford Stone, whose name she had assumed—all these English; also three Americans: Joel Barlow, his wife Ruth; Gustav, Graf von Schlabrendorf, born in Stettin; a happy pair from Zurich, Jean Gaspard Schweizer and his wife Madeleine; Archibald Hamilton

Rowan, an expatriated Irishman; her French intimates Brissot and the Rolands, and—most important of all—Gilbert Imlay.[19]

Her international friendships helped to shape Wollstonecraft's national and domestic feelings of identity, a fuller discussion of which appears in Chapter 7. Among these friends Wollstonecraft met the American businessman Gilbert Imlay. Both her attractions to Imlay and to the Revolutionary ideas in 1793 led Wollstonecraft from a sentimentality of passions to suicidal depression. Imlay represented her anti-institutional ideologies where marriage was considered a corruption of romantic love, and Wollstonecraft cherished their freedom from a formal contract while holding their relationship as one of "the most sacred nature."[20] His intellectual accomplishments and handsome looks made him even more appealing. Perhaps his inclinations toward writing drew Wollstonecraft into a false sense of companionship with a man who had left unfinished business in America and painted himself as a victim of other women's deceits. He published two books over six years, his *Topographical Description of the Western Territory of North America* in London in 1792 and *The Emigrants* in 1793 that advocated divorce and portrayed the husband as a tyrant,[21] a character also developed in Wollstonecraft's novel *Wrongs of Woman, or Maria* (1798) as Maria's husband. Vulnerable to her own excess of emotion and the upheaval of social order produced by the French Revolution, Wollstonecraft turned her quest for happiness inward to discover that her fight for intellectual equality would be compromised by her need to preserve her reputation through the institution of marriage.

In her novel *Wrongs of Woman*, Wollstonecraft contrasts Maria's role as the oppressed wife of an abusive husband with her liberated romantic feelings for Henry Darnford while both are locked away in a madhouse. Her husband has committed her to the madhouse in order to procure her inheritance. Maria, a paradigm of the submissive wife, is denied her individual rights and liberty. Unfairly treated by the legal system, Maria searches for solace in her love for Darnford. Through the honesty of her love arises a natural virtue of feminine sensibility, one unencumbered by the institution of marriage. Within her novels and her life Wollstonecraft investigates a reinvention of marriage that supersedes moral and legal acceptance. Yet, when she conceives a child with William Godwin out of wedlock, she finds herself conceding to the socially sanctioned institution of marriage. Wollstonecraft fictionalizes the traditional role of wife to demonstrate its hardships while acknowledging moral approval for female passion expressed outside the marriage.

As in her fiction, so in her life Wollstonecraft grappled with emotional dilemmas that chartered her course for social reform to the marriage relationship and its institutional counterpart. After some time apart,

Wollstonecraft recognized that Imlay's absences were more of choice than of necessity. She had given birth to his daughter, Fanny, and was prepared to set sail for Scandinavia at Imlay's request to handle his business affairs in Sweden and Norway even though she was heartbroken over their separation. Her life seemed to be overwhelmed by a flood of sentimentalism that dragged her across the seas of despair, and her daughter Fanny became her only symbol of hope and affection in a cruel world. Here again the comparison from her life to her literature finds an obvious parallel to Maria whose only hope to escape from the madhouse is inspired by finding her infant daughter. The dramatic feeling with which Wollstonecraft wrote this tale intensifies the reader's compassion for the characters' impoverished situations, both emotionally and economically. The richness of her rhetoric must have certainly stirred many hearts of the women in the eighteenth century. She writes to Imlay in 1794,

> Believe me, sage sir, you have not sufficient respect for the *imagination* [italics mine]—I could prove to you in a trice that it is the mother of sentiment, the great distinction of our nature, the only purifier of the passions—.[22]

Wollstonecraft's reliance on the imagination as a political act shows her desperation to engage Imlay in her emotional distress. Her use of imagination as a literary and rhetorical device is discussed further in Chapter 3. These remarks to Imlay reveal a personal and political tyranny, one prompted by unsatisfying attempts to secure her relationship with him.

In a letter addressed to Godwin and dated 3 September 1796, Wollstonecraft compares herself to her fictional character Maria to illustrate her own childhood experiences and also to leave a legacy of the truth about her relationship to Imlay for her daughter Fanny. She writes,

> Maria, at the heart of it, has my sensibility, and poor Bess' circumstances [Mary's sister]. Of her marriage it may be said as Mrs. Siddons puts it, when she played Calista: "Hearts like ours were paired ... not matched". Once married, she finds her husband does not wish to become either friend or confidant. I shall take as the basis of character of the husband the most outrageous aspects of Imlay, even some of his business dealings.[23]

Wollstonecraft reveals "the cruel restraints" of her childhood and the "warm sunshine of romance" that blinded her to Imlay's deceptions. In an earlier account Wollstonecraft expresses her fears that Fanny will be deceived as she was, uninstructed in the ways of romance, and be left "to live a life in which her mind—what mind is left to her to have—[she hopes] will not be imprisoned in its own little tenement."[24] Concerned that women are fated to live by the illusion of romance to find their happiness, leaving them in a state of childlike sentimentality, Wollstonecraft declares, "We women are idiots."[25] She furthers her attempt to awaken women to the unlawfulness of a poor marriage in her treatise *Rights of Woman*. Haunted by her sister Bess' loss of her child to her husband, Wollstonecraft endeavors to show the wrongs committed on women: "how flagrant is a system of law that makes a woman unable to divorce an unprincipled man, nor lawfully to obtain custody of her child."[26] She allegorizes the breakdown of marriage and addressing a judge states her case to sue for divorce but receives the following reply:

> How's that? Now, what did she say? We want no new-fangled notions here in our court, if you please.... What virtuous woman ever thinks of her feelings? It is her duty to love and obey the man chosen.... Why, never could too many restrictions be thrown in the way of divorce, if we wish to maintain the sanctity of marriage.[27]

Wollstonecraft insists that the wrongfulness of the present marriage laws must be written about in novels. Apparently, Godwin thinks she is too sentimental in her literary approach; however, she reminds him that a woman of sensibility and education must improve her state of marriage and that cannot be done "under our present system of legal bondage."[28]

In Wollstonecraft's novel *Mary, a Fiction* (1788), she describes a woman living under oppressive conditions in a loveless marriage who struggles to extricate herself while trapped by a rigid legal system. From the beginning of the novel, the protagonist Mary claims her freedom from oppression turning to her passions throughout the story to dramatize the significance of powerful emotions. She writes, "Nothing could be more natural than the developement [sic] of the passions, nor more striking than the views of the human heart."[29] However, her delicate nature and tender care for others are consistently challenged by worldly circumstances where ugly emotions predominate. As a young child she witnesses the dead body of a "poor wretch" who in "a fit of delirium stab[s] herself."[30] This violent scene traumatizes Mary who will experience recurring incidents in the future. The emotional ambivalence of kindness and cruelty persists in Mary's marriage and friendships. Burdened by a loveless marriage Mary represents a powerful opposition to the institution of marriage. With each relationship established in the novel, except the one with her husband, she develops a deep emotional attachment to individuals who will fade from her life. It is the virtuous nature of these friendships that endures because of her pure affection. However, she painfully witnesses the death of each one watching closely by their side as they transition from life to death, first Ann, and then later, Henry. She even takes the sacrament with Henry to demonstrate "a bond of union which was to extend beyond the grave."[31] The loss of her friend Fanny Blood following childbirth and Wollstonecraft's dying mother, whom she cared for through her end-of-life experience, resonate in the loss of human companionship in the novel. Human passions pervade the narrative illustrating their powerful control over the extremities of life and death.

Even though others criticized her zealous outcry for the oppression of married women, Godwin discovered in Wollstonecraft and in her writings a virtuous nature. He describes a new feeling: "I had never loved till now; or, at least, had never nourished a passion to the same growth, or met with an object so consummately worthy."[32] The intellectual respect and dignity of this relationship was in itself a remarkable display of virtue. Godwin describes the early stages of their acquaintance as "friendship melting into love."[33] Their show of personal restraint exhibits a deeper affection that grew from private sentiments unmeasured by social approval. Godwin explains,

> We did not marry. It is difficult to recommend any thing to discriminate adoption, contrary to the established rules and prejudices of mankind; but certainly nothing can be so ridiculous upon the face of it, or so contrary to the genuine march of sentiment, as to require the overflowing of the soul to wait upon a ceremony, and that at which, wherever delicacy and imagination exist, is of all things most sacredly private, to blow a trumpet before it, and to record the moment when it has arrived at its climax.[34]

However, in April 1797 they decided to declare their marriage openly since Wollstonecraft was pregnant with Godwin's child, the future Mary Shelley.[35] During their short-lived marriage of five months, they could not have foreseen Wollstonecraft's unexpected death in September after giving birth to their daughter Mary. Godwin and Wollstonecraft shared a sublime marriage united spiritually, while to the rest of the world, their union was fraught with impropriety, a lawless exhibition of anti-religious sentiment and denigration. Theirs was a poverty of social acceptance and conformity, yet, paradoxically, a relationship of unrecognized innocence hidden by the socially inhibited.

Godwin's love of the intellectual nature of humanity became intertwined with Wollstonecraft's passion for the pleasures of the imagination, and together they enhanced what was most masculine and feminine in both individuals. He admits, "One of the leading passions of my mind has been an anxious desire not to be deceived."[36] With Wollstonecraft, Godwin was reassured by her honesty both in private and in public; she plainly criticized the cunning manipulations of the female sex. On the other hand, in her letter of 1 September 1796, Wollstonecraft describes her quickness to defend the role of women:

> I had been quick to anger, the night before, at his saying [Godwin] that tragedy was too strenuous an exercise for females. Not that I deny the statement—*but must we for ever sit and listen to what all females are like?*[37]

He admired in Wollstonecraft her ability to possess feelings which "had a character of peculiar strength and decision; and the discovery of them," and that "in matters of taste or of moral virtue, she found herself unable to control [these feelings]."[38] Finally, Godwin appreciated Wollstonecraft most for her immeasurable capacity to feel. He writes, "Her taste awakened mine; her sensibility determined me to a careful development of my feelings."[39] Like Godwin, Wollstonecraft's readers are also awakened to an emotional revival that redefines the passions of domestic love as virtue.

In 1793 the publication of Godwin's *Enquiry Concerning the Principles of Political Justice* expounded on the liberties, rights, and personal happiness of individuals just before Wollstonecraft advocated her political theory. When Wollstonecraft was writing her treatise on *An Historical and Moral View of the French Revolution* in 1794, asserting her views on the declaration of rights, Godwin was also writing one of the most terrifying tales of a young man whose individual right to liberty was seized by the distorted and narrow interpretation of the law. Influenced by the terrors of the French Revolution and the destruction of traditions rooted in the medieval age, Wollstonecraft and Godwin set out to change political principles and social standards that inhibited natural principles of justice and equality. As Wollstonecraft explains, "The declaration of rights contains an aggregate of principles the most beneficial; yet so simple, that the most ordinary capacity cannot fail to comprehend their import."[40] The manners and customs of the French under an aristocratic government were yielding to a new identity, a government concerned with the good for all citizens. Furthermore, writes Wollstonecraft,

> In this delineation men may learn, that, in the exercise of their natural rights, they have the power of doing whatever does not injure another; and that this power has no limits, which are not determined by law— the laws being at the same time an expression of the will of the community, because all the citizens of the state, either personally, or by their representatives, have a right to concur in the formation.[41]

Reform that addressed a political and religious system based on aristocratic authority was imminent. Laws that served the interests of one class of citizens over another were subject to the scrutiny and criticism of the growing intellectualism of the middle-class concerned with the underprivileged poor. Happiness could no longer be measured by the economic conditions of the privileged as the awareness of affective individualism grew among the bourgeois.[42]

Among the concerns for individual rights in English society was the marriage relationship as a civil and religious union between a man and a woman. In 1873, a lawyer by the name of James T. Hammick wrote of the matrimonial contract,

> From its consequences as regards property and the rights of husbands and wives, children, &c., matrimony may be correctly designated a civil contract; but as an institution deriving its origin from God, and not from any human legislation, it must also be deemed a divine or religious contract, even when solemnized according to civil forms.[43]

One of the most significant historical moments affecting marriage and family occurred in 1439 during the Middle Ages. The marriage relationship was recognized as a sacrament of the Church, a sacred relationship established by religious doctrine that by 1563 required a clergyman to perform the ceremony in the parish where the couple lived.[44] By the eighteenth century this union was performed in an Anglican church and was considered by eighteenth-century standards to be a regular marriage because acknowledged publicly and with parental consent. Parish records were maintained with fair consistency during this time. However, as more and more couples especially of the lower classes sought to make their choice of a mate without parental consent and from a different religious persuasion than the Church of England (Catholic and Dissenting religions), marriages of the clandestine type began to flourish. Since Scottish marriage laws were less strict in marrying couples based on age and religion, many individuals crossed the border to tie the knot. Others took advantage of quick and inexpensive marriages in the Fleet region of London giving marriages that were potentially problematic because of poorly kept records the name of Fleet marriages. As the issues of property and children arose in the courts, the question of legal inheritance was more difficult to solve where there were no written records and the verbal word of a witness could be easily bought.

Along with the ecclesiastical and civil debates over the marriage contract came the non-conforming trends of individuals such as Wollstonecraft and Godwin who challenged the marriage law on the basis of its political and religious inequities. From their treatises on justice for individual rights and from readers acknowledging the marital struggles of characters in their novels, the widespread influence of non-conforming behavior toward marriage developed more rapidly. Through examples of their fictional characters and excerpts from their political treatises, the reforming influences of Wollstonecraft and Godwin provide clear evidence of their dissenting views. Moreover, their intimate relationship as lovers, and then as husband and wife, provides the emotional strength to reform the thinkers of English society and loosen orthodox Christian views toward the marriage relationship despite the Marriage Act of 1753. Several reasons for the receptivity of these two writers to reform public opinion include their tendency to view social behavior from what is natural, their worldliness, their ability to educate others, and their domestic interests. While the Marriage Act was addressing important legal concerns in clarifying marriage contracts on the possession of property and issue, Wollstonecraft and Godwin engaged readers in the morality of the marriage relationship. The pressing issue focused on how an agreement of marriage secured by the law could allow a husband or wife to suffer abuse (economic, emotional, and physical), abandonment or desertion, or other inequities preventing the achievement of personal happiness. Adherence to the sacrament of marriage and its binding religious law gave an authority to the husband that superseded the individual rights of the individual. From Godwin's upbringing as a Sandemanian, a Church founded by an anti-Establishmentarian Scottish Presbyterian minister in 1730,[45] and from Wollstonecraft's association with Richard Price's liberal views and Dissenting philosophy advocating separation of church and politics,[46] these two writers brought a more rational understanding to the marriage contract.

The very dualistic nature of the marriage contract, the civil and the religious, now being sorted out by Lord Hardwicke's Act of 1753 raised the question of how to regard marriage in terms of the human relationship and the divine. The Act stated

> that all marriages, after the 25th March, 1754, should be solemnized in the parish church or public chapel (in which banns were usually published) of one of the parties, and that all marriages celebrated without publication of banns, or licence duly granted, should be absolutely null and void.[47]

It readily enforced punishment on those individuals who attempted to make claims on a husband or wife with whom there had not been a celebration of the marriage according to the rites of the Church of England. The presence of a priest at the marriage ceremony was mandatory; however, the ceremony itself did not have to take place in a church. For Roman Catholics

Marriage, Passion, and Justice in English Society   13

and Dissenters, the objection continued to be that the power of a legal marriage was still primarily in the hands of the Church. Wollstonecraft's and Godwin's rational treatment of the law as non-conformists exemplifies the conflicts inherent in the law. Godwin's respect for authority can be weighed along with his adherence to an individual's natural right to hold virtues of sincerity and justice in higher esteem than an act of government. In his chapter "Of Promises" in *Enquiry Concerning Political Justice* he states,

> Again, why should I promise, that I will do everything that a certain power, called the government, shall imagine it convenient, or decide that it is fitting, for me to do? Is there in this, either morality, or justice, or common sense?[48]

Godwin defends his argument on the moral grounds of sincerity that he explains is a principle of morality not found in promises but in the indissoluble benefit of living with sincerity in one's life and relationships. Godwin honored sincerity over the promise of marriage until he and Wollstonecraft decided it was better to conform to a conventional marital relationship, a social contract that brought respectability to the woman he loved. However, when hearing of another young woman, Sarah Parr, eloping to Gretna Green with one of her father's pupils, who was just a boy of 18, Godwin "ungallantly reminded Wollstonecraft that marriage for anyone was a gaol sentence,"[49] a remark he uttered once he and Wollstonecraft had become husband and wife.

In addition to their outspoken opposition on the political and religious deficiencies of the marriage contract, Wollstonecraft and Godwin further illustrated the moral and legal entanglements of the marital relationship in their novels, thereby reaching a wider audience of readers. In the preface to her book *The Wrongs of Woman, or Maria*, Wollstonecraft writes that these sketches of women "are not the abortion of a distempered fancy, or the strong delineations of a wounded heart," but rather she has tried to "pourtray passions [more] than manners."[50] She further explains,

> In many instances I could have made the incidents more dramatic, would I have sacrificed my main object, the desire of exhibiting the misery and oppression, peculiar to women, that arise out of the partial laws and customs of society.[51]

Instead, her protagonist Maria finds herself reflecting on her deep passions, of grief and loss, of longing for her four-month-old daughter from whom she has been "torn" while she remains confined in a madhouse. Abused by her tyrant husband who seeks to steal Maria's inheritance, Wollstonecraft attacks the masculine authority figure in this novel while establishing female independence through the powerful exchange of emotions between Maria and her guard in the madhouse, Jemima. She writes,

> Though she failed immediately to rouse a lively sense of injustice in the mind of her guard, because it had been sophisticated into misanthropy, she touched her heart. Jemima (she had only a claim to a Christian name, which had not procured her any Christian privileges) could patiently hear of Maria's confinement on false pretences; she had felt the crushing hand of power, hardened by the exercise of injustice, and ceased to wonder at the perversions of the understanding, which systematize oppression, but, when told that her child, only four months old, had been torn from her, even while she was discharging the tenderest maternal office, the woman awoke in a bosom long estranged from feminine emotions, and Jemima determined to alleviate all in her power, without hazarding the loss of her place, the sufferings of a wretched mother, apparently injured, and certainly unhappy.[52]

The emotional abuse, suffered by the protagonist Maria at the hands of her husband, and the imbalance of the law reinforce the need for social and legal reform in English society.

Wollstonecraft advocates for the rational and intellectual education of women, while she denounces the indulgence of fashionable tastes and feminine delicacy. As illustrated through her novel, Maria receives books from her fellow prisoner Henry Darnford to comfort and instruct her in her miserable and wretched condition. Selectively, Wollstonecraft chooses texts for female instruction from among Dryden's *Fables* and Milton's *Paradise Lost*, not unlike the manner in which the creature in Mary Shelley's *Frankenstein* discovers the history of the world and his own identity as part of the human race. From these sources Maria, too, discovers her inferior social status, the injustices of the law, and the need for reform especially within the marriage relationship. The narrator explains,

> It was a mine of treasure. Some marginal notes, in Dryden's *Fables*, caught her attention: they were written with force and taste; and, in one of the modern pamphlets, there was a fragment left, containing various observations on the present state of society and government, with a comparative view of the politics of Europe and America.[53]

Using literature as an instrument for publicizing her political ideology, Wollstonecraft represents the need for social and legal reform of the marriage covenant.

Since the conditions of English life were predominantly defined by economic policy and constitutional law, Godwin's efforts to reveal the inequities of these policies and laws in the 1790s become essential to understand the changing virtues and philosophical shifts that occurred during the second half of the eighteenth century. Threatened by the upheaval of the French monarchy on English conservatism, statesmen, politicians, and religious leaders in England re-examined the role of the citizen within the governing powers. Not only were these concerns voiced publicly throughout the press but were also preached from the pulpits and published in radical treatises. Godwin further identifies those principles that formed the center of politically and socially complicated issues in his novel *The Adventures of Caleb Williams, or Things As They Are* (1794). The story tells of a poorly educated peasant named Caleb Williams in contrast with the wealthy and educated country squire Mr. Tyrrel. The well-to-do country squire commits injustices against his cousin Emily Melville, thereby causing her untimely death. Asserting his authoritative and superior position, Tyrrel arranges a marriage for his cousin Emily with a brutal and insensitive neighbor, Mr. Grimes. When the marriage plans go awry upon Emily's escape from Grimes, Tyrrel is indignant and searches for her with a vehemence that exhibits the irrational will of a powerful citizen. At the demand of Tyrrel she is arrested while lying in a sick bed and conducted to prison. As the narrator explains, "The forlorn state of these poor women, who were conducted, the one by compulsion, the other a volunteer [her caretaker], to a scene so little adapted to their accommodation as that of a common jail, may easily be imagined."[54] Emily is coerced and manipulated by her cousin Tyrrel but chooses to resist even if it means her death. However, Tyrrel persists in his search for her to bring her to his form of justice. The extremity of the situation is described in the following passage:

> The health of Miss Melville was materially affected, by the surprise and removal she had undergone, at the very time that repose was most necessary for her preservation. Her fever became more violent; her delirium was stronger, and the tortures of her imagination were proportioned to the unfavourableness of the state in which the removal had been effected. It was highly improbable that she could recover.[55]

The brutality inflicted on Emily by her cousin Tyrrel emphasizes the dangerous effect of the law when enforced by the tyranny of those in authority like Tyrrel who ignore the virtue and innocence of others. Her caretaker Mrs. Hammond declares, "Why, you would not tear her from her bed? I tell you, she is in a high fever; she is light-headed; it would be death to remove her! You are bailiffs, are not you? You are not murderers?"[56] The bailiffs reply in their grim ignorance, "The law says nothing about that. We have orders to take her sick or well. We will do her no harm; except so far as we must perform our office, be it how it will."[57]

Godwin carefully injects his characters with values and expectations of justice and reason that are constantly challenged by the old traditions of rank, wealth, and political power. The invasion of politics into everyday life is evident in the manner in which Tyrrel disregards Emily's individual happiness. First, she is prevented from choosing her own marriage partner, and then she is arrested for deserting her prospective husband, a marriage arranged by Tyrrel. Emily has just barely escaped from her prospective husband who attempted to sexually assault her before the wedding ceremony occurred. Godwin draws deep sympathy for his character Emily and, at the same time, a public awareness to his readers for the reform of female oppression experienced by the social mistreatment of wives. He recognized that the marriage laws still lacked protection and equality for women under the current authority.

Instead of protecting individuals, the Marriage Act of 1753 forced those wanting to marry without parental consent to cross the border north into Scotland where people could marry quickly and secretively. As Lawrence Stone explains,

> In 1760 it was claimed that there were boats waiting at Southampton to carry run-aways—for a fee of five guineas—to Guernsey where clandestine marriages were still legal. Whether or not this was true is not known, but Guernsey was soon far outstripped by Scotland as a place in which to get married in a hurry. The Scottish Court of Sessions failed to agree to overthrow the ancient Scottish marriage laws permitting contract and private marriages in order to bring that country into line with its neighbor to the south.[58]

While Stone argues against the positive effects of the Marriage Act, others such as Rebecca Probert indicate that the act fairly represented women's legal interests. She asserts that women were not passive victims of men or of the might of the law even though they had formerly suffered injustices. She states, "The Marriage Act should be seen as part of a gradual progression towards regularity and formality rather than an abrupt shift in the regulation of marriage."[59] However, she emphasizes along with Stone that marriage was moving toward a deregulation of the Church's influence and a secularization of the relationship. Despite some improvement of the Hardwicke Act, marriage celebrations continued to remain "exclusively in the hands of the church, a restriction which gave offence to Roman Catholics and almost every denomination of dissenters."[60] The movement from sacred to secular control over marriage is further detailed in Chapter 8: Marriage Law and the Rights of Woman from Sacred to Secular.

Later on in the nineteenth century, further separation from Church influence occurred when in 1837 Lord John Russell changed the marriage law to allow those who were not members of the Church of England to perform marriage ceremonies according to their own form of worship. Therefore, religious authority over marriage weakened considerably leaving the power to choose a partner within the particular and natural rights of the individual to achieve happiness. Through the protection of the law one's individual freedom to choose a marriage partner was becoming more commonplace as the irrational and unreasonable enforcement of previous laws gave way to the rationalism that enlightened women's rights legally and morally. Through Wollstonecraft's and Godwin's efforts to contextualize the marriage relationship within their novels and essays, the religious sacrament of marriage was subordinated to the civil union of couples who were now freer to accept proposals based on their own affections without parental influence and the ceremonial indoctrination of the church.

As Wollstonecraft recognizes in her insightful comments on the progress of reform,

> People thinking for themselves have more energy in their voice, than any government, which it is possible for human wisdom to invent; and every government not aware of this sacred truth will, at some period, be suddenly overturned. Whilst men in a savage state preserve their independence, they adopt no regular system of policy, nor ever attempt to digest their rude code of laws into a constitution, to ensure political liberty. Consequently we find in every country, after it's civilization has arrived at a certain height, that the people, the moment they are displeased with their rules, begin to clamour against them; and, finally rejecting all authority but their own will, in breaking the shackles of folly or tyranny, they glut their resentment by the mischievous destruction of / the works of ages, only considering them as the moments of their servitude.[61]

The civilizing process of English society through the changes of the marriage laws was largely due to non-conforming individuals like Wollstonecraft and Godwin who sacrificed popularity within their communities for the advancement of personal liberty.

Notes

1. Mary Hays, *Appeal to the Men of Great Britain in Behalf of Women*, introduction by Gina Luria (New York: Garland, 1974), 47.
2. Germaine de Staël, "On the Influence of the Passions," *La Belle Assemblée*, 1813, 109–10.
3. Mary Hays, *The Victim of Prejudice*, edited and with an introduction by Eleanor Ty (Ontario: Broadview Press, 1994), 80.
4. Jean Detre, *A Most Extraordinary Pair: Mary Wollstonecraft and William Godwin* (Garden City: Doubleday, 1975), 45.
5. Detre, *A Most Extraordinary Pair*, 44.
6. Detre, *A Most Extraordinary Pair*, 49–50.
7. Janet Todd, *Sensibility: An Introduction* (London: Methuen, 1986), 28.
8. Todd, *Sensibility*, 22.
9. Roderick Phillips, *Putting Asunder: A History of Divorce in Western Society* (Cambridge: Cambridge University Press, 1988), 279–80.
10. For detailed explanation of these alternatives see Phillips, *Putting Asunder*, 279–313.
11. Mary Wollstonecraft, *The Vindications: The Rights of Men and the Rights of Woman*, eds. D. L. Macdonald and Kathleen Scherf (Ontario: Broadview Press, 2001), 157.
12. Wollstonecraft, *The Rights of Men*, 51.
13. Wollstonecraft, *The Rights of Men*, 55.
14. Janet Todd, *Mary Wollstonecraft: A Revolutionary Life* (New York: Columbia University Press, 2000), 194.
15. Todd, *Mary Wollstonecraft, a Revolutionary Life*, 195.
16. William Godwin, *Memoirs of Mary Wollstonecraft*, ed. W. Clark Durant (New York: Haskell House Publishers, 1969), 220.
17. Godwin, *Memoirs*, 221.
18. Godwin, *Memoirs*, 169.
19. Godwin, *Memoirs*, 223–24.
20. Claire Tomalin, *The Life and Death of Mary Wollstonecraft* (New York: Harcourt Brace Jovanovich, 1974), 147.
21. Tomalin, *The Life and Death*, 146.
22. Janet Todd and Marilyn Butler, eds., *The Works of Mary Wollstonecraft*: Letters to Gilbert Imlay (from Posthumous Works) vol. 6: 365–438 (New York: New York University Press, 1989), 387–88.
23. Detre, *A Most Extraordinary Pair*, 75.
24. Detre, *A Most Extraordinary Pair*, 73.
25. Detre, *A Most Extraordinary Pair*, 73.
26. Detre, *A Most Extraordinary Pair*, 74.
27. Detre, *A Most Extraordinary Pair*, 74.
28. Detre, *A Most Extraordinary Pair*, 80.
29. Janet Todd and Marilyn Butler, eds., *The Works of Mary Wollstonecraft*: Mary, a Fiction vol. 1: 1–74 (New York: New York University Press, 1989), 6.
30. Todd and Butler, eds., *The Works of Mary Wollstonecraft*: Mary, a Fiction, vol. 1: 1–74, 8.

31 Todd and Butler, eds., *The Works of Mary Wollstonecraft*: Mary, a Fiction, vol. 1: 1–74, 51.
32 Godwin, *Memoirs*, 101.
33 Godwin, *Memoirs*, 100.
34 Godwin, *Memoirs*, 101.
35 Mary Wollstonecraft married William Godwin on 29 March 1797, at St. Pancras Church in London.
36 Godwin, *Memoirs*, 131.
37 Detre, *A Most Extraordinary Pair*, 69.
38 Godwin, *Memoirs*, 131.
39 Godwin, *Memoirs*, 132.
40 Todd and Butler, eds., *The Works of Mary Wollstonecraft*: An Historical and Moral View of the French Revolution, vol. 6: 1–236, 221.
41 Todd and Butler, eds., *The Works of Mary Wollstonecraft*: An Historical and Moral View of the French Revolution, vol. 6: 1–236, 221.
42 Affective individualism is defined by Lawrence Stone as

> firstly, a growing introspection and interest in the individual personality; and secondly, a demand for personal autonomy and a corresponding respect for the individual's right to privacy, to self-expression, and to the free exercise of his will within limits set by the need for social cohesion: a recognition that it is morally wrong to make exaggerated demands for obedience, or to manipulate or coerce the individual beyond a certain point in order to achieve social or political ends.
> (*The Family, Sex and Marriage in England 1500–1800* (New York: Harper & Row, Publishers, 1977), 223–24)

43 James T. Hammick, Esq., *The Marriage Law of England: A Practical Guide to the Legal Requirements connected with The Preliminary Formalities, Solemnization, and Registration of the Matrimonial Contract with an Appendix of Statutes, Etc.* (London: Shaw and Sons, Fetter Lane, Law Printers & Publishers, 1873), 2.
44 Stone, *The Family, Sex and Marriage*, 30.
45 Donald Davie, *A Gathered Church: The Literature of the English Dissenting Interest, 1700–1930* (New York: Oxford University Press, 1978), 68.
46 Todd, *Mary Wollstonecraft: A Revolutionary Life*, 163.
47 Hammick, *The Marriage Law of England*, 13.
48 William Godwin, *Enquiry Concerning Political Justice and Its Influence on Morals and Happiness*, vol. 1, ed. F. E. L. Priestley (London: Printed for G. G. and J. Robinson, Paternoster-Row, 1798; Toronto: University of Toronto Press, 1946), 211–12.
49 Todd, *Mary Wollstonecraft: A Revolutionary Life*, 441.
50 Janet Todd and Marilyn Butler, eds. *The Works of Mary Wollstonecraft*: The Wrongs of Woman: or Maria, vol. 1: 75–184 (New York: New York University Press, 1989), 59.
51 Todd and Butler, eds., *The Works of Mary Wollstonecraft*: The Wrongs of Woman: or Maria, vol. 1: 75–184, 59.

52 Todd and Butler, eds., *The Works of Mary Wollstonecraft*: The Wrongs of Woman: or Maria, vol. 1: 75–184, 64.
53 Todd and Butler, eds., *The Works of Mary Wollstonecraft*: The Wrongs of Woman: or Maria, vol. 1: 75–184, 68.
54 William Godwin, *The Adventures of Caleb Williams or Things As They Are* with an introduction by George Sherburn (New York: Holt, Rinehart &Winston, 1960), 98.
55 Godwin, *The Adventures*, 98.
56 Godwin, *The Adventures*, 96.
57 Godwin, *The Adventures*, 96.
58 Lawrence Stone, *Road to Divorce: England 1530–1987* (Oxford: Oxford University Press, 1990), 130.
59 Rebecca Probert, "The Impact of the Marriage Act of 1753: Was it Really 'A Most Cruel Law for the Fair Sex'?" *Eighteenth-Century Studies*, vol. 38 no. 2, Winter 2005, 258.
60 Hammick, *The Marriage Law of England*, 33.
61 Todd and Butler, eds., *The Works of Mary Wollstonecraft*, vol. 6, 223.

References

Davie, Donald. *A Gathered Church: The Literature of the English Dissenting Interest, 1700–1930* New York: Oxford University Press, 1978.

de Staël, Germaine. "On the Influence of the Passions." *La Belle Assemblée*, October 1813.

Detre, Jean. *A Most Extraordinary Pair: Mary Wollstonecraft and William Godwin*. Garden City: Doubleday, 1975.

Godwin, William. *Enquiry Concerning Political Justice and Its Influence on Morals and Happiness*, vol. 1, ed. F. E. L. Priestley. London: Printed for G. G. and J. Robinson, Paternoster-Row, 1798; Toronto: University of Toronto Press, 1946.

---. *The Adventures of Caleb Williams or Things As They Are* with an introduction by George Sherburn. New York: Holt, Rinehart &Winston, 1960.

---. *Memoirs of Mary Wollstonecraft*, ed. W. Clark Durant. New York: Haskell House Publishers, 1969.

Hammick, James T., Esq., *The Marriage Law of England: A Practical Guide to the Legal Requirements connected with the Preliminary Formalities, Solemnization, and Registration of the Matrimonial Contract with an Appendix of Statutes, Etc*. London: Shaw and Sons, Fetter Lane, Law Printers & Publishers, 1873.

Hays, Mary. *Appeal to the Men of Great Britain in Behalf of Women*. New York: Garland, 1974.

---. *The Victim of Prejudice*, edited and with an introduction by Eleanor Ty. Ontario: Broadview Press, 1994.

Phillips, Roderick. *Putting Asunder: A History of Divorce in Western Society*. Cambridge: Cambridge University Press, 1988.

Probert, Rebecca. "The Impact of the Marriage Act of 1753: Was It Really 'A Most Cruel Law for the Fair Sex'?" *Eighteenth-Century Studies*, vol. 38 no. 2, Winter 2005.

Stone, Lawrence. *The Family, Sex and Marriage in England 1500–1800*. New York: Harper & Row, Publishers, 1977.
---. *Road to Divorce: England 1530–1987*. Oxford: Oxford University Press, 1990.
Todd, Janet. *Sensibility: An Introduction*. London: Methuen, 1986.
---. *Mary Wollstonecraft: A Revolutionary Life*. New York: Columbia University Press, 2000.
Todd, Janet, and Marilyn Butler, eds. *The Works of Mary Wollstonecraft*: Mary, a Fiction, vol. 1: 1–74. New York: New York University Press, 1989.
---. *The Works of Mary Wollstonecraft*: The Wrongs of Woman, or Maria, vol. 1: 75–184. New York: New York University Press, 1989.
---. *The Works of Mary Wollstonecraft*: An Historical and Moral View of the French Revolution, vol. 6: 1–236. New York: New York University Press, 1989.
---. *The Works of Mary Wollstonecraft*: Letters to Gilbert Imlay (from Posthumous Works), vol. 6: 365–438. New York: New York University Press, 1989.
Tomalin, Claire. *The Life and Death of Mary Wollstonecraft*. New York: Harcourt Brace Jovanovich, 1974.
Wollstonecraft, Mary.. *The Vindications: The Rights of Men and the Rights of Woman*, eds. D. L. Macdonald and Kathleen Scherf. Ontario: Broadview Press, 2001.

2 Reason and Passion in the Education of Virtue

> "*Educate women like men,*" says *Rousseau* [in *Emile*], "*and the more they resemble our sex the less power will they have over us.*" This is the very point I aim at. I do not wish them to have power over men; but over themselves.[1]
>
> (Mary Wollstonecraft)

The magnitude of Mary Wollstonecraft's writings on liberating female intellectuality and passion is further enhanced by her advocacy of female education as illustrated in her work *Original Stories* published in 1788. Along with examples of Wollstonecraft's moral lessons for children, she teaches the importance of fair treatment toward all classes of English society with particular attention to the middle and lower classes. To further comprehend Wollstonecraft's unique significance as a reformer, we need to position her ideology in proximity to other female writers during this time. From an examination of the conservative Bluestockings among Wollstonecraft's radical group of educators such as Catherine Macaulay and Mary Hays, Wollstonecraft emerges more clearly as a non-conforming thinker whose radicalism did not separate her from strong Christian values. Andrew McKendry points out probable causes for Wollstonecraft's liberal sympathies in her friendships with the Dissenting group of intellectuals:

> Their republican heritage, regularly flaunted in relation to the 1688 revolution, made them amenable to schemes of popular sovereignty, while their subjection to the penal laws animated the anti-authoritarian inflections of natural law and Christian scripture in their polemics—so much so that Dissent was frequently considered a political faction.[2]

Often misunderstood in her adherence to Christian values, Wollstonecraft's advocacy of civil liberty is more aptly aligned with her religious faith as McKendry further explains in his chapter on "Dissenters." In her writings on moral education, Wollstonecraft relies on her Christian values to further

her liberal approach to elevating and instructing female intellectuality as she draws on her personal experiences with children.

As a young woman, Wollstonecraft sought a position as a governess where she witnessed the lack of moral education in upper class homes. In her later treatise on the social education of women, *A Vindication of the Rights of Woman* published in 1792, Wollstonecraft targets the ignorance of upper class women, like her employer Lady Kingsborough, as a contributing factor to the treatment of women as inferior to men and to their personal suffering. She saw her role as a moral instructor of children to be the proper method of educating both genders on becoming intellectual equals, and as a result, to live as moral equals. In her instructional tales to children, *Original Stories*, the protagonist Mrs. Mason closely resembles Wollstonecraft in her role as governess.

In this series of children's tales written in 25 chapters, Wollstonecraft prefers instruction by example as preferable to preaching. Lessons follow the instructions on charity, poverty, the treatment of animals and insects, temperament, lying, folly, indulgence, and idleness to instill good habits of thought. From John Locke's theory of education she shaped her own ideas on the influence of environment and experience.[3] The protagonist, Mrs. Mason, instructs two young girls, Mary and Caroline, aged 14 and 12 respectively, children of wealthy parents who from infancy had been raised by "ignorant" servants. When their mother died, they were given to the charge of Mrs. Mason who recognized her challenge in retraining their vulgar habits into more tolerable ones. In her preface, Wollstonecraft indicates her purpose was to establish a method of moral instruction through the conversations of these characters. She writes, "The tendency of the reasoning [obviously tends] to fix principles of truth and humanity on a solid and simple foundation; and to make religion an active, invigorating director of the affections, and not a mere / attention to forms."[4] In Chapter II, Mrs. Mason teaches Mary and Caroline how to become more tender-hearted and "useful to my fellow-creatures"[5] as they learn how their "superior endowments ward off the [evils] [which] they cannot foresee."[6] Learning they are below the angels but above the animals teaches them about human virtues. Mrs. Mason explains, "[What we call virtue, may be thus explained]:—we exercise every benevolent affection to enjoy comfort here, / and to fit ourselves to be angels hereafter."[7] The children learn they can improve by humanizing their hearts through suffering as Mrs. Mason reminds them, "... if we suffer, we grow humbler and wiser: but animals have not this advantage, ..."[8]

In Chapter VIII, the tale teaches lessons of temperance and self-denial to Mary and Caroline. When on a summer's evening walk Mrs. Mason and the children wandered through a violent thunderstorm, Mrs. Mason reassured them, calming their fears, while teaching them a scientific principle "[that] storms were necessary to dissipate noxious vapours ... ."[9] She also encouraged the children to rely on God's presence ensuring their safety while they learned that virtue overcomes the fear of death. After they climbed a cliff and heard the crashing of the waves against the rocks below, they found safety nearby in a poor woman's cottage. At the cottage the children witnessed the poverty in the lives of others, teaching them control over their own appetites and self-indulgence when sharing a meal with this family. This story illustrates the practicality of virtue that is further applied to employment as virtue and the vulgarity of idleness in Chapter XIII. The children, tired and bored, act foolishly eating from boredom even though they are not hungry or in need. Mrs. Mason instructs Caroline to help her make some clothes for a poor woman while Mary should read them "an entertaining tale."[10] After the clothes are made, the children visit the woman to deliver the clothes. In addition, the children are told to consider what the poor woman is most in need of and to exercise their judgment to provide and act on "immediate relief" for her circumstances. The lesson here teaches more than good habits of behavior but goes beyond obedience to teach right judgment. Mrs. Mason has taught the children that "[A]s the judgment gains strength, so do the passions also; we have actions to weigh, and need that taste in conduct, that delicate [sense of] propriety, which gives grace to virtue."[11] Virtue supersedes an overzealous righteousness based on religious doctrine as passion infiltrates and joins with righteous moral behavior. The purity and innocence associated with children are not exempt from feelings of tenderness and do not exclude emotions of compassion and empathy conventionally held by adults.

Other critics have interpreted these lessons for children from a less favorable perspective. "*Original Stories*, however, is often seen as the antithesis to the nascent Romantic cult of childhood innocence and imagination, and has been typically described as a 'series of harsh moral tales',"[12] writes Alan Richardson. Wollstonecraft's reliance on the writings of educational theorist and historian Catharine Macaulay from *Letters on Education* fueled her desire to lift women's education from a male-dominated system to a rational and independent-minded philosophy for women. This perspective reformed the role of motherhood from one of weakness to strength, from passivity to activity, from dependence to independence in the education of their children, and in their own views of themselves as intellectual equals to men. As Richardson notes, "Such arguments, made by Wollstonecraft in company with a wide range of female reformers, running the ideological spectrum from conservatives like Hannah More to radicals like Macaulay and Mary Hays, were inevitably double-edged."[13] Wollstonecraft's earlier text *Thoughts on the Education of Daughters* (1786) adheres to the accepted eighteenth-century view on developing the moral excellence of children; however, by the time she writes *Original*

Stories (1788), Wollstonecraft has read Rousseau's educational treatise *Emile, or On Education* (1762) and lived as a governess in Ireland employed by Lady Kingsborough. Both experiences shaped and reformed her pedagogical views along with the application of the Socratic dialogue as her primary method to instruct children in a moral way of life that was based on her own lifestyle as a governess.

Yet, the paradox exists in educating women as mothers and wives to feel the intoxicating passions that stir their independent thinking while, at the same time, creating fanciful notions to rise above their traditional domestic roles as obedient wives and ignorant mothers. Her educational and novel writing like her life portray Wollstonecraft's personal contradictions but also demonstrate how she ventured into a realm of complexities in order to improve the position of women in society. As Moira Ferguson and Janet Todd note,

> Like *Mary, A Fiction*, *The Rights of Woman* springs from Wollstonecraft's experience and does not escape its paradoxes: romantic love is seen as both a delusion and the "concomitant of genius"; an unhappy marriage is good for the children when contrasted with a passionate one, but disastrous when contrasted with one based on domestic friendship; sensibility marks the humanitarian and the languishing female.[14]

The improvement of female education and the education of children during the eighteenth century cannot be understood simply by the morality of the age. Instead, the "[g]lory, ambition, fanaticism, and enthusiasm" Germaine de Staël points to in her essay "On the Influence of the Passions" (1813), stimulate the kind of moral excellence Wollstonecraft is seeking to achieve in her pedagogical tracts on education. From fact to fiction, this female author labored to create a new voice for women, for the educated and uneducated alike, that deviated from the conventional view of women as inferior, enslaved by their own emotional weaknesses, and she dramatically affected the norm by which women identified themselves.

As women writers such as Elizabeth Carter, Elizabeth Montagu, and Hester Chapone, along with Hannah More and other learned ladies, voiced their ideas on female education and encouraged other women to develop their intellectual abilities, they became disliked by many men for their accomplishments while, at the same time, they were also supported by respectable literary figures such as Samuel Johnson. Their clever intellect coupled with a deeply religious faith rustled the social feathers of those men who resisted this reform of young women. Yet as Norma Clarke succinctly notes, "Female 'virtue' had been joined to female 'sense'."[15] These changing social attitudes fostered a reconstitution of the ideology of virtue with some radical female reformers attempting to redefine virtue in negating domesticity and others like the conservative Bluestocking Circle of literary women, who maintained morality, self-expression, and intellectual equality as dominant features of domestic virtue. Both points of view challenged the virtues of submission and obedience that characterized the wife as an economic and social possession of the husband. From an examination of these two perspectives, Wollstonecraft's group of radical educators and the conservative Bluestockings, the ambivalence of virtues experienced by these married women in the eighteenth century led to the formation of a new cult of domesticity linking moral, creative, and intellectual virtues within a community of enlightened wives.

Moreover, according to Nancy Armstrong and Mary Poovey[16] along with Susan Yadlon, this normative definition of femininity describes a domestic ideology that was fraught with conflicts while, at the same time, providing women "a space from which to intervene in that paradigm."[17] In fact, Yadlon's metaphor that the feminine ideal of the age was "a vessel of morality" implies the passivity of virtue as an intrinsic characteristic. Even though Yadlon addresses all women in her argument, I prefer to limit my discussion to the married woman since the conventions of this age directly and indirectly inhibit this class of women by legal, moral, economic, and political restrictions designed primarily for the married woman. As the lives of the Bluestockings affirm, these women actively expressed reason, passion, and virtue in their roles of authorship as well as in their social and domestic spheres, thereby challenging the traditional role of domestic passivity. As Sonia Hofkosh explains in her discussion of gender and the Bluestockings,

> When the Bluestockings change the color of their undergarments, wearing blue worsted instead of white, silk stockings at social gatherings, they display their resistance to prescribed materials and modes of gender—and class—specific discourse; they signal closely on their bodies the refashioning of sexual and social categories.[18]

Recognizing the social impositions made on married women, Yadlon argues that the writings of eighteenth-century women (both from personal correspondence and published works) "function not only as a tool of ideological dissemination but also as a site of intervention into domestic ideology's construction of femininity."[19] An examination of some of the writings from the circle of women known as the Bluestockings, a term at first used to describe intellectual men and later identified with educated married women, will reveal the ideological contradiction that these writings have simultaneously established a new female discourse, one that separates women from a non-literary tradition while yet remaining situated within a domestic sphere. Yadlon further contended that the "epistolary friendships, formed in response to the power of dominant ideology, additionally become an act of intervention in it" by asserting that the Bluestockings resisted the dominant ideology by threatening its very definition of femininity. Yadlon suggests, "They [the Bluestockings] do not threaten the institution of heterosexual marriage itself, but rather intervene in certain marital practices."[20] These women who advocated female education did, in fact, also threaten the institution of marriage as it was defined in the eighteenth century not as an intentional act, but nonetheless, as an act of ideological change that occurs based on the dynamics of a changing set of values. As evidenced by their private and public lives, they were responsible for eradicating the social resistance toward married women writers and for significantly fashioning the popularity of female discourse/or power. The domestic strife suffered by the Bluestockings further attests to the reformation of the dominant ideology of the cult of femininity and not merely a change of marital practices within its eighteenth-century cultural definition as asserted by Yadlon.

Despite the conservatism of this group of married women, they can and should be seen as a critical force in creating a new cult of domesticity, a domestic sphere imbued with intellectual acuity. Moreover, the effect of women's writing on the new cult of domesticity becomes even more obvious within the context of another ongoing debate of the eighteenth century, that of the formation of taste in the analysis of beauty. Bringing a woman's virtue under increasing scrutiny, Robert W. Jones describes the social and judgmental use of beauty as a way "to assess the morality or conduct of a woman, her likely authority or the extent of her charms."[21] These concurrent discursive debates helped to define a woman's social place and domestic sphere in relation to her moral nature.[22]

The "learned ladies" of the Bluestocking Circle, while more conservative in their behavior than radical female reformers Mary Wollstonecraft and Mary Robinson, represented an important contribution to not only changing domestic interests in terms of education but also in terms of romantic relationships, aligning female desire with duty in marriage. The significant change in this era is that women were now responsibly instructing women out of the eighteenth-century cult of femininity. Yadlon argues that the Bluestockings' influence was limited during this time because of their privileged class and their marriages to men of social and economic advantage. She suggests that due to their class positioning, they would not side with Wollstonecraft's more radical views on marriage or with the marginal women of lower class and lower moral standing. Yadlon cites critics such as Moira Ferguson, Marilyn Williamson, and Sylvia Myers as undertheorizing the desire of the Bluestockings to maintain the *status quo* of marriage and domestic life while instituting new educational ideas. "All three critics recognize the Bluestockings' conservative politics but miss examining how an insistence on retaining class privilege prevents the Bluestockings from taking up the struggles of the majority of eighteenth-century women," Yadlon claims.[23] However, while their writings may not have dramatically changed the class structure of women, the Bluestockings irreversibly influenced the way women thought about the limitations of their domestic positions, the way women of all classes redefined domestic virtue now to include intellectual equality and creative self-expression, and the way the cult of domesticity enlarged the borders of marital duty in liberating women emotionally as well as socially.

The rigor and success of the writings of the Bluestockings can be seen in the published works of many of these women during the period from 1758 to 1798. Elizabeth Carter translated and published the works of Epictetus (1758) from Greek as well as contributing essays to Samuel Johnson's *The Rambler* on such topics as religion versus superstition, Elizabeth Montagu published *Essay on the Writings and Genius of Shakespeare* (1769), Hester Chapone claimed her success with *Letters on the Improvement of the Mind* (1773) and *Letter to a Married Lady* (1777), and Hannah More's publication of *Cheap Repository Tracts* (1795–98) attests to the scholarship and intellect of a group of women who can be said to have engraved the history of feminism with their presence. As Sylvia Myers notes,

> Their "fame" as scholars and writers, discussed in newspapers and periodicals, combined with interest in and gossip about their social gatherings, brought the idea of eminently respectable women with intellectual interests into public notice; the change in gender reflected an uncomfortable awareness of the breaking of a taboo.[24]

Elizabeth Montagu became known as "the 'queen' of the Bluestockings because of her leading role in the network."[25] In a letter to Elizabeth Carter, 24 November 1759, she writes of the natural and liberating pursuit of the intellect as a virtue rather than as a weakness:

> I am a little fearfull that what you call faults in yourself I have call'd virtues when I have found them in my own mind; particularly when you accuse your self of a wild & untractable love of liberty, because you want a place where you can enjoy some hours every day uninterrupted. This is my own turn, & I thought it an excellence, a perfection & almost a virtue.[26]

Her correspondence emphasizes the discomfort felt in expressing the freedom of an intellectual journey within an antagonistic culture. Further on in the letter Montagu's literary voice and critical awareness of philosophical ideas can be discerned:

> There is a letter from Rousseau to Mr D'Alembert on ye project of settling a Theatre at Geneva which treats of Dramatical performances in general: it is ingeniously written & with great eloquence. The author wrote before to prove the savage state preferable to civil society: He is a stranger to ye sweet civilities of life; whatever is gentle he thinks weak; he seems to have principles of justice & integrity, so we must call him honest Bruin.[27]

While sensitive to Rousseau's linguistic eloquence, Montagu cleverly recognizes the "Bruin" or bear in Rousseau's character along with his honesty.

Not unlike Montagu's generous acknowledgment of Rousseau's morality and Christian forgiveness of his brutish nature, Hester Chapone is acclaimed for her high regard to moral and intellectual acumen. As a poet and epistolary writer she was esteemed as "the female intellectual moralist" from the 1770s until the middle of the nineteenth century according to Rhoda Zuk.[28] As Zuk explains,

> Esteem for Chapone and her work extended from two generations of Bluestockings, the Queen (who modeled the Princess Royal's education on *Letters on the Improvement of the Mind*), men of letters, and a large public: however, the ambivalence reflected in occasional commentary counters the impression that Chapone, a charming yet formidable intellectual personality, was unproblematically welcome.[29]

One has only to look more closely at her writing to acknowledge her contributions to elevate the marital condition of women during the period of the Enlightenment.

> In 'Matrimonial Creed', [Hester] Mulso, [later Chapone], argues that a woman's moral convictions and intellectual capacities should not exclude her from marital happiness, but on the contrary should entitle her to love, honour, and the dignity of freedom within marriage.[30]

Chapone's poignant advice on companionate marriages focused on the virtue of friendship between husband and wife, a virtue which was to be exalted by both male and female writers like Wollstonecraft and others well into the next century and the ramifications of which not only promoted equality and fraternity within the marriage relationship but also discouraged the practice of arranged marriages. Chapone writes,

> Notwithstanding this acknowledged superiority of right of command, I believe it highly conducive, and, to delicate minds, absolutely necessary

to conjugal happiness, that the husband have such an opinion of his wife's understanding, principles, and integrity of heart, as would induce him to exalt her to the rank of his *first* and *dearest friend,* and to endow her, by his own free gift, with all the privileges, rights, and freedoms of the most perfect friendship.[31]

It is no wonder that even Samuel Richardson who maintained a correspondence with Chapone on filial obedience was deeply stirred by her direct and innovative public voice. In the face of other advice literature primarily written by men for women, Chapone's *Letters* challenged authors such as John Gregory, James Fordyce, Thomas Marriott, William Kenrick, and Wetenhall Wilkes. Chapone intended her writing "to construct a course of self-education for girls that would approximate the standard education established and institutionalized for boys."[32] As Zuk notes, these writings served to advance "the intellectual capacities and moral potential of women for the purposes of forming the rational female citizens of an increasingly powerful middle-class social order."[33]

The adherence of the Bluestocking women to a high moral standard while pursuing their intellectual interests propelled this circle of women as literary equals into the realm of an exclusionary masculine tradition but not without controversy. In her discussion of this controversy over literary authority, Deborah Heller cites Habermas' *Structural Transformation of the Public Sphere* (1989) and asks, "But who were the 'authorized participants' of the public sphere?" She responds, "... the Bluestocking salons of later eighteenth-century London...where women appear to be full and active participants in the public sphere."[34] The conservatism of these "learned ladies" was a platform on which they constructed a new cult of domesticity that built on their aspirations to express themselves in a variety of literary modes including letters, marital advice, translations, and original literary works. Hofkosh furthers our understanding of the impact the Bluestockings had on reforming female education both in the higher and lower classes of society. As she explains that they did not confine their works to the drawing room, Hofkosh asserts,

> their eighteenth-century domestication of the venue of literary activity and their concomitant venture into the male-dominated domains of learning and literature—the lecture hall, the bookseller's backroom, the columns of the periodical, the library—together urged nineteenth-century reconsiderations of the status of [female] authorship.[35]

On the progress of education as a means to advance the female character in society, the radical Wollstonecraft and the conservative Bluestockings would agree. On the encouragement of virtuous behavior in women, both viewpoints would be supported; however, for Wollstonecraft, the issue of emotionalism was central to her opposition to women's passivity as legitimized by Edmund Burke's advocation of feminine weakness. Perhaps while More's and Wollstonecraft's religious inclinations as Evangelicals grounded their ideas on a similar moral foundation, nevertheless, Wollstonecraft's need to cultivate reason over passion and her resistance to authority separated these social reformers socially, politically, and historically as the debate over female virtue continued to challenge the feminine ideal. A closer look at Wollstonecraft's early years in the next chapter will attempt to show the environmental forces that shaped her philosophical views on women in society, views that were fundamental to her treatise on *A Vindication of the Rights of Woman*.

When Wollstonecraft wrote her first volume on vindications in 1790, *A Vindication of the Rights of Men*, she framed her argument in the eighteenth-century epistolary form, a letter addressed to Burke in response to his *Reflections on the Revolution in France* (1790). Her manner of speech was so obviously straightforward, filled as it was with contempt and indignation for which she made no polite apology, that she herself considered her own style of language as manly. Consequently, Wollstonecraft wastes neither words nor sentimental manners in informing Burke that his adherence to respect causes a sacrifice of love, suggesting fancy more than reason. She admonishes Burke,

> it is natural to conclude, that all your pretty flights arise from your pampered sensibility; and that, vain of this fancied pre-eminence of organs, you foster every emotion till the fumes, mounting to your brain, dispel the sober suggestions of reason. It is not in this view surprising, that when you should argue you become impassioned, and that reflection inflames your imagination, instead of enlightening your understanding.[36]

She continues to attack Burke's conservatism in her defense of the lower classes who cannot rise up from poverty, who cannot advance as property owners because of the perpetuation of property in families, and who under the laws of the land can even imprison their own children to prevent them from making unsuitable marriages.[37] Wollstonecraft poignantly remarks, "All these circumstances you must have known, yet you talk of virtue and liberty, as the vulgar talk of the letter of the law; and the polite of propriety."[38] It is no wonder that Wollstonecraft's vehement responses to the proprieties of her day led her to reform the nature of virtue and manners too often expressed with insincerity. As she characterizes Burke's lack of sincerity and compassion in his views, Wollstonecraft sharply criticizes his ideas as "the sordid calculations of blind self-love."[39] She expresses her adamant objections in the following passage:

> A brutal attachment to children has appeared most conspicuous in parents who have treated them like slaves, and demanded due homage for all the property they transferred to them, during their lives. It has led them to force their children to break the most sacred ties; to do violence to a natural impulse, and run into legal prostitution to increase wealth or shun poverty; and, still worse, the dread of parental malediction has made many weak characters violate truth in the face of Heaven; and, to avoid a father's angry curse, the most sacred promises have been broken.[40]

Attacking the extreme treatment of parental discipline, Wollstonecraft identifies that the injustices done to children arise from property laws of inheritance.

Wollstonecraft recognized that adherence to a "blind propriety," apparent within an indifference to laws that would sustain the natural rights of a woman, both restrained female nature and threatened the stability of the family. As Poovey notes,

> Throughout this period, then, the dual function the ideal of feminine propriety served was, implicitly if not explicitly, to harness the appetites men feared and associated with women to their own more reliable masculine wills and then, by extension, to protect the property upon which the destiny of both individuals and an entire society depended.[41]

Rejecting the conservative and traditional views of Burke that to protect the family is to protect the nation, Wollstonecraft pursued her objective to free women from the tyranny of a patriarchal authority. Confident in her own theories of virtue and domestic happiness, Wollstonecraft benefited from a growing middle class that relied on individual affection more than on parental control. From her own experiences in becoming a lady's companion at the age of 19, Wollstonecraft understood the difficulties facing young women who were forced to choose low-paying positions and to endure the humility of companioning some rich stranger in order to establish one's independence from home.

Enthusiasm of Virtue

Wollstonecraft's writing instructed and inspired women to express feminine virtue as a natural act of sexual freedom. As Wollstonecraft emphasizes in her feminist treatise, *A Vindication of the Rights of Woman*, "Liberty is the mother of virtue, and if women be, by their very constitution, slaves, and not allowed to breathe the sharp invigorating air of freedom, they must ever languish like exotics, and be reckoned beautiful flaws in nature."[42] Her own passion for freeing women from sexual inhibitions and traditions grew intensely as she was influenced by her friendships with radical thinkers like Michael Faraday, Joseph Priestley, and Richard Price. Michael Faraday (1791–1867) was a nineteenth-century scientist, a natural philosopher, and an elder in the Sandemanian Church,[43] who followed the Dissenting tradition in which William Godwin was raised and from which Wollstonecraft's circle of friends found their religious principles and political affiliations. Wollstonecraft befriended the Dissenting minister Dr. Richard Price in Newington Green in 1784 where she had moved to establish her school for young ladies. His compassion for children and his humanity to animals complimented his radical political and religious views. An American revolutionary sympathizer, Price associated himself with

> the most eminent scientists and philosophers of his day, in England, France and America—men such as Franklin, Jefferson, Condorcet and Joseph Priestley, a fellow-Dissenter—and was looked to with respect by all who were not too blinkered by religious or political prejudice.[44]

Wollstonecraft was profoundly influenced by the non-conforming philosophy of these Dissenters and their strict adherence to sexual modesty for both sexes.

While she never abandoned her Anglican Church, she regularly attended the Dissenting Chapel where Price preached[45] and retained a strong religious conviction that grounded her writing on the morality of the Scriptures. Among these Dissenting voices, Wollstonecraft's voice arises to introduce the ideal notion of enthusiasm as a passionate advocate of virtue that paradoxically silences the moral restraint of virtue. As McKendry notes,

> Domesticity played an integral role in the way that Dissenters conceived of their identity; the proscriptions against public worship situated domestic space not only as a necessary alternative to the Established Church, but correspondingly as a conceptual locus of religious subjecthood, godly community, and even political opposition.[46]

McKendry explains further how Wollstonecraft was drawn to the Dissenters based on their views for domestic concerns, yet she also distanced herself from their extreme views of non-conformity. As Wollstonecraft attempts to reconcile civil and religious values in light of the Dissenting movement,

McKendry recognizes her adherence to the natural right of liberty. He states, "We don't usually think of Wollstonecraft as a champion of religious freedom, but her pairing of 'civil' with 'religious' liberty reflects the concept's ancestry in long-standing debates about 'liberty of conscience', a legacy that acuminated her feminism."[47] Barbara Taylor emphasizes Wollstonecraft's religious faith as well when she remarks, "Admirers of Mary Wollstonecraft are often reluctant to see her as a religious thinker." However, she firmly acknowledges, "The famous call for a 'revolution of female manners' in the Rights of Woman on close inspection proves to be first and foremost a summons to women to a right relationship with their Maker."[48]

The appeal of non-conformist thinking encouraged Wollstonecraft to reject traditional values and rules on the one hand, but on the other hand, fueled her enthusiasm for the expression of passionate emotions natural to both sexes. Faraday was sympathetic to the secular culture of poetry and theatre embracing the passions of the imagination; however, he preached reason as the producer of a calm and patient temperament. He writes,

> That man in his natural state is greatly influenced by his fellow creatures and the forms of emotion which are amongst them, is doubtless true, even when it concerns what he considers his eternal welfare.... Man's natural mind is a very unstable thing, and most credulous, and the imagination often rules it when reason is thought to be there.[49]

Recognizing the influence of the imagination through poetry and the arts, Faraday identified the power these agencies held over the systems of religion and political government that ultimately caused his sympathy toward but also his distrust of enthusiasm. Linking the traditional and dissenting views of religion, Faraday's beliefs embrace both conservative and liberal ideas. Through the intermingling of reason and imagination, a paradox of passion and virtue emerges to create a moral foundation for natural virtue. Through an analysis of Wollstonecraft's *Original Stories from Real Life* (1788), illustrated by William Blake in 1791, this paradox of enthusiasm and virtue is shown to be the pivotal link balancing reason in the age of Enlightenment with passion in the age of Romantic imagination.

In order to situate the eighteenth-century values of enthusiasm and virtue within the philosophical pursuits of Wollstonecraft's writing, it is helpful to begin by defining these terms according to the Oxford English Dictionary. Enthusiasm is characterized by its religious, poetic, and emotional applications in the following three ways:

1 "Possession by a god, supernatural inspiration, prophetic or poetic frenzy;"
2 "Fancied inspiration; 'a vain confidence of divine favour or communication' (J.). In eighteenth-century often in vaguer sense: Ill-regulated or misdirected religious emotion, extravagance of religious speculation;"
3 "The principal current sense: Rapturous intensity of feeling in favour of a person, principle, cause, etc.; passionate eagerness in any pursuit, proceeding from an intense conviction of the worthiness of the object."[50]

As Priestley suggested in 1782, "Enthusiasm [makes us] imagine that we are the peculiar favorites of the divine being," and Shaftesbury wrote in 1737, "Inspiration is a real feeling of the Divine Presence, and Enthusiasm a false one."[51] Understood as a description of religious devotion, enthusiasm begs the sincerity and persistence of inspiration while as a poetic feeling or intense emotion for another, enthusiasm more resembles the passions of the human soul. To elucidate this paradox of the passions, enthusiasm here asserts a moral primacy where human passion and moral law together become the embodiment of female nature as Wollstonecraft advocates the restraint of human passion, not its repression. She explains,

> Let the honest heart shew [sic] itself, and *reason* teach passion to submit to necessity; or, let the dignified pursuit of virtue and knowledge raise the mind above those emotions which rather imbitter [sic] than sweeten the cup of life, when they are not restrained within due bounds.[52]

In this manner of passionate restraint, Wollstonecraft furthers her position as a moralist while she allows for the sentimental tradition as natural affection. She asserts, "Let their faculties [women] have room to unfold, and their virtues to gain strength, and then determine where the whole sex must stand in the intellectual scale."[53] Wollstonecraft taught that children and uneducated women naturally embrace morality because unlike men they are not educated to rationalize purity in their basic nature. The concept of the sentimental as it embraces the passions becomes an even clearer expression of the emotions when examined by other female critics. Mary Patterson Thornburg explains the sentimental myth of this age:

> The superiority of feeling, of intense personal, emotional knowledge, was repeatedly asserted by the early romantic writers—in conjunction, often, with the idea that the person closest to his own unschooled feelings, like the child, the peasant, the "noble savage", was better able to make correct judgments than those who had learned to distort their native impulses with an excess of rationality.[54]

However, natural purity and active female sentiment oppose representations of chastity and passive religious purity in socially defined roles as mother, wife, and teacher. Wollstonecraft insists, "Do passive indolent women make the best wives?"[55] Advice and didactic literature authors such as Dr. Gregory, a Christian moralist, taught women passive restraint, however, from a perception of weakness. Inspired by unrestrained emotions, Wollstonecraft "recommends 'active sensibility' and 'positive virtue' to women,"[56] as Claudia Johnson notes in her explanation of the sentimental. Johnson further explains,

> To tell women to exercise "active" (as opposed to passive) sensibility and "positive" (as opposed to negative) virtue is to immasculate their affective lives, to assert their legitimacy as affective and quite explicitly as erotic subjects, a position which subverts heterosexual orthodoxy.[57]

For women to submit to men sentimentally suggests an indulgence with chivalric ideals rather than cultivating themselves as "erotic subjects," to use Johnson's phrase. Johnson's argument supports an assertion that when enthusiasm pervades virtue, it results in the natural behavior of women formed by passion, not duty. According to the *Oxford English Dictionary*, "virtue" is primarily defined as:

1 the "Conformity of life and conduct with the principles of morality; voluntary observance of the recognized moral laws or standards of right conduct; abstention on moral grounds from any form of wrong-doing or vice;"
2 "The possession or display of manly qualities; manly excellence, manliness, courage, valour."[58]

Both the moral and masculine aspects of the dictionary definition of virtue inhibit natural female emotions and supplant Wollstonecraft's advocacy of natural virtue in women as a moral attribute.

In the next chapter, Wollstonecraft's marriage to William Godwin and their sympathies toward the common person, along with her educational writings, novels, and essays will elucidate the moral virtues critical to the individual growth of the Romantic wife as a paradigm of social reform.

Notes

1 Mary Wollstonecraft, *The Vindications: The Rights of Men and the Rights of Woman*, eds. D. L. Macdonald and Kathleen Scherf (Ontario: Broadview Press, 1997), 80.

2 Andrew McKendry, "Dissenters," *Mary Wollstonecraft in Context*, eds. Nancy E. Johnson and Paul Keen (Cambridge: Cambridge University Press, 2020), 146–54, 148.
3 Moira Ferguson and Janet Todd, *Mary Wollstonecraft* (Boston: Twayne Publishers, 1984), 17.
4 Janet Todd and Marilyn Butler, eds. *The Works of Mary Wollstonecraft*: Original Stories, vol. 4: 353–450 (New York: New York University Press, 1989), 360.
5 Todd and Butler, eds., *The Works of Mary Wollstonecraft*: Original Stories, vol. 4: 353–450, 373.
6 Todd and Butler, eds., *The Works of Mary Wollstonecraft*: Original Stories, vol. 4: 353–450, 322.
7 Todd and Butler, eds., *The Works of Mary Wollstonecraft*: Original Stories, vol. 4: 353–450, 371–72.
8 Todd and Butler, eds., *The Works of Mary Wollstonecraft*: Original Stories, vol. 4: 353–450, 373.
9 Todd and Butler, eds., *The Works of Mary Wollstonecraft*: Original Stories, vol. 4: 353–450, 394.
10 Todd and Butler, eds., *The Works of Mary Wollstonecraft*: Original Stories, vol. 4: 353–450, 414.
11 Todd and Butler, eds., *The Works of Mary Wollstonecraft*: Original Stories, vol. 4: 353–450, 415.
12 Alan Richardson, "Mary Wollstonecraft on Education," *The Cambridge Companion to Mary Wollstonecraft*, ed. Claudia L. Johnson (Cambridge: Cambridge University Press, 2002), 24–41, 28.
13 Richardson, "Mary Wollstonecraft," 25.
14 Ferguson and Todd, *Mary Wollstonecraft*, 71.
15 Norma Clarke, *Dr. Johnson's Women* (London: Hambledon and London, 2000), 157.
16 Mary Poovey extends her definition of ideology beyond the Marxist and Freudian assumptions:

> Although the prevailing system of values at any given historical moment inevitably serves to protect the interests of a powerful class or social group, it does not necessarily follow that simply identifying the social function of ideology will enable one to escape or even to challenge it. Ideology, as I use the term, governs not just political and economic relations but social relations and even psychological stresses as well.
> (*The Proper Lady and the Woman Writer* (Chicago: The University of Chicago Press, 1984), Preface)

17 Susan M. Yadlon, "The Bluestocking Circle: The Negotiation of 'Reasonable' Women," *Communication and Women's Friendships: Parallels and Intersections in Literature and Life*, eds. Janet Doubler Ward and Joanna Stephens Mink (Bowling Green: Bowling Green State University Popular Press, 1993), 113–31, 113.
18 Sonia Hofkosh, "A Woman's Profession: Sexual Difference and the Romance of Authorship," *Studies in Romanticism*, vol. 32 (Summer 1993), 245–72, 246.

38 *The Social Imagination of the Romantic Wife in Literature*

19 Yadlon, "The Bluestocking Circle," 113.
20 Yadlon, "The Bluestocking Circle," 119.
21 Robert W. Jones, *Gender and the Formation of Taste in Eighteenth-Century Britain* (Cambridge: Cambridge University Press, 1998), 2.
22 Virtue in its relationship to beauty during the eighteenth century was a significant part of the discussions on changing values within the domestic and cultural spheres. According to Robert W. Jones,

> Not only can the question of beauty be discovered occupying a prominent position in debates about the nature of taste, but it can also be found within texts covering art criticism, moral philosophy, and social commentary. The term, though, was perhaps most strikingly deployed in relation to the role of women in cultural and social debate.
> (*Gender and the Formation of Taste in Eighteenth-Century Britain* (Cambridge: Cambridge University Press, 1998), 1)

23 Yadlon, "The Bluestocking Circle," 130.
24 Sylvia Myers Harcstark, *The Bluestocking Circle: Women, Friendship, and the Life of the Mind in Eighteenth-Century England* (Oxford: Clarendon Press, 1992), 285.
25 Gary Kelly, ed., *Bluestocking Feminism: Writings of the Bluestocking Circle 1738–1785*. 6 vols. (London: Pickering & Chatto, 1999), x.
26 Kelly, ed., *Bluestocking Feminism*, 150.
27 Kelly, ed., *Bluestocking Feminism*, 151.
28 Kelly, ed., *Bluestocking Feminism*, 181.
29 Kelly, ed., *Bluestocking Feminism*, 181.
30 Kelly, ed., *Bluestocking Feminism*, 249.
31 Kelly, ed., *Bluestocking Feminism*, 252–53.
32 Kelly, ed., *Bluestocking Feminism*, 257.
33 Kelly, ed., *Bluestocking Feminism*, 258.
34 Deborah Heller, "Bluestocking Salons and the Public Sphere," *Eighteenth-Century Life*, vol. 22 (May 1998), 59.
35 Hofkosh, "A Woman's Profession," 247.
36 Wollstonecraft, *The Rights of Men*, 37.
37 Wollstonecraft, *The Rights of Men*, 52–53.
38 Wollstonecraft, *The Rights of Men*, 52.
39 Wollstonecraft, *The Rights of Men*, 52.
40 Wollstonecraft, *The Rights of Men*, 52–53.
41 Poovey, *A Proper Lady*, 6.
42 Wollstonecraft, *The Rights of Woman*, 147.
43 Donald Davie explains the origins of the Sandemanian Church:

> The Sandemanian Church came into being in 1730, founded by an anti-Establishmentarian Scottish Presbyterian minister, John Glas (b. 1695). It was greatly strengthened in 1760 when it was joined by the Inghamites, followers of Benjamin Ingham (1712-72) who, though one of Wesley's

earliest associates, broke away and evangelized on his own account, chiefly in the West Riding.
(*A Gathered Church: The Literature of the English Dissenting Interest, 1700–1930* (New York: Oxford University Press, 1978), 68)

44 Claire Tomalin, *The Life and Death of Mary Wollstonecraft* (New York: Harcourt Brace Jovanovich,1974), 31.
45 Tomalin, *The Life and Death of Mary Wollstonecraft*, 32.
46 McKendry, "Dissenters," 151.
47 McKendry, "Dissenters," 148. McKendry references Wollstonecraft's use of "civil," "religious," and "liberty of conscience" from her writings on the *Rights of Men*. See Mary Wollstonecraft, *A Vindication of the Rights of Men* in *The Works of Mary Wollstonecraft*, eds. Janet Todd and Marilyn Butler (London: W. Pickering, 1989), 5: 8–9.
48 Barbara Taylor, "The Religious Foundations of Mary Wollstonecraft's Feminism," *The Cambridge Companion to Mary Wollstonecraft*, ed. Claudia L. Johnson (Cambridge: Cambridge University Press, 2002), 99.
49 Davie, *A Gathered Church*, 70–71.
50 "Enthusiasm." *Oxford English Dictionary* (OED). Second Edition. Vol. 5 (Oxford: Clarendon Press, 1989), 296.
51 "Enthusiasm." *OED*, 296.
52 Wollstonecraft, *The Rights of Woman*, 141.
53 Wollstonecraft, *The Rights of Woman*, 145.
54 Mary Patterson Thornburg, *The Monster in the Mirror* (Ann Arbor: UMI Research Press, 1987), 22.
55 Wollstonecraft, *The Rights of Woman*, 145.
56 Claudia L. Johnson, *Equivocal Beings: Politics, Gender, and Sentimentality in the 1790s: Wollstonecraft, Radcliffe, Burney, Austen* (Chicago: University of Chicago Press, 1995), 63.
57 Johnson, *Equivocal Beings*, 63.
58 "Virtue," *Oxford English Dictionary*, Second Edition. Vol. 5 (Oxford: Clarendon Press, 1989), 676.

References

Clarke, Norma. *Dr. Johnson's Women*. London: Hambledon and London, 2000.
Davie, Donald. *A Gathered Church: The Literature of the English Dissenting Interest, 1700–1930*. New York: Oxford University Press, 1978.
"Enthusiasm." Oxford English Dictionary (OED). Second Edition. Vol. 5, Oxford: Clarendon Press, 1989.
Ferguson, Moira, and Janet Todd. *Mary Wollstonecraft*. Boston: Twayne Publishers, 1984.
Harcstark, Sylvia Myers. *The Bluestocking Circle: Women, Friendship, and the Life of the Mind in Eighteenth-Century England*. Oxford: Clarendon Press, 1992.

Heller, Deborah. "Bluestocking Salons and the Public Sphere." *Eighteenth-Century Life*, vol. 22, May 1998, 59–82.

Hofkosh, Sonia. "A Woman's Profession: Sexual Difference and the Romance of Authorship." *Studies in Romanticism*, vol. 32, Summer 1993, 245–72.

Johnson, Claudia L. *Equivocal Beings: Politics, Gender, and Sentimentality in the 1790s: Wollstonecraft, Radcliffe, Burney, Austen*. Chicago: University of Chicago Press, 1995.

Jones, Robert W. *Gender and the Formation of Taste in Eighteenth-Century Britain*. Cambridge: Cambridge University Press, 1998.

Kelly, Gary, ed., *Bluestocking Feminism: Writings of the Bluestocking Circle 1738–1785*, 6 vols. London: Pickering & Chatto, 1999.

McKendry, Andrew. "Dissenters," *Mary Wollstonecraft in Context*, eds. Nancy E. Johnson and Paul Keen. Cambridge: Cambridge University Press, 2020, 146–54.

Poovey, Mary. *The Proper Lady and the Woman Writer*. Chicago: The University of Chicago Press, 1984.

Richardson, Alan. "Mary Wollstonecraft on Education." *The Cambridge Companion to Mary Wollstonecraft*, ed. Claudia L. Johnson. Cambridge: Cambridge University Press, 2002, 24–41.

Taylor, Barbara. "The Religious Foundations of Mary Wollstonecraft's Feminism." *The Cambridge Companion to Mary Wollstonecraft*, ed. Claudia L. Johnson. Cambridge: Cambridge University Press, 2002, 99–118.

Thornburg, Mary Patterson. *The Monster in the Mirror*. Ann Arbor: UMI Research Press, 1987.

Todd, Janet, and Marilyn Butler, eds. *The Works of Mary Wollstonecraft*: Original Stories, vol. 4: 353–450. New York: New York University Press, 1989.

Tomalin, Claire. *The Life and Death of Mary Wollstonecraft*. New York: Harcourt Brace Jovanovich, 1974.

"Virtue." Oxford English Dictionary (OED), Second Edition. Vol. 5, Oxford: Clarendon Press, 1989.

Wollstonecraft, Mary. *The Vindications: The Rights of Men and the Rights of Woman*, eds. D. L. Macdonald and Kathleen Scherf. Ontario: Broadview Press, 1997.

Yadlon, Susan M. "The Bluestocking Circle: The Negotiation of 'Reasonable' Women." *Communication and Women's Friendships: Parallels and Intersections in Literature and Life*, eds. Janet Doubler Ward and Joanna Stephens Mink. Bowling Green: Bowling Green State University Popular Press, 1993, 113–31.

3 Portrait of an Intellectual Wife
Mary Wollstonecraft Godwin

Sing, O daughter of Zion; shout, O Israel; be glad and rejoice with all the heart, O daughter of Jerusalem.[1]

(Zephaniah 3:14)

The rise of women as intellectual "creatures" was indeed a revolutionary idea as much as dignifying the female emotions became Mary Wollstonecraft's primary ambition. Eighteenth-century culture experienced a revolution of sentiments affecting the social structure of society as more and more women began reading novels that no longer treated the subject of romantic love as taboo for the rising middle class. The dangerous passions against which Wollstonecraft cautioned women in her *Vindication of the Rights of Woman* (1792) grew, ironically, from the very sentiments that inspired her epistolary novel *Mary, a Fiction* (1788), her *Original Stories* (1788), and her unfinished novel *The Wrongs of Woman: or, Maria* (1798). This chapter attempts to unearth the causes that contributed to the revolution of sentiments particular to the role of women as seen through Mary Wollstonecraft's intimate experiences as daughter, mother, and wife, as well as her role as friend.

From fact to fiction Wollstonecraft endeavored to create a new voice for women, for the educated and uneducated alike, a voice that would acknowledge the equality of women. Voicing her adamant conviction that unchecked emotions shackle women rather than liberate them, Wollstonecraft reveals her own confessions of sentimentalism in her literature. As other eighteenth-century writers treated the concept of sentimentality, particularly in several epistolary novels that defined the passions such as Samuel Richardson's *Clarissa* (1747–48), Jean-Jacques Rousseau's *Julie ou la nouvelle Héloïse* (1757), and Germaine de Staël's *Corinne, or Italy* (1807), it encompassed a refinement of emotion and taste.[2] Jean H. Hagstrum explains the term sentimental as it applies to love and

DOI: 10.4324/9781003504238-3

friendship as a reconciliation of "the physical-emotional and the ethical-religious" elements of romantic relationships.[3]

Notably, Wollstonecraft achieved her recognition as an advocate of intellectual equality for women; however, she must also be acknowledged as the forerunner of women's emotional equality. Critical to this perspective on emotional equality is her personal struggle with the sentiments, characterized as feminine weakness of the emotions, and the importance her writing brings to enlarge the sensibilities of her readers. The *Oxford English Dictionary* defines sensibility as "emotional consciousness" and "in the 18th and early 19th century: [a] capacity for refined emotion; delicate sensitiveness of taste; also, readiness to feel compassion for suffering, and to be moved by the pathetic in literature or art."[4] Wollstonecraft reveals these eighteenth-century sensibilities in her relationships, through her correspondence and novels, and in her efforts for political and social reform. In Figure 3.1, the portrait of Mary Wollstonecraft reflects her calm demeanor of an ordinary wife, yet a wife with extraordinary ideas.

Figure 3.1 Portrait of Mary Wollstonecraft (1759–97) at age 39.
James Heath after John Opie.
Public Domain. *Wikimedia Commons*.

Her contributions to women's writing and to an enlarged domestic sphere have altered perceptions about ordinary women within this patriarchal culture. As Roxanne Eberle observes about women's writing during the eighteenth century,

> The two primary forces vying for the power to define the British woman were those voices aligned with "conservative" social forces intent upon positioning the virtuous British woman and her voice of moral rectitude within the private sphere and, on the other hand, "radicals" interested in seeing well-educated women enter the public sphere with a new authority.[5]

Wollstonecraft is uniquely seen here through a biographical and literary nexus that defines the ordinary woman, wife and mother, as an intellectual reformer for domestic women. From this perspective, Wollstonecraft's fervency for the social reform of marriage is expressed when she states, "but what I have in mind is to show the lack of liberty in the lives of ordinary women… ."[6] She explains further,

> Our language is hesitancy. When we speak from experience, we are told to speak of other less trivial things. In the end, we conform to what is expected of us, resigning ourselves to silence; or, like slaves, exchanging our stories in secret among ourselves—changing nothing in the every-day world. This is the way it has been for as long as history—but avaunt! ye waking dreams! It need not be so![7]

Wollstonecraft's voice of reform re-envisions the virtuous woman from a broader perspective that retains the conservative nature of Christian morality, while radically rejecting social restraints on women's intellectual and domestic advancement.

Throughout her daily life from childhood through adolescence, Wollstonecraft's feminist ideology developed, as she became a voice for other less outspoken women. Her intimate relationships with family members and her early friendships with young women described here paint a portrait of Mary Wollstonecraft as an impressionable young girl who evolves into an intellectual thinker and writer among poets like Samuel Taylor Coleridge. Coleridge and Wollstonecraft share their public voices in writing about domestic cares, family, and nature through an ideal perspective of the Romantic imagination. Philosophical writers like Jean-Jacques Rousseau and Edmund Burke, who examine the social roles of men and women, contribute to Wollstonecraft's debate on natural virtue and tradition in her feminist approach to intellectual equality. From within a circle of women's independent voices, Hannah More emerges as a contrast to

Wollstonecraft as the more conservative thinker while, like Wollstonecraft, she is also an avid proponent for the intellectual education of young girls. Other political voices and religious figures, like William Godwin, Richard Price, and Joseph Priestley, shape Wollstonecraft's political attitudes through the revolutionary era and influence her Christian beliefs as her moral philosophy on virtue and passion is explained here. Her portrait as an intellectual wife when studied in light of these literary, political, and religious influences brings Wollstonecraft's feminist ideology to a recognition that the eighteenth-century woman was emerging intellectually not only as a writer but more importantly, as an independent wife.

As Wollstonecraft publicizes the feminine voice within a masculine sphere of literary and political writers, her rhetoric penetrates the lives of ordinary women like Sara Fricker Coleridge. While Sara's independence and intellectual yearnings emerge within her domestic environs among the privacy of intimate friends and family members, Wollstonecraft's intellectualism asserts itself publicly through her essays, letter writing, and her fiction. Sara's self-expression remains within the traditions of marriage; on the other hand, Wollstonecraft's advice for female independence instructs married women from their position outside the marriage contract. As an unmarried woman, Wollstonecraft encourages married women to educate themselves within the boundaries of their current status. Remarkably, the unmarried Wollstonecraft significantly impacts the role of wives from her status as a single woman and unwed mother. Yet, Wollstonecraft engages in an intimate relationship with the American Gilbert Imlay without the formality of a legal contract. Through her roles as spiritual wife and mother to their daughter Fanny, Wollstonecraft cherishes the affections of a family and longs for a relationship with Imlay that disappoints her. From this vantage point, Wollstonecraft desires the intimacies of a husband/wife relationship unhampered by moral or legal standards. For Wollstonecraft, virtue is a natural expression of goodness and passion.

After her return to England in 1786 from her stay with the Kingsboroughs as their governess in Dublin, Wollstonecraft writes to her sisters about a new philosophical idea of virtue. She has been reading William Paley's philosophy and shares his definition of virtue that incorporates moral goodness with personal happiness: "Virtue is the doing good to mankind in obedience to the will of God, and for the sake of everlasting happiness."[8] Her attraction to Paley's philosophy aids Wollstonecraft's discovery of how the conservative view of virtue blends with the radical view toward a feminine independence. As Janet Todd explains, "William Paley, a kind of theological utilitarian, put morality within life and supported women's education and independence."[9] Wollstonecraft naturally aligns her perspective of virtue with Paley's utilitarian view, a view that popularized virtuous behavior for ordinary women like herself.

Wollstonecraft spent her childhood in the environs of London, moving with her family from Spitalfields to Essex to Yorkshire. She was born on 27 April 1759, 11 years earlier than Sara Fricker. Neither religion nor education was of particular importance to her mother, Elizabeth Dixon who was of Irish descent, nor her father, Edward John Wollstonecraft whose family had settled in Spitalfields from a rather poor and meager people.[10] Among her brothers and sisters, Mary was the oldest daughter followed by Eliza (1763) and Everina (1765). Her older brother Ned (Edward), who was born in 1757, was the family's favorite and in line to inherit their resources from farming and the weavers' trade. Another son was born, Henry Woodstock, who died in infancy in 1761, and then came the birth of a third son, James in 1768 and Charles in 1770, who was the youngest of the seven children.

As an adolescent between the ages of 12 and 14, Wollstonecraft's desire to separate from the rest of her family led to her attachment to another young 14-year-old girl named Jane Arden. Wollstonecraft had been schooled in the local village but found the Arden family's contentment with reading enviable. Biographer Claire Tomalin describes Wollstonecraft's dissatisfaction with her own family:

> Drinking was the general male habit, but he [her father] took his drink badly, and Mary's stories of sleeping on the landing and shielding her mother from his blows convey her view of him. Her willpower was strengthened in the process no doubt, but at the cost of learning to despise her father and pity her mother.[11]

The instability of her family relationships was a constant motivation for Wollstonecraft to formulate new conceptions of satisfying family relations.

Tomalin characterizes Wollstonecraft's relationship with Jane Arden as a stormy one that intensifies Wollstonecraft's emotional conflict throughout her life from the early age of 14. She writes to her friend Jane describing the intensity of her girlhood love:

> If I did not love you I should not write so;—I have a heart that scorns disguise, and a countenance which will not dissemble: I have formed romantic notions of friendship… . I am a little singular in my thoughts of love and friendship; I must have the first place or none.[12]

Declaring her "romantic notions of friendship," Wollstonecraft confesses her deepest emotions for her friend Jane expecting this love to be returned with the same ardor. However, she was to be disappointed that Jane did not express the same singularity of affection. Instead, through her writing Wollstonecraft found her singular expression of emotion in the lives of her characters. It was while living in Beverley that Wollstonecraft began to recognize the difficulties of the poor and uneducated which continued as an explicit theme in her novels. Suffering from her own family's uneven economic lifestyle, Wollstonecraft had developed her doubts about a happy and content family life and deeply considered the problems of achieving domestic happiness.

Several biographers of Mary Wollstonecraft, including Claire Tomalin, Janet Todd, Moira Ferguson, and Jean Detre, have provided a comprehensive and detailed portrait of her life. However, I will focus here on those relationships and biographical details that primarily shaped Wollstonecraft's conception of femininity. Her brand of femininity is a paradigm of self-directed womanhood that pervades the social construct of the eighteenth-century wife. Her attachments to young women such as Jane Arden and Fanny Blood show just how deeply Wollstonecraft yearned for the bonds of sisterhood. From within her own family relationships, Wollstonecraft experienced a sisterly affection for Eliza and Everina whom she nurtured and protected more as a mother would than as a sister. The formation of her thinking as an educator stemmed from experiences she had in her life as a companion to Mrs. Sarah Dawson, as a governess for Mrs. Kingsborough's children, and as the caretaker of her dying mother. It is no wonder that Wollstonecraft's endeavors as a nurturer and her own desires for affection led her to become a determined social reformer for wives. Tracing Wollstonecraft's history of female friendship provides critical insights into her development as an early feminist who defined femininity as a strength, not a weakness.

In 1774, while struggling to adjust to her family's move to Hoxton near London, Wollstonecraft once again yearns for the emotional comfort from a female friendship with another young woman, Fanny Blood. Both young girls were educated in the Clare household, an elderly couple who had no children of their own. They were taught to read literary authors and to develop the proper manners of a young lady: "… sewing, drawing, a little music, poetry reading and the art of writing a pretty letter."[13] In this female friendship, Wollstonecraft poured her sentimental and romantic notions of love, a love she had declared earlier for Jane Arden. As with most of her early attachments, Wollstonecraft was to experience disappointment, jealous of Fanny's affection for Wollstonecraft's sisters Eliza and Everina, and later for a young man, Hugh Skeys, with whom Fanny had fallen in love. As Tomalin remarks, "Fanny was no more able than Jane to sustain a passionate sentimental relationship of the kind Mary wanted; she found her eagerness greeted with an increasingly cool response."[14] It was just two years later when Wollstonecraft turned 18 that her family moved once again, this time to a farm in Laugharne, Wales, all the while planning her own future with Fanny. However, this female friendship was to end in sorrow for Wollstonecraft, and instead, she would turn her affections toward young men. Her emotional attachments for young women would reappear in her fictional stories illustrating how deeply Wollstonecraft's identity was indelibly engraved by strong relationships with women in her early life.

The cultural lifestyle of fashionable Bath with its emphasis on upper class manners and dress provided Wollstonecraft with a perspective on frivolous women that would be the center of her criticism. As a companion to Mrs. Sarah Dawson, the widow of a rich merchant who lived in the elegant shopping area of Milsom Street, Wollstonecraft experienced the social mobility of the upper class gentry. Even though she was enjoying the English countryside, she continued to yearn for the simpler lifestyle of her home. Todd explains, "But still the untasted gaieties oppressed her, still she longed for a 'more retired situation' where people did not dress 'amazingly' and she was not thought 'a very poor creature'."[15] By the fall of 1781 Wollstonecraft returned home to care for her dying mother, Elizabeth Wollstonecraft. The difficulties of caring for her dying mother under these unpleasant circumstances weighed on her sensibilities even more over months of painful and restrictive activities. Her mother died in April 1782 with no eulogy from Wollstonecraft. This tenuous mother–daughter relationship impressed Wollstonecraft with little desire to be a mother herself. As Todd suggests, "Mary's sense of herself as a mother to the younger children could not overwhelm her desire to be free of them all again: mothering was never quite as fulfilling a role in practice as she imagined."[16]

When her brother Ned agreed to take their sisters Eliza and Everina into his home, Wollstonecraft was finally free to pursue her life with Fanny Blood. The Bloods were a poor family and survived economically through the occupation of sewing. Wollstonecraft lived with the Blood family in Walham Green for over a year endearing herself to Fanny's brother George and her parents. Todd describes Wollstonecraft's experience with Fanny as "her emotional stay in the world" while others in her life had disappointed her. In her attempt to establish her life with Fanny, Wollstonecraft asserted her female independence on her frail friend just as she was to do with her sister Eliza. When Hugh Skeys finally proposes to Fanny and sends for her to come to Lisbon, Wollstonecraft has every intention of accompanying Fanny.

Wollstonecraft's dominating personality becomes aggressively harmful to her sister Eliza as well as to her friend Fanny. When Eliza marries Meredith Bishop in October 1782, Wollstonecraft is skeptical of the union. Her doubts about the marriage increase as she becomes progressively anxious about the dominant role of Eliza's husband and her sister's submissive response as his wife. Shortly after Eliza gives birth to a baby girl, she suffers from postpartum depression, a condition not readily understood at this time. Impulsively, Wollstonecraft rescues her sister from what she perceives to be a domineering husband; however, sadly, the situation reaches a grave ending. With the abandonment of Eliza's child to her husband and Wollstonecraft's accusations against Meredith Bishop, Eliza was forced to succumb to her sister's compelling advice. Despite Bishop's urging to reconcile with his wife, Wollstonecraft maintains a stronghold on her sister that keeps her estranged from her husband and child. Eliza's child died "… just days before her first birthday and was buried by her father in the Bermondsey church where she had been baptized."[17] While Wollstonecraft had justified her own actions assuming a defensive posture against Bishop and other men, she had also caused a calamity in Eliza's marriage and life. Despite her decisions that imposed on the marital relations of other women, Wollstonecraft persisted in the advocacy of female liberties and independence of mind and heart.

With new plans to establish a school in Newington Green among her dissenting friends, Wollstonecraft gathers her sisters, Everina and Eliza, along with Fanny Blood, to begin a life in educating young women. As Todd explains, "Mary, Eliza, Fanny and their friends bustled round and at the end of two or three weeks had attracted nearly twenty pupils while augmenting their income by two families of lodgers."[18] Her ingenuity and determination brought Wollstonecraft to northern London as a teacher in her own school where she accomplished her aspirations for independence. Her friendship with dissenting minister Dr. Richard Price encouraged the intellectualism of thought Wollstonecraft so eagerly desired. "Through Price, Mary learnt that, while faith helped the individual soul, reason aided the individual in society, and that morality and liberty were welded together," remarks Todd.[19] Wollstonecraft's theories on educating daughters grew from her two and half years running the Newington Green school along with her experiences as companion and governess in upper class society. She may have compensated for her own deprivation of family life through these friends and experiences, but she also offered young women the opportunity to exercise freedom of intellectual thinking uncommon to the female population. As Todd notes, "… Mary managed to play two roles for which she yearned: mother and daughter. She was the head of her all-female household, while acting the intellectual daughter outside."[20] Todd points to Dr. Price as the intellectual father Wollstonecraft needed in order to satisfy her intellectual growth. Her educational theories are further explored in the previous chapter through her writings on *Thoughts on the Education of Daughters* published in 1787 by Dissenter and publisher Joseph Johnson. Wollstonecraft expounds on John Locke's theory of the mind as a blank slate while she asserts that the passions must follow the rule of reason. As a young educator, Wollstonecraft recognized in herself and other women how critically the roles of reason and passion operate to elevate young women into independent and intellectual partners as wives.

As a domestic wife, Wollstonecraft embodies three aspects of the marriage partner that redefine the Romantic role of the wife—the passionate, the spiritual, and the literary. Contrary to traditional traits of modesty and submissiveness identified with the wife, Wollstonecraft re-imagined the role of the wife with feminine virtues of intellect and independence. Through each of her significant relationships with men, Wollstonecraft derived her notion of the idealization of the feminine that exists in society today. However, vulnerable to her own passions and the upheaval of social order produced by the French Revolution, Wollstonecraft turned her quest for happiness to reform the role of the wife for all women. The problem, she suggests, is in denying a woman her natural ability to think intelligently. In Chapter 4 of *The Rights of Woman*, she concludes, "Thus understanding, strictly speaking, has been denied to woman; and instinct, sublimated into wit and cunning, for the purposes of life, has been substituted in its stead."[21] While Wollstonecraft's voice of impropriety was silenced in an atmosphere of righteous conservatism, her ideas on educating women were heard through the fictional lives of her characters with whom the women in society could safely empathize without further disrupting the balance of domestic engagement between husband and wife. As Mary Poovey asserts,

> Wollstonecraft's refusal to abandon the ideal of "true sensibility", even after she had recognized that the romantic expectations endemic to such sensibility were agents of the very institutions she was trying to criticize, reflects her persistent yearning for some connection between spiritual values and real, everyday experience.[22]

As a result, women in eighteenth-century society discovered in their individuality a spiritual nature uncommon to their sex and contradictory to their domesticity.

In the midst of an unstable social and political climate, Wollstonecraft projected her disdain for women who identified themselves as creatures of instinct and whose reliance on feminine charms and beauty could be traced to the submissive female, a model of femininity characterized in John Milton's poetic treatise *Paradise Lost*. Paradoxically, in Wollstonecraft's own romantic undoing of the intellectual wife, she pursued an American lover, Gilbert Imlay, with whom she could express "the depths of a passionate, reciprocal exchange of love."[23] Recreating the same image of a passionate woman in her protagonist Maria in *The Wrongs of Woman: or, Maria*, Wollstonecraft justifies the sensibilities of love as virtuous. Her fictional character Maria, wrongly imprisoned in a madhouse and oppressed in an unloving marriage, finds romance with another unfortunate soul,

Henry Darnford, whom she meets while locked away. Maria exemplifies a feminine sensibility thought to be excessive in women and in romantic novels, which sparked the conflict between reason and passion evidenced in Wollstonecraft's life.

The intimate events of Wollstonecraft's life found their home in her literature. While Wollstonecraft never formally wrote her confessions in an autobiographical genre, like Jean-Jacques Rousseau, she pursued a similar literary journey that was to reveal her intimate relationships with family and friends and provide a channel for self-understanding. In 397 AD St. Augustine introduced the confessional genre when he recorded his transgressions in order to cleanse himself for a life of spiritual grace. From the historical publication of *The Confessions* came not only an enlivened hope in Christian faith and duty but also a paradigm for self-discovery that precedes modern psychology and one that Rousseau emulated in his *Confessions* in 1782. Rousseau further expanded a revival of the personal diary with an emphasis on education and nature in order to explain human behavior in his *Emile*, a didactic text on how to educate boys and girls from infancy to adulthood. However, as an individual woman, Wollstonecraft exposed her personal sins in her writings, for the sake of all women, which unfortunately tainted her success as a social reformer of feminine virtues. As Poovey suggests, "Perceptive, intelligent writers like Mary Wollstonecraft continued to envision social change and personal fulfillment primarily in terms of individual effort, and therefore they did not focus on the systemic constraints exercised by such legal and political institutions as marriage."[24]

Wollstonecraft insisted that women disengage themselves from the domestic limitations imposed on married women, limitations compromising their intelligence and keeping them inferior. As Cynthia L. White notes, "The eighteenth century began with an intellectual revival in which women participated, but it ended with Mary Wollstonecraft's impassioned denunciation of sexual discrimination showing that the intervening years had witnessed a marked change in social attitudes."[25] Early social reformers like Wollstonecraft and Rousseau significantly shaped the subjective identity of the wife, mother, and independent woman and together with the women's periodicals provided a deeper understanding of gendered spaces and domains. The ideological opposition that these two writers represent on the social and moral behavior of women is central to the ambivalence of eighteenth-century virtues. Rousseau's philosophical perspective of the natural man and woman asserts that a woman's ability to reason and her physical constitution are inferior to a man's intelligence and physicality, but she is superior in her ability to attract a man. Yet, despite the fundamental differences in Rousseau's and Wollstonecraft's ideologies on feminine virtue, both appealed to married women to become their husbands' intellectual partners as well as acknowledge their own sensibilities. Janet Todd writes, "Now, with the help of Rousseau ..., Wollstonecraft embraced the individualist and self-gratifying values of sensibility, its preference for moral fineness over social rank and birth, its compensatory élitism of mind and exquisite physical feeling."[26]

With the publication of *The Rights of Woman* in 1792 came opposition to Wollstonecraft's radical view of women even though its audience ranged from "Glasgow to Blackburn and Lichfield."[27] Many refused to even read it and its sales were considerably low in comparison to Hannah More's *Strictures on the Modern System of Education* which sold "11,000 copies in the three years between 1799 and 1801" and advocated the type of conduct literature Wollstonecraft challenged in her book.[28] "By contrast *The Rights of Woman* sold only about 1500 to 3000 copies in its first five years in print and very little throughout the next fifty," explains Todd. Opposition came also from within her own family as "Wollstonecraft's sister quoted a popular view of the book as 'the most indecent Rhapsody that ever was penned by man or woman'."[29] As evidenced by the unconventional circumstances of her life over the five years that followed the publication of *The Rights of Woman*, Wollstonecraft also experienced scathing recriminations of her social behavior and her artistic endeavors from Edmund Burke and other conservative thinkers: "Horace Walpole classed Wollstonecraft with Paine as one of 'the philosophizing serpents we have in our bosom', ..."[30] Her ineluctable assertions of women's equality fostered the demise of her reputation as a writer and of her character as a proper lady. Finally, when William Godwin published her memoirs exposing her scandals with Henry Fuseli and Gilbert Imlay, the reviews of *The Rights of Woman* increasingly admonished readers against the liberties advocated in the book. Her affairs with the Swiss artist and American businessman are treated in more detail in the next chapter as I examine Wollstonecraft's romantic feelings and legal bonds of matrimony.

Resistance to Wollstonecraft's idea of natural female virtue provoked a feminist outcry to sunder traditional bands of oppression, an outcry that was later stifled by the French. The current was turning against feminist activities as Claire Tomalin notes:

> In January 1793 an article in *Révolution de Paris* alleged that the women's clubs had become the bane of domestic happiness. A Madame Blandin-Demoulin of Dijon was so angered by this that she sat down and composed an answer, which the editor had the grace to print. It was thoughtful and articulate; she was a republican, and well-read, and she quoted Montesquieu and called on her countrymen to renounce despotism towards women, since no virtue could be expected

of slaves. Some of her expressions suggest that she had been reading Wollstonecraft as well as Montesquieu.[31]

With the Reign of Terror, Wollstonecraft witnessed the imprisonment and deaths of many friends who supported revolutionary ideas: Helen Williams and Stone with his wife were arrested, Schlabrendorf imprisoned, Brissot and other Girondins executed as well as Madame Roland. As evidence of the further deterioration of women's rights, divorce laws were repealed in 1816, signifying a return to an oppressive social condition for women.[32]

Through her novel *Wrongs of Woman, or Maria,* Wollstonecraft illustrates female oppression, especially of the married woman, finding sympathetic reception from an audience of female readers. Maria suffers from a deep resentment toward her husband who was responsible for her incarceration. The narrator explains,

> Now she endeavoured to brace her mind to fortitude, and to ask herself what was to be her employment in her dreary cell? Was it not to effect her escape, to fly to the succour of her child, and to baffle the selfish schemes of her tyrant—her husband?[33]

The parallels between Wollstonecraft's and Imlay's romantic relationship and her fictionalized Maria, imprisoned by her husband's consent, suggest that Wollstonecraft had awakened to Imlay's mistreatment of her. Her character's adultery, for which she is later tried by a judge in her own defense, challenged the unscrupulous customs of society and the inadequacies of marriage laws that protected a tyrannical husband. A wife was left with little choice either to submit to the tyranny of an unloving husband or to face a life of impoverishment. To exercise moralistic virtue and remain chaste meant that women would be subject to an oppressive patriarchal system.

In the beginning of Chapter VI the narrator writes,

> Active as love was in the heart of Maria, the story she had just heard made her thoughts take a wider range. The opening buds of hope closed, as if they had put forth too early, and the happiest day of her life was overcast by the most melancholy reflections.[34]

Here Maria has just heard the tragic circumstances of Jemima's life—the young servant girl attending Maria in prison—a life of forced prostitution, poverty, and hard labor. As her compassion for the young girl deepens, Maria's fears heighten:

Sleep fled from her eyelids, while she dwelt on the wretchedness of unprotected infancy, till sympathy with Jemima changed to agony, when it seemed probable that her own babe might even now be in the very state she so forcibly described.[35]

Maria's horror over a separation from her own child mirrors Wollstonecraft's fear for her child, Fanny, named for her friend Fanny Blood who died from consumption in Portugal after giving birth to a baby boy. Neither an infirm Fanny Blood nor her child survived the ordeal of the mother's childbirth. Struggling as a young mother on her own, abandoned by her child's father, Imlay, Wollstonecraft suffered emotional wounds that led her to attempt suicide. Consequently, her relationship with Imlay caused Wollstonecraft to experience emotional conflict through an intense array of passions—love, grief, joy, and despair.

Plagued by her own inability to transcend the sentimentalism in her life, Wollstonecraft sought to express these passions in fictional tales as well as rhetorical arguments to find a solution to the vulnerability of women. At times Wollstonecraft succumbed to her own sentimental vulnerabilities in her attraction to men. Through her reading of *Paradise Lost,* she was drawn to scenes of sensuality between Adam and Eve. As Todd notes, "In *Paradise Lost* in those scenes which so fascinated and disturbed Wollstonecraft, wise Adam and lovely Eve punctuated their conversation with 'kisses pure'."[36] While Wollstonecraft invoked sensual Miltonic tones in her romantic conversations with both Imlay and Godwin, she disparaged the same vulnerability of sentiments in other women. Her adversaries often harshly criticized her rhetorical style in *The Rights of Woman* "as flowery, flowing, weak, and confused."[37] In fact, as Ferguson and Todd remark, "The *Critical Review* concluded that there must be something rotten in Wollstonecraft's reasoning since her results were so offensive, and it advised the author to seek delicacy, elegance, and sensibility so that she might grow pleasing and achieve happiness."[38] As Wollstonecraft historicizes the degradation of women, she assumes a cynical tone exaggerating the weakness of women as pleasure-givers:

> Pleasure is the business of woman's life, according to the present modification of society, and while it continues to be so, little can be expected from weak beings. Inheriting, in a lineal descent from the first fair defect in nature, the sovereignty of beauty, they have, to maintain their power, resigned the natural rights, which the exercise of reason might have procured them, and chosen rather to be short-lived queens than labour to obtain the sober pleasures that arise from equality.[39]

54 *The Social Imagination of the Romantic Wife in Literature*

Here Wollstonecraft designs her argument around the weakness of the very first woman, Eve, with a reference to Milton's Book 10 of *Paradise Lost*, "the first fair defect in nature." Her vehement attack on the supposed inferiority of women strikes at the heart of Rousseau's argument, that women are inferior by nature because of an extreme dependence on their emotions. The emotional frailty of women rouses the educated reader to think of the first woman, the original weak female, Milton's Eve who is content in her submissiveness to Adam. Wollstonecraft exhorts women to unshackle themselves from the submissive Eve and claim their equality to men through exercising their natural rights. Reason, asserts Wollstonecraft, restores women to an equal stature with men and awakens them from the mythical Eve.

In contrast to her indelicate rhetoric in *The Rights of Woman*, Wollstonecraft's language softens in her later work *Letters Written During a Short Residence in Sweden, Norway and Denmark* published in 1796. In Letter VIII she writes,

> You have sometimes wondered, my dear friend, at the extreme affection of my nature—But such is the temperature of my soul—It is not the vivacity of youth, the hey-day of /existence. For years have I endeavoured to calm an impetuous tide—labouring to make my feelings take an orderly course.—It was striving against the stream.—I must love and admire with warmth, or I sink into sadness. Tokens of love which I have received have rapt me in elysium—purifying the heart they enchanted.— My bosom still glows.—Do not saucily ask, repeating Sterne's question, "Maria, is it still so warm?" Sufficiently, O my God! has it been chilled by sorrow and unkindness—still nature will prevail—and if I blush at recollecting past enjoyment, it is the rosy hue of pleasure heightened by modesty; for the blush of modesty and shame are as distinct as the emotions by which they are produced.[40]

As Wollstonecraft blushes from modesty derived through an understanding of her own feminine virtues, at the same time, she confesses her transgressions against her own sex, aware of the shame of excessive sentimentality. Her most notable social and sexual transgressions are: Wollstonecraft's strong emotional attachment to the married Swiss artist Fuseli, her affair with Imlay, and the birth of Imlay's child out of wedlock. Yet, perhaps even more egregious was Wollstonecraft's artistic transgression. Her writings express the astute intellect and bold rhetoric of a man juxtaposed with the powerful emotions of a woman, reinforcing the autonomy of individual self-expression in eighteenth-century society.

Wollstonecraft's *Vindication of the Rights of Woman* combines both the fervor of a passionate and independent woman and the sensibility and reason of an enlightened female. Couched within the restraints of a society that applauded a woman's propriety, and in Wollstonecraft's words a "blind propriety," she risked her personal reputation to insist that women were the immortal heirs of a "nobler spring" than most women dared to contemplate for themselves. Unafraid to attack a woman's view of herself as a product of beauty, designed by man and for man's pleasure, Wollstonecraft removed the façade of woman as the inferior sex. Paradoxically, the passions Wollstonecraft challenged in herself and in other women as inferior feelings were also the impetus for reforming the duties of the virtuous woman. Wollstonecraft's life was devoted to the improvement of women in society, and in particular, to the social, emotional, and intellectual stature of the wife. As we explore the development of her goal to liberate women from cultural restraints, the changing roles of political, economic, social, religious, and literary ideologies will demonstrate a climate conducive to its accomplishment. Powerful shifts in concepts of virtue, happiness, and enthusiasm underlie the domestic gains achieved.

In order to better understand the evolution of the married woman during the late eighteenth century, the life of Wollstonecraft shows her struggle between virtue and passion that characterizes the changing ideologies of this period. The scholarly debate that distinguishes the convictions of the Neoclassical view from the Romantic perspective also contrasts virtue with passion, virtue as modesty seen by writers such as Samuel Johnson and other rational thinkers, and passion as emotion characterized by Romantic writers such as Samuel Taylor Coleridge. According to this schism of thought, passion belongs to the imagination of the Romantic Age as ideas of fancy and instability, while virtue belongs to the rationalism of the Enlightenment ensuring order through a grounded empirical system of ideas.[41] Several scholars including W. J. Bate in the mid-1900s and, more recently, James Engell have shown that many thinkers during the eighteenth century were fascinated with the power of the imagination and its influence on the domestic sphere. As L. J. Swingle notes, "This yoking of the Romantic age with imagination and of the preceding age with an anti-imaginative bias flies in the face of considerable scholarly evidence."[42] The relationship between these two eras, and therefore, between these two distinct ideologies, is more complicated than it seems at first. Wollstonecraft's emphasis on virtue as a natural expression of feminine identity, unrestrained by institutional parameters, critically attacks Edmund Burke's association of female virtue with the rationalism of the age.

The purpose here is not to debate the ideas of the Romantics, but rather to recognize prevalent ideologies in this literary and historical period such as Neoclassicism, humanism, and individualism, systems of thought counteracted by a "second powerful cultural movement of the age" as defined by Edmund Burke in his 1790 text *Reflections on the Revolution in France*. Marilyn Butler describes Burke's views on family, marriage, and parenting as positive ideas:

> The Burkean positives are family affections and loyalties, hearth and home; hence, by extension, the greater family made by the nation, a hierarchy with the king at its head; and continuity with the past, especially with the inherited creed which it is the Church's business to preserve.[43]

This widespread concern to preserve the value of domesticity confines the role of the wife to a sense of duty and the home to a sense of responsibility. The national and domestic identities of wives will be more fully explored in Chapter 7 to show how the female identity links the interrelationship of home and nation. As the individuality of the wife becomes more respected, her role and household attain a new freedom that modifies virtue independently of established conventions. One example of domestic happiness is illustrated in the Romantic poetry of Samuel Taylor Coleridge. In Coleridge's poem "Frost at Midnight" (1798) where he pauses to notice the sleeping babe, we encounter a new freedom of domestic insights that exalts the mundane aspect of child-raising and praises the natural growth of the child:

>   Dear Babe, that sleepest cradled by my side,
> Whose gentle breathings, heard in this deep calm,
> Fill up the intersperséd vacancies
> And momentary pauses of the thought!
> (lines 44–47)

Recognizing the continuity of life that connects growth to nature and God, Coleridge imagines the infant in pantheistic terms, thereby breaking through a logical conception of growth:

> But thou, my babe! Shalt wander like a breeze
> By lakes and sandy shores, beneath the crags
> Of ancient mountain, and beneath the clouds,
> … so shalt thou see and hear
> The lovely shapes and sounds intelligible
> Of that eternal language, which thy God
> Utters, who from eternity doth teach
> Himself in all, and all things in himself.[44]
> (lines 54–62)

The calm creates an atmosphere in which the infant can be heard breathing, a focus on the individual child, and yet Coleridge also establishes this individualism within the magnitude of nature's forms, comparing the babe's growth to a breeze. While Coleridge's vision of the child advances beyond the moment, in contrast, Burke's views of family and home are more narrowly established in the religious and political institutions of the period. For Wollstonecraft, Coleridge's poetic exaltation of the child in a domestic setting furthers her argument against Burke's conventional attachment to home.

For Wollstonecraft, moving away from her family was both an emotional need for independence and a need for financial survival. As Janet Todd notes,

> Didactic fiction of the early nineteenth century showed the moral value of paid employment for females, but this was not so when Mary was growing up, and the novelists of her day routinely portrayed the horror of ladies earning bread outside the family.[45]

A domineering father, Edward Wollstonecraft, and a submissive mother, Elizabeth, marked Wollstonecraft's early family life. "The pains of marriage were engraved on Mary's mind in this demeaning tie of father-tyrant and mother-slave, and the authority this mother naturally had over her was tainted by the vision of improper submission," explains Todd.[46] In addition, the traditional roles of a domineering father and submissive mother that governed Wollstonecraft's life were historically established by the rise of first Puritan and then Evangelical principles during the seventeenth and eighteenth centuries.[47] During this period in Wollstonecraft's life, her separation from family and the formation of her emotional relationships with both men, for instance, Joshua Waterhouse, and women, her close ties to Fanny Blood, began to shape her social philosophy of reforming the ideology of a proper lady, influencing others to rethink and redefine virtue in the married woman.

Several disparate political and religious views that permeated the eighteenth century and impacted the proprieties of married women polarized Christian duty with feminist thinking. The most obvious controversy existed between radical Dissenters, or Unitarians, and Evangelicals. Wollstonecraft's relationships with Dr. Richard Price and later on, Joseph Priestley, both radical Dissenters, began when she established a school with her sisters, Eliza and Everina, and her close friend Fanny Blood, for the education of young girls in Newington Green, a village situated in the country near to Islington. The individualism that characterizes early feminist ideology was also an attribute of the Dissenting movement linking democratic ideals with the reform of feminine virtue based on the intellectualism of women. As Claire Tomalin indicates, it was during this period in Wollstonecraft's life that she developed her idea of individualism as a critical element in her later philosophy: "Mary wanted to believe that individual willpower and energy could better the state of the world, and that human nature was improving, as Price and his friends thought."[48] However, like Hannah More, a leading figure in the Evangelical movement, Wollstonecraft focused her social concerns on the poverty-stricken and the oppressed; therefore, both women had more deeply in common than many scholars have acknowledged. As Norma Clarke notes, Hannah More was

> a social activist: passionately anti-slavery (much of Bristol's wealth came from the hugely profitable slave trade), she urged people to boycott sugar, wrote a poem, "The Slave Trade", and carried about a shocking picture showing the slaves crammed in the holds of ships which she brought out at tea parties.[49]

Furthermore, not only was More educated at "a successful school for girls" which was established by her sisters, Mary and Elizabeth, but later, she also became a teacher there and wrote a play, "The Search after Happiness," which was "written for, performed by and attended on its first production by an audience exclusively female."[50]

Despite a glaring contradiction in their adherence to religious doctrine, both women also embraced a close faith in the virtues taught through the Holy Scriptures. While Wollstonecraft chose not to leave her Anglican faith for the beliefs of the Dissenters, she did, however, identify the oppression of women with the oppression of this radical group of intellectuals because they each attacked the traditions of their society. As Tomalin explains,

> The Dissenters in fact had turned their disabilities to good purpose; debarred from the universities, for instance, they had set up their own academies which proved markedly superior to anything Oxford or Cambridge had to offer: in particular, and alone, they taught history, science and economics, suggested a critical approach to the text of the Bible and encouraged speculative thought and debate on points of religion.[51]

Even though Wollstonecraft heralded many unconventional views that challenged institutional principles, she held chastity of high importance for both sexes. Yet, she incurred the disdain of the middle classes because her opposition to the convention was viewed as immoral even though she herself was not an advocate of immorality. Wollstonecraft's outspoken ways challenged the conventional view of sexuality with an understanding that sexuality was a natural behavior. As More and other women in the bluestocking circle advanced a sisterhood among women based on their intellectual abilities and their purity, so did Wollstonecraft in her writings. She states,

> Yet, if love be the supreme good, let woman be only educated to inspire it, and let every charm be polished to intoxicate the senses; but, if they be moral beings, let them have a chance to become intelligent; and let love to man be only a part of that glowing flame of universal love, which, after encircling humanity, mounts in grateful incense to God.[52]

While Wollstonecraft often despaired at her own emotional weakness, especially when it came to falling in love with Gilbert Imlay, she persisted in conquering these feminine frailties. Relying on her sensibility of nature to uplift her spirits, Wollstonecraft struggled to resolve a painful love affair. On her way to visit a family in Gothenburg, Sweden, she writes,

> I had forgot the horrors I had witnessed in France, which had cast a gloom over all nature, and suffering the enthusiasm of my character, too often, gracious God! damped by the tears of disappointed affection, to be lighted up afresh, care took wing while simple fellow feeling expanded my heart... .I walked on, still delighted with the rude / beauties of the scene; for the sublime often gave place imperceptibly to the beautiful, dilating the emotions which were painfully concentrated.[53]

Her discernment of the beauty around her amplified the strain of loneliness and separation she experienced while traveling without her lover. She intuitively felt the purity of nature wash over her while distraught from a want of human affection. Yet, some scholars, such as Todd and Poovey, in their efforts to dichotomize virtue and passion argue that Wollstonecraft was unable "to achieve genuine freedom" in her effort to transcend her femaleness. Todd suggests that Wollstonecraft "underestimated the power of polarization and physical difference,"[54] while Poovey criticizes Wollstonecraft's unresolved issue of "a fundamentally nonsexual human essence."[55] Despite these criticisms of Wollstonecraft's failure to achieve freedom from her own romantic weakness, she demonstrated through her personal struggles and social concerns for married women "a paradigm of femininity [that] had come to dominate the experience of most middle-class Englishwomen by the last half of the eighteenth century,"[56] and this paradigm continues to evolve, reshaping the nature of propriety as the married woman achieves her rightful inheritance.

From within Wollstonecraft's circle of dissenting friends, she found a non-conforming spirit that fortified her reliance on natural virtues. Her marriage to William Godwin was a promising outcome although one that both writers resisted as an institutional imposition on marital relations. In his reply to Burke's *Reflections*, Godwin wrote a political treatise on *An Enquiry Concerning the Principles of Political Justice, and Its Influence on General Virtue and Happiness*, begun in 1790 and published in 1793. The dissenting views of Godwin, as a moralist and philosopher, challenged the established views on religion and the monarchy as well as conventional morals that Burke and others held in support of the established Church and the King. In fact, as Butler explains,

> *Political Justice* (1793), by the former dissenting minister, William Godwin, can be viewed as a pioneering work in a new intellectual movement, anarchism; but, with its emphasis on the "sacred and indefeasible right of private judgement", it also draws deeply on the old feeling inherited from the Commonwealthmen and the sects.[57]

Moreover, as Godwin developed his moral doctrine and radical stand against the institution of marriage in *Political Justice* and in his novel *Caleb Williams; or Things as They Are* (1794), he also became a writer of sentimental novels and children's literature. As Marilyn Gaul notes, "… Godwin's radicalism was primarily an inevitable working out of basic and familiar concepts that had informed the most respectable eighteenth-century thinkers: Reason, Equality, Perfectibility, and Necessity."[58]

As he explored the domestic roles of family relationships in his writing, he also encountered a sudden conflict between his ideology of social freedom and the practicality of a wife and child. In his personal life, Godwin's decision to marry Mary Wollstonecraft in March of 1797 demonstrates a more pragmatic approach to impending fatherhood and husbanding than his radical beliefs allowed. The reality of family life, however, did not abate his political views altogether as evidenced in the political undertones of his daughter's novel, Mary Shelley's *Frankenstein; Or, the Modern Prometheus* (1818). Butler recognizes the political attack in Shelley's gothic novel "on the current alliance between conservative politics and High Church or Catholic religion," which she also acknowledges "revive[s] the conscious liberalism of Gothic in the 1790s, and run[s] counter to the strongest trend in immediately contemporary Romantic writing from the Continent."[59] Consequently, the pervading attention to contradictory beliefs and values of domestic tranquility, fostered by the political and religious views in Godwin's writing and his age, can also be seen as a central focus in the shifting ideologies on the passions in Wollstonecraft's *Vindications*. In Figure 3.2, William Godwin appears in a sketch as confident and stately, asserting his role as a political author.

Portrait of an Intellectual Wife 61

Figure 3.2 Portrait of William Godwin (1756–1836).
From *Illustrations of Phrenology* (1820) by Sir George Steuart Mackenzie.
Public Domain. *Wikimedia Commons.*

Along with the acknowledgment that women were by nature moral and rational creatures came the harsher awareness that wives and mothers should repress feelings of pleasure to indulge in suffering. Mary Patterson Thornburg states, "Certainly, suffering is considered in Christian tradition to be a purging and purifying experience, and sentimental tradition retains this sense of it; … ."[60] In Wollstonecraft's novels *Mary, a Fiction* and *The Wrongs of Woman: or, Maria*, both female protagonists suffer in circumstances that challenge their delicate natures and sensibilities by a society that imposes unfair social and legal impositions on women. Wollstonecraft's philosophy on the passions can be compared to another powerful feminist writer, Germaine de Staël who wrote, "Compared with the sufferings which sentiment occasions, the external circumstances which may disturb the union of hearts, are of inferior importance…. Nevertheless, souls of a sublime virtue have experienced in themselves invincible struggles."[61] Wollstonecraft's adamant resistance to the social

62 *The Social Imagination of the Romantic Wife in Literature*

and moral limitations imposed on wives is coupled with a sentimentalism of the female spirit that enhances intellectualism through passion and enthusiasm. As she encounters difficulties in her romantic relationships, first as an unmarried and then as a married woman, her intellectualism and benevolence serve to liberate her from a tradition of oppression. The next chapter attempts to draw a comparison of two wives, as Sara Fricker Coleridge's own married life with its disappointments elevates the ordinary role of the wife to the literary status achieved in Wollstonecraft's life as an extraordinary one.

Notes

1. From Zephaniah 3:14, King James Version of the Bible.
2. The *Oxford English Dictionary* defines sentimental as "characterized by or exhibiting refined and elevated feeling." Also from the *OED*, sentiment is defined as an "exercise or manifestation of 'sensibility'; emotional reflection or meditation."
3. Jean H. Hagstrum, *Sex and Sensibility: Ideal and Erotic Love from Milton to Mozart* (Chicago: University of Chicago Press, 1980), 161.
4. See the online version of the *Oxford English Dictionary* (www.oed.com).
5. Roxanne Eberle, *Chastity and Transgression in Women's Writing, 1792–1897: Interrupting the Harlot's Progress* (New York: Palgrave, 2002), 6.
6. Jean Detre, *A Most Extraordinary Pair: Mary Wollstonecraft and William Godwin* (New York: Doubleday, 1975), 81.
7. Detre, *A Most Extraordinary Pair*, 81.
8. Janet Todd, *Mary Wollstonecraft: A Revolutionary Life* (New York: Columbia University Press, 2000), 110.
9. Todd, *Mary Wollstonecraft*, 110.
10. Claire Tomalin, *The Life and Death of Mary Wollstonecraft* (New York: Harcourt Brace Jovanovich, 1974), 2.
11. Tomalin, *The Life and Death*, 7.
12. Tomalin, *The Life and Death*, 8.
13. Tomalin, *The Life and Death*, 13.
14. Tomalin, *The Life and Death*, 14.
15. Todd, *Mary Wollstonecraft*, 35.
16. Todd, *Mary Wollstonecraft*, 40.
17. Todd, *Mary Wollstonecraft*, 57.
18. Todd, *Mary Wollstonecraft*, 56.
19. Todd, *Mary Wollstonecraft*, 60.
20. Todd, *Mary Wollstonecraft*, 61.
21. Mary Wollstonecraft, *The Vindications: The Rights of Men and the Rights of Woman*, eds. D. L. Macdonald and Kathleen Scherf (Ontario: Broadview Press, 2001), 168.
22. Mary Poovey, *The Proper Lady and the Woman Writer* (Chicago: University of Chicago Press, 1984), 108.

23 Poovey, *The Proper Lady*, 82.
24 Poovey, *The Proper Lady*, 109.
25 Cynthia L. White, *Women's Magazines 1693–1968* (London: Michael Joseph, 1970), 33.
26 Todd, *Mary Wollstonecraft*, 103.
27 Todd, *Mary Wollstonecraft*, 184.
28 Todd, *Mary Wollstonecraft*, 185.
29 Moira Ferguson and Janet Todd, *Mary Wollstonecraft* (Boston: Twayne Publishers, 1984), 72.
30 Ferguson and Todd, *Mary Wollstonecraft*, 72.
31 Tomalin, *The Life and Death*, 157.
32 Tomalin, *The Life and Death*, 165.
33 Janet Todd and Marilyn Butler, eds., *The Works of Mary Wollstonecraft*: The Wrongs of Woman: or, Maria, vol. 1: 75–184 (New York: New York University Press, 1989), 86.
34 Todd and Butler, eds. *The Works of Mary Wollstonecraft*: The Wrongs of Woman: or, Maria, vol. 1: 75–184, 120.
35 Todd and Butler, eds., *The Works of Mary Wollstonecraft*: The Wrongs of Woman; or Maria, vol. 1: 75–184, 120.
36 Todd, *Mary Wollstonecraft*, 396.
37 Ferguson and Todd, *Mary Wollstonecraft*, 73.
38 Ferguson and Todd, *Mary Wollstonecraft*, 73.
39 Wollstonecraft, *The Rights of Woman*, 170.
40 Janet Todd and Marilyn Butler, eds., *The Works of Mary Wollstonecraft*: Letters Written in Sweden, Norway and Denmark, vol. 6: 237–348 (New York: New York University Press, 1989), 280.
41 To better explain the theoretical views of the late eighteenth century, L. J. Swingle argues,

> One type of Romantic theory—what Morse Peckham has termed the "attributional construction of Romantic theory"—involves seeing the eighteenth century as an age dominated by a relatively stable ideology. Romanticism, then, when it is viewed as a "movement" in revolt against eighteenth-century thinking, seems a competing ideology. Hence we arrive at a Romantic philosophy set off against an Augustan or Neoclassical philosophy.
> (*The Obstinate Questionings of English Romanticism* (Baton Rouge: Louisiana State University Press, 1987), 14)

42 Swingle, *The obstinate questionings*, 15.
43 Marilyn Butler, *Romantics, Rebels and Reactionaries: English Literature and Its Background 1760–1830* (New York: Oxford University Press, 1982), 180.
44 Ernest Hartley Coleridge, ed., *Coleridge: Poetical Works* (Oxford: Oxford University Press, 1988), 242.
45 Todd, *Mary Wollstonecraft*, 28.
46 Todd, *Mary Wollstonecraft*, 5.
47 Poovey, *A Proper Lady*, 6–7.

48 Tomalin, *The Life and Death*, 34.
49 Norma Clarke, *Dr. Johnson's Women* (London: Hambledon and London, 2000), 155.
50 Clarke, *Dr. Johnson's Women*, 156.
51 Tomalin, *The Life and Death*, 43.
52 Wollstonecraft, *The Rights of Woman*, 185.
53 Todd and Butler, eds., *The Works of Mary Wollstonecraft*: Letters Written in Sweden, Norway and Denmark, vol. 6: 237–348, 247.
54 Todd, *Mary Wollstonecraft*, 186.
55 Poovey, *A Proper Lady*, 81.
56 Poovey, *A Proper Lady*, 30.
57 Butler, *Romantics*, 44.
58 Marilyn Gaul, *English Romanticism: The Human Context* (New York: W. W. Norton, 1988), 132.
59 Butler, *Romantics*, 161.
60 Mary Patterson Thornburg, *The Monster in the Mirror* (Ann Arbor: UMI Research Press, 1987), 23.
61 Germaine de Staël, "On the Influence of the Passions," *La Belle Assemblée* (October 1813), 109–10.

References

Butler, Marilyn. *Romantics, Rebels and Reactionaries: English Literature and Its Background 1760–1830*. New York: Oxford University Press, 1982.
Clarke, Norma. *Dr. Johnson's Women*. London: Hambledon and London, 2000.
Coleridge, Ernest Hartley, ed. *Coleridge: Poetical Works*. Oxford: Oxford University Press, 1988.
de Staël, Germaine. "On the Influence of the Passions." *La Belle Assemblée*, October 1813.
Detre, Jean. *A Most Extraordinary Pair: Mary Wollstonecraft and William Godwin*. New York: Doubleday, 1975.
Eberle, Roxanne. *Chastity and Transgression in Women's Writing, 1792–1897: Interrupting the Harlot's Progress*. New York: Palgrave, 2002.
Ferguson, Moira, and Janet Todd. *Mary Wollstonecraft*. Boston: Twayne Publishers, 1984.
Gaul, Marilyn. *English Romanticism: The Human Context*. New York: W. W. Norton, 1988.
Hagstrum, Jean H. *Sex and Sensibility: Ideal and Erotic Love from Milton to Mozart*. Chicago: University of Chicago Press, 1980.
Poovey, Mary. *The Proper Lady and the Woman Writer*. Chicago: University of Chicago Press, 1984.
Swingle, L. J. *The Obstinate Questionings of English Romanticism*. Baton Rouge: Louisiana State University Press, 1987.
Thornburg, Mary Patterson. *The Monster in the Mirror*. Ann Arbor: UMI Research Press, 1987.

Todd, Janet. *Mary Wollstonecraft: A Revolutionary Life*. New York: Columbia University Press, 2000.

Todd, Janet, and Marilyn Butler, eds. *The Works of Mary Wollstonecraft*: The Wrongs of Woman: or, Maria, vol. 1: 75–184. New York: New York University Press, 1989.

---. *The Works of Mary Wollstonecraft*: Letters Written in Sweden, Norway and Denmark, vol. 6: 237–348. New York: New York University Press, 1989.

Tomalin, Claire. *The Life and Death of Mary Wollstonecraft*. New York: Harcourt Brace Jovanovich, 1974.

White, Cynthia L. *Women's Magazines 1693–1968*. London: Michael Joseph, 1970.

Wollstonecraft, Mary. *The Vindications: The Rights of Men and the Rights of Woman*, eds. D. L. Macdonald and Kathleen Scherf. Ontario: Broadview Press, 2001.

4 Portrait of a Lake Poet's Wife
Sara Fricker Coleridge

> *When C. [Coleridge] was here in Feb'ry he was cheerful & good natured & full of fair promises—he talked of our setling [sic] finally in London...* [1]
>
> (Mrs. S. T. Coleridge)

The legacy of the lake poet Samuel Taylor Coleridge emerges through his literary genius, a legacy established through his daughter Sara and a legacy encouraged by his wife Sara through her perseverance as a mother and wife educating and nurturing the literary interests of her family. His daughter Sara Coleridge is described as "an image of grace and intellectual beauty that time can never tarnish."[2] As family friend and correspondent Aubrey De Vere writes, "But in the daughter, as in the father, the real marvel was neither the accumulated knowledge nor the literary power. It was the spiritual mind."[3] Sara's daughter Edith continues the lineage as she prepares a book of her mother's recollections. In her preface to *Memoirs and Letters*, Edith quotes from her mother's poetry apologetically: "Poor is the portrait that one look portrays, / It mocks the face on which we loved to gaze" (Lines from *Phantasmion*[4]). One look is not sufficient to provide a complete picture of an individual; however, gathered moments of a life shape a timeless portrait. Through a look at Samuel Taylor Coleridge and his wife Sara, and their children, moments of their lives spent together and apart paint an intimate view of their marital relationship, his poetic genius, and its legacy. De Vere captures the spark of inherited genius in Coleridge's daughter, Sara, as he writes,

> Great and various as were your mother's [Sara's] talents, it was not from them that she derived what was special to her. It was from the degree in which she had inherited the feminine portion of genius. She had a keener appreciation of what was highest and most original in thought than of subjects nearer the range of ordinary intellects.[5]

DOI: 10.4324/9781003504238-4

Certainly, the measure of an individual's genius has been debated through an examination of tradition and invention, in order to determine the highest attribute of an intellectual gift, and this very debate provides an essential ingredient in the discovery of the Romantic wife, an invention of the eighteenth century and its literary identity.

Looking at the wife of poetic genius Samuel Taylor Coleridge and mother of young Sara Coleridge, Sara Fricker Coleridge evolves in the eyes of a sincere reader from a common domestic partner and sacrificial mother to the intellectual equal, educated thinker, and imaginative linguist whose roles as wife and mother left her potential as a writer untapped. Through the eyes of her children, sisters, family, and friends a more profound view of this woman will supplant one that has remained only a superficial glimpse, thereby conveying a more comprehensive view of the woman—mother and sister—that composes the image of the wife. While the most significant relationship to examine is the husband/wife relationship, other significant figures in Sara's life contribute to a complementary understanding of the wife more accurately as an individual. However, beginning with her husband's views on marriage, in general, and on Sara's personality will help to establish a basis for the role of the particularities of the wife, Coleridge's wife, and the literary identity of the Romantic wife in its more ideal portrayal. In his poetic fragment "The Happy Husband" (?1802),[6] Samuel Taylor Coleridge praises the name of *wife*, a name honored by contract and commitment. In Figure 4.1, the miniature portrait of Sara Fricker Coleridge as the wife of Samuel Taylor Coleridge illustrates her gentle nature.

Only his commitment to establishing an ideal Pantisocratic community could compete with his insistence on domestic happiness. Marriage is "a promise," he proclaims, describing it as "a pledge" between two individuals to love, honor, obey, and cherish each other, and as Coleridge so insightfully acknowledges in his fragment, marriage is also a "mystery."

Perhaps marriage to a poetic husband appears romantic at first glance; however, Sara Fricker Coleridge embarked on a life journey with Samuel that not even the sweetest poetry could have faithfully uttered its most intimate moments or soothed its most bitter disappointments. Coleridge compares marriage to a mystery and leaves his reader wondering whether he was resigned to accept this enigma and remain ambivalent throughout his own marriage or striving to resolve his uncertain feelings. Yet, in his search for a compatible wife, he was attracted to several women: Mary Evans, an early object of his affection; Sara Fricker, his wife; Dorothy Wordsworth, his literary friend and companion; and Sara Hutchinson, his imaginative ideal and poetic love. From letters Coleridge exchanged with his wife, letters written to Sara Hutchinson, and letters written by Dorothy

68 *The Social Imagination of the Romantic Wife in Literature*

Figure 4.1 Portrait of Sara Fricker Coleridge (1770–1845) at 39 years of age.
Painted by Mary Matilda Bentham in 1809.
Public Domain. *Wikimedia Commons.*

Wordsworth, the intimate world of the Coleridges is revealed. More than a rehearsal of biographical details, these letters along with letters from such friends as Thomas Poole and Robert Southey form an epistolary and literary connection that shapes the portrait of the Romantic wife, literally and figuratively, since the wife, friend, and writer are intermingled among these relationships for the poet Coleridge.

Coleridge encouraged education for women, so he naturally gravitated toward Sara Fricker and her family. Describing Sara's background, biographer Stephen M. Weissman explains,

> Coming from a prosperous and cultivated family, Mrs. Fricker had taken great pains to ensure that her vivacious daughters [Sara, Mary, and Edith] attained a higher level of education than most young women in their sagging circumstances managed to achieve.[7]

In fact, even Sara's two unmarried sisters, Martha and Elizabeth, are remembered in her daughter Sara Coleridge's letters as women who managed their lives by their own labors as dressmakers. She describes her aunts as women with "sterling qualities" contributing to characters of "high respectability" who were

> [w]ithout talent, except of an ordinary kind, without powerful connections, [but] by life-long perseverance, fortitude, and determination, by prudence, patience, and punctuality, they not only maintained themselves, but, with a little aid from kind friends, whom their merits won, they laid by a comfortable competency for their old age.[8]

It is no wonder that in October of 1795, Coleridge chose Sara Fricker for his wife, a woman sympathetic to his philosophical ideal of Pantisocracy. Sara was raised in Bath and in Bristol where Hannah More, a member of the Bluestocking Club, founded a school of education for girls that revolutionized female education through higher instruction in intellectual pursuits. These methods of education promoted freedom of thinking yet still retained a sympathetic outlook toward a conservative morality. Not only was Sara schooled in English and French as well as mathematics, but she was brought up in the fashionable surroundings of Bath, a resort city where privileged young men and women met their future husband or wife. Molly Lefebure describes Sara as "a daughter of Bath"[9] where she was brought up during her most impressionable teenage years. Lefebure explains, "... Bath in its fashionable heyday [was] one of the most elegant and sophisticated spas in Europe, where everyone vied to dazzle with all the latest refinements of *bon ton.*"[10] In this sophisticated atmosphere Sara spent her youth from age 10 to 16, as she grew fond of seeing other people's homes, drawing-rooms, furniture and equipages.

In contrast to the highly stylish life of Bath in which Sara was raised, the Frickers had also made their home in Bristol where Sara's father Stephen Fricker pursued several business ventures. He was the landlord of The Fountain Tavern in Bristol High Street and a partner with his brother in a pottery business in Westbury which was just two miles outside of Bristol.[11] Sara's mother Martha Rowles was from a "genteel" Bristol family and with her father Samuel Rowles as bondsman for the marriage license, she married Stephen Fricker at the St. James Church in Bristol in 1764. Of their ten children only six survived, Sara—born on 10 September 1770, Mary—born 1771, Edith—born 1774, Martha—born 1777, Elizabeth—born 1778, and George—born 1785. At the age of 16, Sara was sent to Chewton Keynsham, the country residence of a Mr. Kirby, a Bristol attorney, after her father went bankrupt and lost his possessions. Sara,

Mary, and eventually Edith were sent out to do needlework to help with the family income.[12]

Situated along the Avon River, Bristol was an attractive seaport for merchants and tradesmen who helped to build its economy from foreign and domestic commerce. The city lies at the southern end of Gloucestershire and the northern section of Somersetshire some 115 miles west of London and 12 miles northwest of Bath. Nestled among picturesque downs, thriving valleys and green hills, watered by the rivers, springs, brooks, and rivulets, Bristol was found to be a comfortable climate with its sublime rocks and natural beauty which drew travelers and foreigners to its surroundings. The city itself was constructed in a circular manner with the heart of the city seated on a hill and the streets intersecting each other at right angles in several places. Bristol was described as an ancient Roman city built on seven hills with its principal river, the Avon, similar to the Tyber in "width, color and rapidity." Bristol culture thrived on the slave trade for many years until its abolition caused the economic crisis of 1793.[13]

While living in Bristol, Mrs. Fricker ran a dame school after her husband's bankruptcy and death in 1786. Sara and her sisters had to take up sewing to provide income for their family. Sara would have been exposed to prevalent ideas of non-conformist thinking in this environment among Dissenters and the Society of Friends in Bristol who advocated for the abolition of the slave trade.[14] Just about ten years earlier Mary Wollstonecraft worked as a companion for Mrs. Dawson in Bath where she began to experience the social pressure of the upper class women of fashion. She later wrote about how repugnant this fashionable scene was as she warned women in her *Vindication of the Rights of Woman* in 1792 to avoid flattery and infantile behavior to attract men. As Kathleen Jones explains,

> For Sarah [sic] its ideals of sexual equality accorded with her own passionate nature... . The idea of being a loving friend to your husband rather than a 'humble dependent' was very attractive, and what Wollstonecraft wrote about female independence and self-reliance had become so evidently necessary by the time Sarah [sic] read the book, it seemed a fundamental truth.[15]

Inspired by her love for Coleridge early in their relationship, Sara wrote several poems recorded in letters from Coleridge to Joseph Cottle. Her poem entitled "Silver Thimble" was described by Coleridge as "remarkably elegant and would do honor to *any* Volume of *any* Poems."[16] Coleridge tells Cottle, "There is a beautiful little poetic Epistle of Sara's, which I mean to print here—... 'And you, dear Sir! the arch-magician![']—were likewise printed—so as to have two of her Poems?"[17] Her letters and daily conversations in the home offered Sara a private location in which to express her cleverness and imagination in an inventive language the family called "Lingo Grande."[18] However, despite her creative attempts at poetry and inventive language, "Coleridge went to great lengths to deny Sarah [sic] any creative or perceptive powers at all, and it was one of the Wordsworths' most damning criticisms of her that she had no 'creative sensibility'."[19] Of course, this denial occurred as soon as the marriage relationship began to dissolve, and any recognition of Sara's literary ability was belittled by Coleridge when he found his literary companions in other women such as Dorothy Wordsworth and Sara Hutchinson.

Thomas Poole, a close friend of both Sara and Samuel, remained loyal to Sara throughout her years of ordeal with her husband. He saw Sara "as possessing just the elements of practicality and common sense that her husband needed to function as a poet."[20] In February 1796 Tom Poole wrote to his friend Henrietta Warwick about his deep concern for how Coleridge would maintain his kind of extraordinary poetic genius and intellectual acumen within an ordinary and common domestic habitation on Redcliff Hill in Bristol, where he lived with his wife's mother. Poole compares Coleridge's predicament with Wollstonecraft's struggle for recognition as a writer and the sad effects on their personal lives. As Poole prophetically exclaims,

> It is a sublime though melancholy instance of the justice of Providence, that we seldom see great talents, particularly that class which we peculiarly denominate genius, enjoying an even tenour of human happiness … . What a striking instance of this is Mrs. Wolstonecraft! What a striking instance is my beloved friend Coleridge! … Is genius a misfortune? No. But people of genius ought imperiously to command themselves to think *without* genius of the common concerns of life.[21]

Despite her acute awareness of and training by Wollstonecraft's radical ideas on female education, Sara chose to enhance a domestic environment for Coleridge, a decision which later proved to be detrimental instead of supportive for their relationship. Even though Coleridge's third issue of *The Watchman*, published on 17 March 1796, advocated Wollstonecraft's ideas that wives should become their husbands' intellectual equals,[22] his personal life did not advance this kind of gender equality between husband and wife.

Coleridge lived his life inconsistent with his philosophical ideals and appears to have been caught in the snare of rhetorical hypocrisy, a hypocrisy not personal to himself only but one that surfaced in the late eighteenth century as writers such as Rousseau and Wollstonecraft earnestly explored the problems of virtue in a troubled society. As social reformers, Rousseau and Wollstonecraft significantly shaped the subjective identity of the wife, mother, and independent woman. New concepts of virtuous behavior for middle-class women emerged, concepts that Coleridge embraced in his writing but which he could not reconcile in his relationship with his wife. Paradoxically, Rousseau reinforces the superiority of men over women depicting a social environment where the subordination of women, intellectually and politically, continued as long as they were educated by men and not by nature.[23] Wollstonecraft counteracts Rousseau's denigration of women by attacking the source of virtue, not as Rousseau would have it, as originating in the natural construct of women, but by asserting that virtue relies on "immutable principle," as Catherine Macaulay affirms in her *Letters on Education* published in 1790. Coleridge acknowledges freedom for those women who choose intellectual equality over feminine charm, and he approves of Wollstonecraft's "philosophy of sensuality" as stated in the third issue of *The Watchman* mentioned earlier. As Coleridge notes, "The women of Germany were the free and equal companions of their husbands: they were treated by them with esteem and confidence, and consulted on every occasion of importance."[24] He also recognizes the problem inherent in this debate over virtue when he continues, "What then, is this love which woman loses by becoming respectable?"[25] On the one hand, women were treated with esteem and respect, while on the other hand, it would appear that their passionate nature was sacrificed for this respectability as individual thinkers. The identity of the wife began to include not just intellectual freedom but political and civil freedoms as well, and the ideal marriage became a partnership based on liberty and equality. A more thorough examination of the debate on political and religious freedoms and how these controversies impacted the Romantic wife is discussed further in Chapter 8 on the marriage laws and rights of women.

The ideal community that Coleridge and his brother-in-law Robert Southey imagined rested on their marriages to the Fricker sisters, Sara and Edith, respectively. Coleridge writes to Southey around the end of October 1794,

> Should not all, who mean to become members of our Community, be incessantly meliorating their Tempers and elevating their Understandings? ... Whether our Women have not been taught by us habitually to contemplate the littlenesses of indiv[id]ual Comforts, and a passion for the *Novelty* of the Scheme, rather than the generous enthusiasm of Benevolence? Are they saturated with the Divinity of Truth sufficiently to be always wakeful? ...

These questions are meant *merely* as motives to you, Southey! to be strengthening the minds of the Women and stimulating them to literary Acquirements......[26]

Before Coleridge considers the significance of his marriage choice, he has already united his Pantisocratic ideals with a commitment to Sara. In preparation for his wedding in October 1795, Coleridge leased a cottage at Clevedon, Somerset, on the Bristol Channel. He writes to Joseph Cottle, his friend and publisher,

There are some old *Prints*, I believe—belonging to us in the room above the shop / if you would be so kind as to put one above the other and send them to Miss Fricker's, Red Cliff Hill, before 9 to-morrow morning I shall deem myself obliged to you as by that time the cart will be setting off with our goods [to Clevedon cottage].[27]

The cottage remains his place of domestic comfort until his literary obligations draw him back to Bristol. According to Cottle's own recollections of Coleridge's marital well-being in his book *Reminiscences*, Coleridge expresses sincere happiness:

He had, in good truth, discovered the grand secret; the abode of happiness, after which all are so sedulously inquiring; and this accompanied with the cheering assurance, that, by a merely pleasurable intellectual exertion, he would be able to provide for his moderate expenses, and experience the tranquillizing joys of seclusion, while the whole country and Europe were convulsed with war and changes.[28]

However, while he immerses himself fully in the romantic moments with Sara, worldly cares move quickly to dominate his mind and disturb his quiet intimacy with his wife. He composes "The Eolian Harp" as he writes, "My pensive Sara! thy soft cheek reclined / Thus on mine arm, most soothing sweet it is / To sit beside our Cot..." (lines 1–3).[29] The idyllic setting of Clevedon and his rose-bud cottage, his ideal community and home, are displaced by pressing literary endeavors. In Figure 4.2, a sketch of Samuel Taylor Coleridge in his later years reflects his life as an accomplished poet.

Coleridge's attention to the momentary experiences in his life overshadowed his ability to maintain consistency in his relationships, especially his most intimate ones. As his discontent with his marriage loomed larger, he wrote to Robert Southey in October 1801 when he was turning 29 "that his marriage, though indissoluble, was unendurable; 'for what is life,' he cried on the last day of the year, 'gangrened, as it is with me, in its

74 *The Social Imagination of the Romantic Wife in Literature*

Figure 4.2 Portrait of Samuel Taylor Coleridge (1772–1834).
Project Gutenberg.
Public Domain. *Wikimedia Commons.*

very vitals, domestic tranquility?'"[30] Southey had encouraged Coleridge to marry Sara as the two men planned their ideal community in the Susquehanna Valley across the ocean. He, too, honored the commitment to marriage as a duty but by 1799 Southey tells Coleridge, "I had rather have somebody to be happy with and think myself well off" than to accept the pleasant surroundings and society of agreeable neighbors.[31] Southey's compassion for Sara appears in his letter to Coleridge on 16 January 1800 where he expresses his admiration for Mary Wollstonecraft and Mary Hays, two literary women whose intellectual accomplishments and temperaments define an elevated view of women in society. Southey describes Mary Hays as

> a woman of talents, and I believe of a good and warm heart... Mary Hays is one of those persons whom twenty years hence it will be pleasant and gratifying to have seen. Moreover Sarah [sic] may wish for some female acquaintance.[32]

However, Sara Coleridge was to suffer within a marriage that refused to recognize her as an equal to these free-thinking women.

As tensions heightened between Sara and Samuel, any endeavor to become an intellectual equal to her husband, was thwarted by the immediate needs of her family. She chose to be the traditional wife, incapable of becoming his friend, to maintain a comfortable home environment and to protect Coleridge from the trivial needs of the home and the financial deprivations that turned her to others for support. Elizabeth Sanford describes the close relationship between Tom Poole and the Coleridges as neighbors and friends in Nether Stowey during 1796 and the early years of their marriage. "Nevertheless, Mrs. Coleridge was not altogether wrong when she remembered the house as a 'miserable cottage,' and, indeed, the day was not far distant when Coleridge himself would write of it as 'the old hovel,'" writes Sanford.[33] Years later in April 1819, Sara addresses a letter to Poole where she reminisces about the conditions of their home environment:

> I scarcely could have ventured this long and egotistical epistle, if I could ever forget that he whom I address is the same person who, in days of long past, made so many and so friendly exertions to render a miserable cottage an abode of comparative comfort.[34]

During the early years of their marriage Sara and Samuel grew apart. His poetic disposition and failing efforts to support his family increased the stress a wife and children naturally produce. Sara was frequently left to resolve financial issues for the household while unable to reconcile her own emotional strain of a distant husband. With their separation upon Coleridge's decision to pursue his studies in Germany, the marriage was to suffer irreparable damage. Coleridge's voyage to Germany began on 14 September 1798 leaving London with John Chester of Stowey and the Wordsworths and setting sail on 16 September. He was not to return until ten months later in July 1799. In his earlier letter dated 3 August 1798, Coleridge explains his intentions to Tom Poole:

> I still think the realization of the scheme of high importance to my intellectual utility; and of course to my moral happiness. But if I go with Mrs C. & little ones, I must *borrow*—an imprudent, perhaps an immoral thing--: and the uncertainties attendant on all human schemes; the uncertainty of our happiness, comfort, cheap living &c when in Germany; ... .[35]

However, despite his insatiable desire to study the language and culture of Germany, he struggles with his long absence from his wife. Sara writes to Poole on 2 April 1799:

—My poor Samuel seems to be quite tired of that place, yet says nothing in his last letter of returning but I shall continue to expect him in May, but I suppose it will be the end of it rather than the beginning—I pray to God that nothing may keep him later! For I am weary of this long long absence! ... My principal reason for troubling now, is to beg you will send me ten Guineas, for I expected Coleridge would have thought of it, but he has not probably thinking I can do without untill he arrives.[36]

Later that month on 23 April, Coleridge writes to Sara,

Surely it is unnecessary for me to say, how infinitely I languish to be in my native Country & with how many struggles I have remained even so long in Germany! ... Nothing could support me but the knowledge that if I return now, we shall be embarrassed & in debt; & the moral certainty that having done what I am doing, we shall be more than *cleared*: / not to add that so large a work with so great a variety of information from sources so scattered, & so little known even in Germany, will, of course, establish my character—for industry & erudition, certainly; & I would fain hope, for reflection & genius.[37]

Justifying his long absence Coleridge tries to assuage Sara's discomfort relying on the importance of his work to become a noted genius. Sara, on the other hand, maintains her longing for Samuel through a quiet desperation as she shares her emotional and financial worries with Tom Poole. Always sounding apologetic in her letters to Poole, Sara presents herself as the practical yet distressed wife whom Poole describes as the "pretty young Mrs. Coleridge" who appeared like "a poetic embodiment of the idea of Woman, bringing with her the 'smile of home' to complete the charm of that delicious day."[38] Even Samuel enjoyed the serenity of his home at that time when he writes:

We are very happy, and my little David Hartley grows a sweet boy.... I raise potatoes and all manner of vegetables; have an orchard; and shall raise corn (with the spade) enough for my family. We have two pigs, and ducks and geese. A cow would not answer to keep; for we have whatever milk we want from T. Poole.[39]

Of course, as in every marriage, the day-by-day activities of the home are far less poetic and more tedious, too tedious for the poetic genius of Samuel Taylor Coleridge. Try as he would to embrace the common pleasures of married life, Coleridge sought his companionship from literary friendships that developed with William Wordsworth and his sister Dorothy beginning in June 1797 with his visit to Racedown.

Coleridge's poetic sensibility inspired Dorothy Wordsworth's affection for her brother's friend, and his admiration for her "quick romantic mind— what he called her 'eager soul', her creative gifts, and her quicksilver personality and 'the ascendancy of imagination over intellect' " attracted Coleridge more to Dorothy than to his wife's independent inclinations and intellectual accomplishments.[40] In his letter to Joseph Cottle *circa* 3 July 1797 Coleridge describes Dorothy as Wordsworth's "exquisite sister" and with "her eye watchful in observation of nature—and her taste a perfect electrometer—it bends, protrudes, and draws in, at subtlest beauties & most recondite faults"[41] which further defines the growing intimacy between the two. Drawing on the sensitivity of Coleridge's language in his essay "Coleridge's Poetic Sensibility," George Whalley discerns these poetic ties between Coleridge and Dorothy as he examines how sensory perception is rendered in the language of the poet. Whalley asserts, "That Coleridge's sensibility was in fact, like Dorothy's, 'a perfect [goldleaf] electrometer' there can be no question."[42] In her journal of 20 January 1798, written from Alfoxden, Dorothy describes her observations of nature with a poetic delicacy:

> The green paths down the hill-sides are channels for streams. The young wheat is streaked by silver lines of water running between the ridges, the sheep are gathered together on the slopes. After the wet dark days, the country seems more populous. It peoples itself in the sunbeams. The garden, mimic of spring, is gay with flowers. The purple-starred hepatica spreads itself in the sun, and the clustering snow-drops put forth their white heads, at first upright, ribbed with green, and like a rosebud when completely opened, hanging their heads downwards, but slowly lengthening their slender stems.[43]

As she personifies her surroundings of the hillsides, the young wheat, the peopled sunbeams, the gay garden, and the searching heads of purple-starred hepatica stretching their stems, Dorothy reveals that her affinity to nature is compatible with Coleridge's expression of figurative language in his own poetry. Coleridge writes in a notebook entry of 1797 probably during the autumn,

> Describe—
> —the never-bloomless Furze—
> & the transi to the Gordonia Lasianthus.
> Its thick foliage of a dark green colour is flowered over with large milkwhite fragrant blossoms: on long slender elastic peduncles at the extremities of its numerous branches—from the bosom of the leaves,

& renewed every morning—and that in such incredible profusion that the Tree appears silvered over with them & the ground beneath covered with the fallen flowers.[44]

With his references to the colors and fragrances of the blossoms on their long slender stems among the foliage, Coleridge's sensual description ("bosom of the leaves") provides Dorothy with similar language in her later description at Alfoxden. Whether or not Dorothy was privileged to see Coleridge's notebooks, she would certainly have heard much of this same language in his poetry. In his conversation poem *The Nightingale* written in April 1798, Coleridge refers to the poet's creative spirit within a setting of "vernal showers / That gladden the green earth, …" (lines 9–10) as the poet composes his rhyme "Beside a brook in mossy forest-dell, / By sun or moon-light, to the influxes / Of shapes and sounds and shifting elements / Surrendering his whole spirit, …" (lines 26–29).[45] The leaves or foliage mentioned in the notebook entry slowly turn their colors "from green to a golden yellow, from that to a scarlet; from scarlet to crimson; & lastly to a brownish purple, & then fall to the ground. So that the Gordonia Lasianthus may be said to change & renew its garments every morning thro'out the year"[46] in the same way the poet surrenders his spirit to share in "Nature's immortality" (line 31).[47] With an endowed literary companion as Dorothy to share his sublime thoughts, it becomes apparent how Coleridge's disappointment with the lack of his wife's literary friendship chills his domestic affections. His imagined ideal of the Romantic wife blending domestic cares and literary fortitude cannot be achieved in the ordinary image of his wife Sara whose needs are confined to the family and household.

Dorothy's appealing temperament can be attributed in part to her upbringing. In contrast to Sara Fricker, she was educated with Erasmus Darwin's *Plan for the Conduct of Female Education* and Dr. Gregory's *A Father's Legacy to His Daughters*, both imparting traditional virtues of submission and obedience as the Conduct Books of the seventeenth and eighteenth centuries were intended to do and which provoked Mary Wollstonecraft into an avid refutation of these ideas in her *Vindication*. As Jones explains, "The only object of female education at that time, wrote Mary Wollstonecraft, was to train girls to be a 'fit companion for a man of sense' and to make them 'agreeable and useful'."[48] Dorothy learned to sublimate her own desires and inclinations thereby making her a more "fit companion" for someone like Coleridge and perhaps also establishing her susceptibility to the use of laudanum that plagued Coleridge as well.

Among Coleridge's circle of friends were the Hutchinson sisters, Mary and Sara, who were distant relatives of William and Dorothy Wordsworth as well as childhood friends. The closeness of the Wordsworths as brother and sister is again evidenced in the Hutchinson family where Mary kept the household for her brother Tom in Sockburn while Sara and her sister Joanna kept the household for another brother, George Hutchinson, near Durham at Bishop's Middleham.[49] The continuation over the years of sisters caring for the households of unmarried brothers, exchanging households and positions, set the tone for a wider definition of "wife" that Coleridge longed to incorporate into his own experience. After William Wordsworth's marriage to Mary Hutchinson in October of 1802, seven years to the date of Coleridge's marriage to Sara Fricker, the Wordsworth household included William, Mary, and Dorothy. Weissman characterizes Coleridge's marital strife as symptomatic of his envy of William Wordsworth's happiness in having a compatible marriage partner in Mary and, at the same time, a literary companion in his sister Dorothy.[50] For Coleridge the image of the Romantic wife was evolving into an ideal visionary love that embodied the intimacy of a brother–sister relationship, an attraction both chaste and pure, binding the sentimental with an ordinary human need for friendship. As J. Robert Barth affirms, "Coleridge's paradigm [for marriage] is friendship, and he represents 'sexual love as an especially intense form of confraternity'."[51]

Coleridge's visit to Sockburn in November of 1799 cultivated his emotional attachment to Sara Hutchinson and his friendship with her at a gathering of the Wordsworths and Hutchinsons "around the hearth … enjoying conundrums, puns, stories, and laughter, while Samuel furtively held Sarah's [sic] hand for a long time behind her back, and 'for the first time was wounded by Love's dainty but deadly poisoned dart'."[52] Inspired by these feelings of love, Coleridge wrote his *Introduction to the tale of a Dark Ladie*, a fragment published in the *Morning Post* on 21 December 1799, and which was later published as a poem entitled *Love* in 1810:

> All thoughts, all passions, all delights,
> Whatever stirs this mortal frame,
> All are but ministers of Love,
>   And feed his sacred flame [53]

From a notebook entry of November 1799, Coleridge's inscription describes "The long Entrancement of a True-love's Kiss."[54] Whether this single sentimental line is an expression of his fanciful imagination or an accurate representation of his true feelings for Sara cannot easily be determined.[55] However, when examining Coleridge's description of the "guileless" woman, her "modest grace" and "virgin-shame" in his poem *Love*, it becomes apparent that Coleridge is attracted to a union of romantic and Platonic sentiments. Coleridge poetically paints the portrait of a woman honored for her chastity and forgiveness, virtues embedded in the submissive and obedient wife.

On the one hand, he saw his marriage to Sara Fricker as an essential component in his Pantisocratic scheme; and then becoming discouraged with the relationship only four years later, falls in love with another ideal, that of a literary admirer and friend. For Coleridge, perhaps this new relationship redefines his initial sense of love, becoming now a capital "R" Romantic love that integrates wife, friend, and literary companion in contrast with the virtues of submission and obedience that characterize the eighteenth-century values of domestic love. When first married to Sara Coleridge, he exclaimed, "Mrs. Coleridge—MRS. COLERIDGE!!—I like to *write* the name."[56] Determined that he had found happiness, he declared, "I love and am beloved and I am happy."[57] However, in his notebook entry of 1796 Coleridge begins to question the nature of marriage: "Marriage—sole Propriety In Paradise. The thorn in the flesh—vide St. Paul—reason on this//."[58] Whether he was discovering the human or the divine purpose for marriage may depend on what he meant by "the thorn in the flesh" (II Cor 12:7) which J. R. Dummelow's *Commentary on The Holy Bible* explains as a painful bodily disease recurring at intervals.

During times of doubt in his marriage which led to his absenteeism as a father and husband, Coleridge tried to unify himself with his literary friends looking for an antidote to his emotional conflict. Yet, he was to continue this struggle within himself as Griggs notes, "Believing, however, in the 'indissolubleness' of marriage, Coleridge was thrown into a state of constant turmoil and a dependence on laudanum for relief."[59] For Coleridge his conflicts deepened and his physical condition worsened: "Continuing ill-health, frustration over his love for Sara Hutchinson, and knowing that he could not live with his wife reduced him to a pitiable condition."[60] Coleridge was driven by the need to unify his feelings into an organic wholeness that he philosophically and poetically embraced yet was unable to experience with any sense of satisfaction in his domestic life.

For a man who spent his life sorting through problems with his own brothers and sisters, as the youngest of nine children, Coleridge longed for and embraced a brotherly affection for both William Wordsworth and his sister Dorothy. As John Worthen remarks, "It is clear that in Wordsworth and Dorothy, he had found a relationship both complementary to, and offering something different from, his marriage."[61] Like most married couples, Sara and Samuel had periods of discord and other periods of relative calm in their marriage leading up to the moment of the Wordsworth wedding in 1802. The Coleridge children were a central focus of their lives despite the growing episodes of Samuel's absences Sara experienced. Their sons, Hartley, Berkeley, and Derwent, were born during the years 1796—1800. Hartley was the first born in September 1796, Berkeley in May

1798, and Derwent in September 1800. A daughter Sara was conceived in the spring of 1802 "... exactly when Coleridge was working on his extraordinary *Letter* mourning the end of his marriage" and was born in December 1802.[62] The death of their infant son Berkeley in February 1799 caused a devastating blow to their marriage while Samuel was in Germany. Sara's despair over the loss of their child was experienced without her husband's presence and without his knowledge. Her emotions were poured forth in poetry, two sonnets written during this period of suffering which will be more fully addressed in Chapter 5 through a closer view of Sara's literary expressions.

Perhaps Sara's plight evokes further sympathy as the sacrificial mother and abandoned wife while Samuel's weaknesses as a father and husband are less acceptable from a contemporary perspective. Yet to judge the situation fairly, the individualities of both Sara and Samuel need to be examined and considered on their own merit before judging their relationship to each other. According to Worthen, Coleridge attempted to understand his wife's anger with Coleridge's friends as "a problem with her 'real self'..." and as "the victim of what she hears and sees."[63] Coleridge apparently believed that Sara relied more on the opinions of others and could not think for herself. For Coleridge, Sara's shortcoming as an independent thinker explains the incompatibility of their relationship, and in fact, Coleridge believed that Sara was not up to his level as his emotional and intellectual equal. He wrote in a notebook entry in September 1801:

> coldness perhaps & paralysis in all *tangible* ideas & sensations—all that forms *real Self*—hence <the Slave of her> she creates her own self in a field of Vision & Hearing, at a distance, by her own ears & eyes—& hence becomes the willing Slave of the Ears & Eyes of others.
>
> — Nothing affects her with pain or pleasure as it is but only as other people will *say it is*—nay by an habitual absence of *reality* in her affections I have had an hundred instances that the being beloved, or the not being beloved, is a thing indifferent; but the *notion*—of not being beloved—that wounds her pride deeply.[64]

Just the mere thought of not being loved, suggests Coleridge, was enough to chill Sara's affections toward him. He defends himself as one wrongly accused of not loving his wife and in turn accuses Sara of listening too sharply to the opinions of others instead of trusting her own heart. The contradiction between the real and the ideal wife imitates Coleridge's poetic theory and ultimately shapes the image of the Romantic wife from the extraordinary to the ordinary, exalting the familiar and bringing the individual traits of wife, friend, and literary companion into an organic union. At the heart of this unity remains a burning conflict of eighteenth-century virtues, submission and obedience, enveloped by the hue of imagination, the tone of fancy, and the form of familiarity. The next chapter will further explore Sara's emotional turmoil and financial difficulties to provide deeper insights into the social and personal constraints that define her role as a wife.

Notes

1. Sara Coleridge writes to her neighbor Thomas Poole from Greta Hall, Keswick, on October 30th, but sent the letter on 14 November [1812]. She goes on to say,

    I listened, I own, with incredulous ears, while he was building these 'airy castles' and calmly told him that I thought it was much better that I and the children should remain in the country until the Boys had finished their School-education … & in the meantime, a regular correspondence *was* to be kept up between himself, and me, and the children; and *never more* was he to keep a letter of mine, or the Boys', or Southey's *un*opened—his promises, poor fellow, are like his Castles,--airy nothings!— … .
    (*Minnow among Tritons: Mrs. S. T. Coleridge's Letters to Thomas Poole 1799-1834,* ed. Stephen Potter (Bloomsbury: Nonesuch Press, 1934), 17)

2. Aubrey De Vere contributes his description of Sara Coleridge to her daughter's compilation of her mother's recollections in *Memoirs and Letters* (New York: Harper & Brothers, 1874), 64.
3. Edith Coleridge, ed., *Memoirs and Letters of Sara Coleridge* (New York: Harper & Brothers, 1874), 65.
4. Sara Coleridge, daughter of Samuel Taylor Coleridge, composed the drama *Phantasmion* inspired by her vision of a fairy-land (First published London: William Pickering, 1837). See *Memoirs and Letters* edited by her daughter Edith Coleridge for more details.
5. Coleridge, E., ed., *Memoirs and Letters*, 65.
6. Ernest Hartley Coleridge, ed. *Coleridge: Poetical Works* (Oxford: Oxford University Press, 1988), 388.
7. Stephen M. Weissman, *His Brother's Keeper: A Psychobiography of Samuel Taylor Coleridge* (Madison: International Universities Press, 1989), 54.
8. Coleridge, E., ed., *Memoirs and Letters*, 40.
9. Molly Lefebure, *The Bondage of Love: A Life of Mrs. Samuel Taylor Coleridge* (New York: Norton, 1987), 24.
10. Lefebure, *The Bondage of Love,* 24.
11. Lefebure, *The Bondage of Love,* 23.
12. Lefebure, *The Bondage of Love,* 23–24.
13. New History, Survey and Description of the City and Suburbs of Bristol, or Complete Guide, (Bristol: W. Matthews, 1794), 2.
14. Lefebure, *The Bondage of Love,* 24.
15. Kathleen Jones, *A Passionate Sisterhood: The Sisters, Wives and Daughters of the Lake Poets* (London: Virago, 1998), 4.

16 Samuel Taylor Coleridge, *Collected Letters of Samuel Taylor Coleridge*, vol. I, 1785-1800, ed. Earl Leslie Griggs (Oxford: The Clarendon Press, 1956), Letter 92, 162.
17 Coleridge, S. T., *Collected Letters*, vol. I, Letter 92, 162.
18 Lefebure, *The Bondage of Love*, 22.
19 Jones, *A Passionate Sisterhood*, 48.
20 Jones, *A Passionate Sisterhood*, 49.
21 Elizabeth Sandford, *Thomas Poole and His Friends* (Over Stowey, Somerset: The Friarn Press, 1996), 84.
22 Jones, *A Passionate Sisterhood*, 50; Samuel Taylor Coleridge, *The Collected Works of Samuel Taylor Coleridge*, vol. 2: *The Watchman*, ed. Lewis Patton, ([London], [Princeton]: Routledge and Kegan Paul; Princeton University Press, 1969), 91.
23 Rousseau's contribution to the debate on female education can be summarized in the following explanation from his novel *Emile* (1762):

> As I see it, the special functions of women, their inclinations and their duties, combine to suggest the kind of education they require. Men and women are made for each other but they differ in the measure of the dependence on each other.... .To play their part in life they [women] must have our willing help, and for that they must earn our esteem. By the very law of nature women are at the mercy of men's judgments both for themselves and for their children.
> (*The Emile of Jean Jacques Rousseau Selections*, ed. and trans. William Boyd (New York: Teachers College Press, Teachers College, Columbia University, 1962), 135)

24 Samuel Taylor Coleridge, *The Collected Works of Samuel Taylor Coleridge*, vol. 2: The Watchman, ed. Lewis Patton, ([London], [Princeton]: Routledge and Kegan Paul; Princeton University Press, 1969), 91.
25 Coleridge, S. T., *Collected Works*, vol. 2: The Watchman, 91.
26 Coleridge, S. T., *Collected Letters*, vol. I, Letter 66, 119.
27 Coleridge, S. T., *Collected Letters*, vol. I, Letter 89, 159.
28 Joseph Cottle, *Reminiscences of Samuel Taylor Coleridge and Robert Southey* (New York: Wiley & Putnam, 1848), 47–48.
29 Coleridge, E. H., ed., *Coleridge: Poetical Works*, 100.
30 George Whalley, *Coleridge and Sara Hutchinson, and the Asra Poems* (London: Routledge & Paul, 1955), 41.
31 Kenneth Curry, ed. *New Letters of Robert Southey*, vol. 1, 1792–1810 (New York: Columbia University Press, 1965), 201
32 Curry, ed., *New Letters of Robert Southey*, vol. 1, 215.
33 Sandford, *Thomas Poole and His Friends*, 115.
34 Sandford, *Thomas Poole and His Friends*, 114.
35 Coleridge, S. T., *Collected Letters*, vol. I, Letter 252, 414.
36 Potter, ed., *Minnow*, 4–5.
37 Coleridge, S. T., *Collected Letters*, vol. I, Letter 276, 484.
38 Sandford, *Thomas Poole and His Friends*, 115.

84 *The Social Imagination of the Romantic Wife in Literature*

39 Sandford, *Thomas Poole and His Friends*, 115.
40 Jones, *A Passionate Sisterhood*, 60.
41 Coleridge, S. T., *Collected Letters*, vol. I, Letter 195, 330.
42 Whalley, *Coleridge and Sara Hutchinson*, 7.
43 Dorothy Wordsworth, *Journals of Dorothy Wordsworth*, vol. 1, ed. William Knight (London: Macmillan, 1897; Project Gutenberg, 2013), 3. www.gutenberg.org.
44 Kathleen Coburn, ed., *The Notebooks of Samuel Taylor Coleridge*, vol. 1, 1794–1804 (New York: Pantheon Books, 1957), 222 G.218.
45 Coleridge, E. H., ed., *Coleridge: Poetical Works*, 264–65.
46 Coburn, ed., *The Notebooks*, vol. 1, 222 G.218.
47 Coleridge, E. H., ed., *Coleridge: Poetical Works*, 265.
48 Jones, *A Passionate Sisterhood*, 30.
49 Whalley, *Coleridge and Sara Hutchinson*, 35–36.
50 Weissman, *His Brother's Keeper*, 212.
51 J. Robert Barth, *Coleridge and the Power of Love* (Columbia: University of Missouri Press, 1988), 115.
52 Oswald Doughty. *Perturbed Spirit: The Life and Personality of Samuel Taylor Coleridge* (Rutherford [N.J.], East Brunswick, N.J.: Fairleigh Dickinson University Press; Associated University Presses, 1981), 191.
53 Coleridge, E. H., ed., *Coleridge: Poetical Works*, 330.
54 Coburn, ed., *The Notebooks*, vol. 1, 578 5.73.
55 Conceivably, Coleridge is trying to achieve in his art what he is seeking in his life, a union of friendship and marriage, but he also seems to recognize the fancifulness of poetic expression when he remarks in an earlier notebook entry of 1796 that "Poetry—excites us to artificial feelings—makes us callous to real ones" (Kathleen Coburn, ed., *The Notebooks of Samuel Taylor Coleridge*, vol. 1, 1794–1804 (New York: Pantheon Books, 1957), 87 G.81.
56 Coleridge, S. T., *Collected Letters*, vol. I, Letter 91, 160. See letter to Thomas Poole dated 7 Oct. 1795.
57 Coleridge, S. T., *Collected Letters*, vol. I, Letter 93, 164. See letter to Robert Southey dated [13] Nov. 1795.
58 Coburn, ed., *The Notebooks*, vol. 1, 79 G.73.
59 John B. Beer, *Coleridge's Variety: Bicentenary Studies* (Pittsburgh: University of Pittsburgh Press, 1974), 40.
60 Beer, *Coleridge's Variety*, 41.
61 John Worthen, *The Gang: Coleridge, the Hutchinsons, and the Wordsworths in 1802* (New Haven: Yale University Press, 2001), 73.
62 Worthen, *The Gang*, 14.
63 Worthen, *The Gang*, 74.
64 Coburn, ed., *The Notebooks*, vol. 1, 979 21.131.

References

Barth, J. Robert. *Coleridge and the Power of Love*. Columbia: University of Missouri Press, 1988.

Beer, John B. *Coleridge's Variety: Bicentenary Studies*. Pittsburgh: University of Pittsburgh Press, 1974.
Boyd, William, ed. and trans. *The Emile of Jean Jacques Rousseau Selections*. New York: Teachers College Press, Teachers College, Columbia University, 1962.
Coburn, Kathleen, ed. *The Notebooks of Samuel Taylor Coleridge, Vol. 1, 1794–1804*. New York: Pantheon Books, 1957.
Coleridge, Edith, ed. *Memoirs and Letters of Sara Coleridge*. New York: Harper & Brothers, 1874.
Coleridge, Ernest Hartley, ed. *Coleridge: Poetical Works*. Oxford: Oxford University Press, 1988.
Coleridge, Samuel Taylor. *Collected Letters of Samuel Taylor Coleridge*, vol. I, 1785–1800, ed. Earl Leslie Griggs. Oxford: The Clarendon Press, 1956.
---. *Collected Letters of Samuel Taylor Coleridge*, vol. II, 1801–1806, ed. Earl Leslie Griggs, Oxford: The Clarendon Press, 1956.
---. *The Collected Works of Samuel Taylor Coleridge*, vol. 2: 1–375. The Watchman, ed. Lewis Patton. [London], [Princeton]: Routledge and Kegan Paul; Princeton University Press, 1969.
Cottle, Joseph. *Reminiscences of Samuel Taylor Coleridge and Robert Southey*. New York: Wiley & Putnam, 1848.
Curry, Kenneth, ed. *New Letters of Robert Southey, Volume 1: 1792–1810*. New York: Columbia University Press, 1965.
---. *New Letters of Robert Southey, Volume 2: 1811–1838*. New York: Columbia University Press, 1965.
Doughty, Oswald. *Perturbed Spirit: The Life and Personality of Samuel Taylor Coleridge*. Rutherford, NJ, East Brunswick, NJ: Fairleigh Dickinson University Press; Associated University Presses, 1981.
Jones, Kathleen. *A Passionate Sisterhood: The Sisters, Wives and Daughters of the Lake Poets*. London: Virago, 1998.
Lefebure, Molly. *The Bondage of Love: A Life of Mrs. Samuel Taylor Coleridge*. New York: Norton, 1987.
New History, Survey and Description of the City and Suburbs of Bristol, or Complete Guide. Bristol: W. Matthews, 1794.
Potter, Stephen, ed. *Minnow among Tritons: Mrs. S. T. Coleridge's Letters to Thomas Poole 1799–1834*. Bloomsbury: Nonesuch Press, 1934.
Sandford, Elizabeth. *Thomas Poole and His Friends*. Over Stowey, Somerset: The Friarn Press, 1996.
Weissman, Stephen M. *His Brother's Keeper: A Psychobiography of Samuel Taylor Coleridge*. Madison, Conn.: International Universities Press, 1989.
Whalley, George. *Coleridge and Sara Hutchinson, and the Asra Poems*. London: Routledge & Paul, 1955.
Wordsworth, Dorothy. *Journals of Dorothy Wordsworth*, ed. William Knight, vol. 1: 1–255. London: Macmillan, 1897; Project Gutenberg, 2013.
Worthen, John. *The Gang: Coleridge, the Hutchinsons, and the Wordsworths in 1802*. New Haven: Yale University Press, 2001.

5 Idyllic Marriage, Motherhood, and Literary Genius

Oh! my dear Mr Poole, I have lost my dear dear child![1]
(Sara Fricker Coleridge)

In 1775 transatlantic tensions were quickly rising among Britons on both sides of the ocean, stretching across the Atlantic from seaport to seaport. At the center of commercial activity was the English provincial town of Bristol whose merchants and tradesmen were responsible for building the prosperity of this Georgian port in Western England. New business enterprises as well as families hoping for fresh opportunities and freedom from economic pressures looked westward to the American colonies which were on the brink of rebellion from an oppressive monarch, George III. Bryan Little marks the account of Bristol's history in his introduction to James Sketchley's record in the first of Bristol's Directories, as "a turning point, in the history of a city which had, for over half a century, been England's second most populous town."[2]

Among the celebrated merchants was a group of Bristolians who traded across the Atlantic, specializing in timber, iron, linen, and wine with American concerns in Carolina and Virginia. Two important Bristolians included the brothers, Robert and Thomas Southey, drapers and lacemen on Wine Street. Of particular interest was Robert Southey, the father of England's future poet laureate, the younger Robert Southey who was to become a co-collaborator with Samuel Taylor Coleridge in a transatlantic scheme of "Pantisocracy" in 1795. On a more local level, the city's weekly newspaper *Felix Farley's Bristol Journal* had been reporting on the business dealings of Stephen Fricker. This historical view of the father becomes even more newsworthy when two of his daughters marry renowned poets. A journal description highlights Stephen Fricker:

> two of whose daughters were in twenty years' time to become Mrs. Coleridge and Mrs. Southey, [and who] announced his move from the

DOI: 10.4324/9781003504238-5

keeping of the "Fountain" tavern to the running, in the outlying village of Westbury on Trym, of the Sugar House Pottery where he planned to make sugar pans, chimney, flower, and garden pots.[3]

As a critical economic description of the 1770s, the account of Stephen Fricker's business dealings defined the period in which Sara Fricker was raised and educated. The culture that shaped the manners and intellectual interests of the Fricker sisters arose from among variable economic conditions, fostering and encouraging the marriages of Sara and her sister Edith to men of letters rather than tradesmen. Moreover, the economic and political instability of this Bristolian community, among other towns in England, reflected the period from the American Revolution in 1776 through the French Revolution in 1789, contributing as well to the instability of marital and family relations, especially among the rising middle class.

The state of marriage during this period had become more focused on the legality of the marriage contract through the courts in order to eliminate the untidiness of multiple marriages, or polygamy, and the care of bastard children. During the medieval period, marriage law was primarily motivated by property ownership and inheritance; however, as the middle-class population increased, the reasons for marrying centered on companionship as well as producing heirs. During the sixteenth and seventeenth centuries, marriage occurred in several ways for couples with property, either through a written legal contract involving the parents' financial arrangements, or spousals, a formal exchange of oral promises before witnesses which also constituted a contract. By declaring intentions to marry as a public display, either with or without a church wedding ceremony, couples were considered to be legally married. Another important criterion that established a legal marriage was the sexual consummation of the marriage once public notice was given of the intent to perform a legal written or oral contract. After 1754 the marriage contract was more highly regarded when a church ceremony also occurred as Lawrence Stone explains,

> Alone among the Christian Churches of Europe, the Anglican Church retained unaltered the medieval law of marriage, and continued to leave matrimonial litigation in the hands of ecclesiastical courts. As the Anglican Church tightened its grip on society in the sixteenth and seventeenth centuries, both the laity and the clergy came increasingly to regard the wedding in church as the key ceremony, but the civil lawyers who ran the courts continued to recognize the spousals before witnesses.[4]

While the legalities of marriage had been vaguely defined in past centuries, by the eighteenth century both the civil and ecclesiastical courts took actions to ensure that accurate records were kept and couples were protected under the law. Stone further illustrates these legal changes and their emotional impact on the marital relationship. He states,

> It was not until 1753 that Lord Hardwicke's Marriage Act was passed, which at last brought coherence and logic to the laws governing marriage. From 1754 only the church wedding, not the verbal spousals, was legally binding, so that a prior oral contract was no longer a cause for the annulment of a later marriage in church; secondly, all church marriages had to be entered in the parish register and signed by both parties; thirdly, all marriages which occurred at times or in places defined as illegal by the 1604 canons were now also declared invalid; fourthly, no marriage of persons under twenty-one was valid without the consent of parents or guardians; and fifthly, enforcement of the law was transferred from the feeble control of the Church courts to the secular courts, which were empowered to impose up to fourteen years' transportation on clergymen who disobeyed the law.[5]

As these laws suggest, marriage was a binding contract both legally and religiously, ties not easily severed, and so any relationship between couples from which one or the other partner wanted to extricate himself required the means and the desire to risk not only public reproach but legal, moral, and religious entanglements as well.[6] Along with the advancement of more lawful enforcement of marriage came the social counterpart of a flourishing of literary, didactic advice books for eligible young women on how to be a virtuous and proper lady.

On a red, sandy cliff stands the Church of St. Mary in Bristol, known as St. Mary's at Redcliff, where on 4 October 1795 Sara Fricker and Samuel Taylor Coleridge were married. Witnesses at the marriage ceremony were the bride's mother and Josiah Wade, a Bristolian tradesman and radical friend of Coleridge. Mrs. Martha Fricker, a widow, had taken refuge on Redcliffe Hill in Bristol where she opened a small dame school after her husband's bankruptcy and subsequent death in 1786. Her younger daughter Edith married Robert Southey in the following month of November of the same year. Another sister Mary, one year younger and closer in age to Sara, had previously married Robert Lovell, a young poet from a Quaker family with whom Robert Southey intended to publish a joint volume of short poems.[7] These three sisters chose marriages that would bring them into a mutual plan intending to establish the family in an ideal community living in America.

Southey and Coleridge coined the term "Pantisocracy" from the Greek word meaning the equal rule of all, based on a shared or common property, and hoped to establish this society on the banks of the Susquehanna

Idyllic Marriage, Motherhood, and Literary Genius 89

River. In this ideal, society the role of a woman serves to create the kind of independent spirit and aspiration for individuality, uncommon to the passivity of the traditional wife. According to Thomas Poole, a close friend and neighbor to Coleridge, this plan defines the roles of men and women so that productivity is shared equitably with an emphasis on education:

> The regulations relating to the females strike them as the most difficult; Whether the marriage contract shall be dissolved if agreeable to one or both parties, and many other circumstances, are not yet determined. The employments of women are to be the care of infant children, and other occupations suited to their strength; at the same time the greatest attention is to be paid to the cultivation of their minds.[8]

The need to educate not only the children but also the women attracted the Fricker sisters who had learned the importance of self-reliance after their father's business failure. While the Pantisocratic scheme to emigrate to America was developing in their conversations and shaping their intimate relationships, Coleridge writes to Southey on 18 September 1794:

> Well, my dear Southey! I am at last arrived at Jesus [College]. My God! how tumultuous are the movements of my Heart—Since I quitted this room what and how important Events have been evolved! America! Southey! Miss Fricker!—Yes—Southey—you are right—Even Love is the creature of strong Motive—I certainly love her. I think of her incessantly & with unspeakable tenderness—with that inward melting away of Soul that symptomatizes it. Pantisocracy—O I shall have such a scheme of it![9]

Often uncertain in his affection for Sara Fricker, Coleridge's enthusiasm for the Pantisocratic scheme reinforced his wavering desire to experience a deep bond of love, one tied to his intellectual inspiration and idealism. This emotional bond to both his idealistic scheme and his wife would unravel through Coleridge's self-doubt and inconsistencies in his literary accomplishments. Yet, Sara's emotional bond would remain strong weathering years of despair, abandonment, and separation, as she was motivated by a personal and social need to identify herself as a wife and as a married woman, with a tenacity to remain within the literary circle that originally attracted her to Coleridge and his friends.

Through those individuals closest to the Coleridges, their relationship can be documented beginning with their neighbor at Nether Stowey, Thomas Poole. Only a few days after the Coleridge wedding at St. Mary's, Tom Poole writes in a letter dated 10 October 1795:

I do congratulate you—most heartily I do. I wish I knew Mrs. Coleridge—remember me most kindly to her. May you both long, long be happy, and may the lowering morning of your days precede a *meridian* serenely bright and cloudless, leading in due time, naturally, to the soft close of a tranquil evening... . The world is all before you; your road seems yet to choose. Providence has been pleased, if I may so express myself, to drop you on this globe as a *meteor* from the clouds, the track of which is undetermined [italics mine].[10]

Poole's enthusiasm for Coleridge's prosperity and happiness in marriage reveals how deeply enamored he is with Coleridge's intellectual and imaginative endeavors. He makes reference to this union between Samuel and Sara as a zenith or meridian in time, the highest point at which a celestial body achieves its power. To further his metaphor of the astronomical configuration of the universe, Poole compares Samuel to a meteor appearing from the clouds whose direction in life is not yet known but whose future with this marriage holds the promise of imaginative genius. Poole expresses his admiration for Coleridge and his genius while he naturally embraces his wife Sara with whom he will develop an enduring friendship. He continues his admiration in the following poem:

> Hail to thee, Coldridge, youth of various powers!
>   I love to hear thy soul pour forth the line,
> To hear it sing of love and liberty
>   As if fresh breathing from the hand divine.[11]

Poole's poetic expression reveals his praise for Coleridge as he recognizes Coleridge's unique philosophical pursuit of individual freedom. He finds in Sara the vision of his own ideal for a companion and wife, one that supports the poetic genius of his friend. In the last verse of this poem written on 12 September 1795, Poole creates this image of Coleridge's wife before he has ever met her:

> Anon thy Sarah's [sic] image cheers thy soul,
>   When sickening, at the world, thy spirits faint;
> Soft balm it brings—thou hails't the lovely maid,
>   Paint'st her dear form as Love alone can paint.[12]

The form of Sara's image is defined by Love with a capital L, a divine Love that incorporates Poole's understanding of the creator. While this "dear form" was meant to describe Sara in particular, the rhetoric draws on a universal concept that shows how the "lovely maid" is painted by the hand of Love itself. Poole's exaltation of Sara lifts the individuality of one woman, one wife, to the universality of all women in their budding roles as wives. Poole's depiction of the Romantic wife is echoed in Samuel's earnest desire for the three poet husbands to marry three sisters and fulfill his Pantisocratic scheme of an idyllic community. Yet, this poetic ideal conceived in the poetic imagination of Coleridge and Southey never achieves its pragmatic reality. He later remarks how Sara remembered her Nether Stowey cottage home as a "miserable cottage" and even Coleridge would refer to it as "the old hovel."[13] Yet, the rustic cottage setting, while not particularly charming because of its smallness and closeness to the street, found its warmth and friendliness in the nature of Sara's "smile of home," as noted by Elizabeth Sandford.[14] However, Samuel's idealism kept the concept of home alive in his poetic imagination when he referred to his cottage as his "Elysium." He wrote to Tom Poole on 11 April 1796:

> I love to shut my eyes, and bring up before my imagination that Arbour, in which I have repeated so many of these compositions to you. Dear Arbour! An Elysium to which I have often passed by your Cerberus, and Tartarean tan-pits![15]

Within the countryside neighborhood of Nether Stowey where the young married couple had settled, the friendship between Thomas Poole and Sara grew even stronger through the early years of the Coleridge marriage. Poole became an indispensable support for the young wife, particularly while the poet Coleridge pursued his literary interests in Germany. A few years later, when the Coleridges moved from Nether Stowey in the southwest to the north of England, Sara diligently wrote to Tom Poole providing all the news of family life and her personal concerns. Charting the course of the Coleridge marriage, these 42 letters written during the period 1799–1834 have been preserved in a volume edited by Stephen Potter and titled *Minnow Among Tritons*. The earliest letter was written on 11 February 1799 and was sent by Mrs. Coleridge while residing in Bristol to care for her mother and during the illness of her son while Samuel was in Germany. Sadly, Sara writes of the tragic death of her infant son Berkeley who died from smallpox:

> Oh! my dear Mr. Poole, I have lost my dear dear child! at one o'clock on Sunday Morning a violent convulsive fit put an end to his painful existence, myself and two of his aunts were watching by his cradle. I wish I had not seen it, for I am sure it will never leave my memory; sweet babe! what will thy Father feel when he shall hear of thy sufferings and death![16]

92   *The Social Imagination of the Romantic Wife in Literature*

Despite her emotional despair over the death of her son, Sara maintains her role as the obedient wife subservient to her husband's needs while he is traveling in Germany. She is advised by Poole not to disturb Coleridge with the upsetting news:

> I am perfectly aware of every thing you have said on the subject in your letter; I shall not yet write to Coleridge, and when I do—I will pass over all disagreeable subjects with the greatest care, for I well know their violent effect on him—but I account myself most unfortunate in being at a distance from him at this time, wanting his consolation as I do, and feeling my griefs almost too much to support with fortitude.[17]

Left to depend on others for her emotional and financial support, Sara yearns for the kind of masculine strength usually provided by a husband during the traumatic loss of their son. The magnitude of her grief seems hardly able to manage alone through her own strength. As she mentions to Poole, she feels her "fortitude," an eighteenth-century stoic trait ascribed to the propriety of wives, is incapable of supporting her. Instead, she feels like the unfortunate wife who desires her husband's consolation, an absent husband with whom she cannot share her grief, a husband who is in pursuit of philosophical interests in Germany.

Through her written correspondence, Sara illustrates how a traditional feminine upbringing of passive resistance severely handicaps her emotional distress. Perhaps this traumatic loss that Sara endures alone in the marriage fosters her sense of individuality that begins to strengthen after the death of her son Berkeley in 1799. At present her only choice is to resign herself to further desperation to save her husband from "all disagreeable subjects." Instructed in the moral virtues of female submission, Sara understood the propriety of such feminine virtues as restraint and compliance that paradoxically enhanced her sufferings.

The letter continues to express her financial worries while she manages to send her kind thoughts to Tom's mother and kind respects to Mr. Ward. Sara demonstrates an ability to use language not only to communicate in her letters but also to pour out her heartfelt emotions with clarity of thought, precise rhetoric, and descriptive phrasing. Her writing is a natural outpouring of her educated and intellectual accomplishments as well as an intimacy found in the literary forms of the letter and the poem. She then writes two sonnets that shape her fear and despair into a poetic structure. At the time Coleridge was still traveling in Germany, Sara composed one sonnet written during Berkeley's illness, and a second sonnet that was composed after his death.[18]

On the lamentable sickness of little Berkeley in his father's absence in Germany in 1799:

Ah, why that languid look & parting breath—
Devoted baby,—art thou doomed to death?
Are all my watchings, progress, & tears in vain,
To late recovered dost thou droop again?
Must the dear hope created by thy smile
Which gave to Oblivion all my care & toil
So soon be dashed? Must my tears flow anew,
And all my cares be centred, sweet, in you?
Yes, I will watch thee from the morning light
Till setting sun, and all the long, long night;
Close in my arms my tender babe shall lie.
While thou art here my progress shall ascend
Oh, interpose kind heaven, thy succour hand:
Put forth thy hand, my drooping infant save;
In mercy spare what thou in mercy gave.—
But if his doom is that of David's son;
I from the earth, rise, & say, Thy will be done!
(Sara Coleridge)

On the death of Berkeley Coleridge 11 months old:

I pressed thee close to hear thy and foretold
"as rumoured robberies endear our gold"
Thou'st gone! My boasted resignations fled
My impious wishes snatch thee from the dead.
Lamented Babe? When shall I bless the blow?
When will these bitter tears forget to flow?
Two babes my all,--and must I <u>one</u> resign?
Cease, weeping Mother—hear the voice divine--!
"Of such as these heaven's glorious kingdom is"
Can'st thou not <u>one</u> child yield to Life and Bliss?
The Almighty bade him lay his burden down;
His mother, thou wouldst lay it heavier on.
Samuel,--thy dire forebodings are fulfilled:
Death's Clay-cold hand our beauteous boy hath chilled.
Ah, where art thou, unconscious father, where?
Whilst thy poor Sara weeps in sad despair!'
(S. C. 1799)

Sara chose to express her sadness in a poetic form familiar to the English poets of her time, but even more significantly, she chose the sonnet to lament the illness and loss of her child perhaps as her way to emotionally connect with her absent husband. Poetry was Samuel's instrument through which to reveal his nature; poetry possessed his identity and his spirit. It is no wonder that Sara would seek to embrace poetry as she also sought solace from Samuel, especially when she was experiencing the loss of their child alone, a child created through their union and bond of love. With Poole's admonition for Sara to refrain from disturbing Samuel's literary and intellectual pursuits in Germany with such tragic news that might distract him, Sarah sought the only means of communication open to her. She suffered in silence and remained obedient to Poole's request, yet her deep emotional wounds found a voice in her poetic soul: "Ah, where art thou, unconscious father, where? / Whilst thy poor Sara weeps in sad despair."[19]

Unlike her sister Edith, Sara loved to express herself through her letters, and this love of language found another intimate form of expression in her clever communication with members of her family. Sara developed an imaginative use of names and descriptive phrases to identify individuals and their actions which her family referred to as "Lingo Grande."[20] Just as her letters to Tom Poole express her concerns and fears for the health and welfare of her family and others over the course of her married life, her inventive language of "portmanteau words" and this "kaleidoscopic compression of verbal impressions and fancies" show the lighter side of her personality.[21] The familiarity and uniqueness of this language to her own family brought laughter and wit into their daily conversations and lives. Robert Southey was particularly taken with Sara's "Lingo Grande" when he wrote to his close friend Grosvenor Charles Bedford in September of 1821 from his study at Greta Hall in Keswick:

> Dear Stumparumper, Don't rub your eyes at that word, Bedford, as if you were slopy. The purport of this letter ... is to give you some account (though but an imperfect one) of the language spoken in this house by Mrs Coleridge, and invented by her. I have carefully composed a vocabulary of it by the help of her daughter and mine, having my ivory tablets always ready when she is red-raggifying in full confabulumpatus. True it is that she has called us persecutorums, and great improprietors for performing this meritorious task, and has often told me not to be such a stuposity; threatening us sometimes that she will never say anything that ends in lumpatus again; and sometimes that she will play the very dunder; and sometimes bidding us get away with our toadymidjerings. And she asks me, how I can be such a Tomnoddycum (though my name, as she knows, is Robert), and calls me detesty, a maffrum, a goffrum, a chatterpye, a sillycum, and a great mawkinfort.[22]

Southey recognizes the imaginative expression and intelligence of Sara's ability to play with language and even suggests later in his letter that

"... It is much to be regretted that Mrs Coleridge's new language is not ... investigated by some profound philologist. Coleridge, perhaps, by the application of Kant's philosophy, might analyze and discover the principles of its construction."[23]

Admiring Sara's linguistic creativity, Southey shares his own lack of invention with Grosvenor Bedford that further exemplifies the uniqueness of Sara's poetic gift. He expresses his frustration at trying to find a linguistic structure to Sara's invention:

> But I should in vain seek to discover the *rationale* of other parts of this speech, though I were to study the subject till I were as tired as a dog's detested hinder. And when I get at the meaning by asking an explanation, still no clue to the derivation is afforded.[24]

When Southey refers to the children in their home, he explains how Sara creatively interprets the children's behavior about the house: "If the children—the childeröapusses I should say—are bangrampating about the house, they are said to be rudderish and roughcumtatherick."[25] It is uncanny that Southey recognizes Sara's creative use of language, whereas during the incompatibility of her marriage to Coleridge, her husband criticizes her for a lack of poetic sensibility.

In her later years, Sara continued to hide her individuality and her intellect as she dictated her past experiences to her daughter Sara. In this way, she was able to record her memories of her life before her marriage to Coleridge under the pseudonym of Mrs Codian. On a small marbled covered notebook of eight pages is written: "Remembrances of STC and RS by Mrs STC" and on the inside title: "Mrs Codian Remembrances of RS & STC."[26] These pages contain information about the Fricker family, Robert Southey, and Samuel Taylor Coleridge. Sara's attempts to keep her identity as the writer secret show her desire for privacy but also her reluctance to involve her name in public discourse. Women like Sara would not have been able to envision themselves as literary writers in the same circle with educated male poets such as Southey, the poet laureate, and Coleridge, the poet genius.

However, the attention given to women writers and uneducated poets in the eighteenth century was growing even more rapidly as the writers of high culture acknowledged them and their works. It becomes evident that to have a writer of Southey's esteem acknowledge Sara's intellect coupled with her imagination opened the way for the public to also acknowledge Sara Coleridge as a literary figure. Moreover, Southey addressed the importance of identifying writers of low cultural background, like laborers whom he compared to uneducated women, in his 1831 text *Lives of Uneducated Poets*. According to Kurt Heinzelman, Southey used the word "uneducated" to identify the working-class people whose lives and voices were "an abiding concern of the romantic writer."[27] As Heinzelman states,

> Their commonality [the uneducated poets] depends not just upon their social origins but also on the artisanal quality of their writing, which is as much a function of how they write—that is, how they actually compose their works, and for whom—as it is a function of what they write about.[28]

How Sara Coleridge composed her inventive language, for whom she composed this language, and the content of this language can and should be considered in acknowledging her place as a literary author. Locating Sara's poetic ability in this way allows the critic to include her writings as the production of an accomplished author, one especially motivated by her role as a wife instead of confining her rhetorical uniqueness to the private realm of home and personal letters.

A debate over the cultural values of writing permeated the literary population of mainstream and radical thinkers like Southey, Coleridge, and Wordsworth. As Southey maintained his view "of a historical fissure within a culture, which significantly distances the language of the uneducated classes and their artistic productions from the mainstream voices that possess the power to acknowledge and so to legitimize cultural works,"[29] Coleridge, on the other hand, argued against the symbiosis of language and culture through an explanation of the lack of imagination in the uneducated man. He writes in *Biographia Literaria*,

> The best part of human language, properly so called, is derived from reflection on the acts of the mind itself. It is formed by a voluntary appropriation of fixed symbols to internal acts, to processes and results of imagination, the greater part of which have no place in the consciousness of uneducated man; though in civilized society, by imitation and passive remembrance of what they hear from their religious instructors and other superiors, the most uneducated share in the harvest which they neither sowed or reaped.[30]

Coleridge's argument underlies his belief that one's cultural position, formed through economics and education, distinguishes the ability of the mind to exercise poetic imagination. He acknowledges that the "uneducated man" may not have the ability to originate "fixed symbols" of the imagination; however, he can, by "imitation and passive remembrance," exchange these ideas with others. This distinction of an "educated" versus an "uneducated" human mind established a narrow view of intellectuality that was widely accepted in his day and restricted women within the public discourse. Furthermore, examining the role of the wife within this cultural setting serves to confirm Coleridge's limited view of his own wife, Sara.

On the other hand, it did not necessarily limit his appreciation for the literary accomplishments of other women who were not wives. His fondness for William Wordsworth's sister-in-law Sara Hutchinson and his ease among the Wordsworth family members which included the unmarried Dorothy Wordsworth corroborate his desire for female companionship with unmarried women. Dorothy wrote extensively in her journals but never associated herself as an author of literature; Sara Hutchinson listened to Coleridge's poetry and transcribed his writing without making wifely demands on him. After joining the domestic felicity of the Hutchinsons and Wordsworths, Coleridge began writing verses and sent them to Sara Hutchinson, verses that eventually became part of a book titled *Sarah Hutchinson's Poets*. George Whalley, author of *Coleridge and Sara Hutchinson and the Asra Poems*, explains,

> The *Soliloquy* is very similar in tone and treatment to a verse letter of seventy-six lines (unpublished), written to Joanna Hutchinson and Isabella Addison on 19 August 1801 when Coleridge was on his way home from Gallow Hill by way of Bishop's Middleham; ... I incline to the view that the *Soliloquy* was written (?in Keswick) at about this time, was sent by letter to Sara and became the first entry in her book....[31]

For Coleridge, these women express the nature of the submissive wife, the charitable and benevolent female, unlike the independent Sara Fricker whose creative spirit made her a less appealing wife. "Sarah [sic] and her sisters (with the exception of Edith) all revealed strong characters; they were all possessors of a proper pride and natural dignity; and all shared hot tempers, quickly provoked, but as quickly subsiding,"[32] explains Molly Lefebure in her description of the Fricker family. Sara's strong personality and quickness of temper, especially concerning domestic needs, financial struggles, and a philosophical husband, lessened her attractiveness as a literary companion to Coleridge.

Growing up Sara faced hard financial times that made her a practical wife rather than a poetic partner. More than likely the economic downturn of the Fricker family due to the bankruptcy and subsequent death of their father, as mentioned earlier in the chapter, placed the daughters in the unenviable position of "returning home to cheap lodgings at night, with no male presence in their household to protect them or buttress them in a society and era which held poor and unprotected women in contempt, ...,"[33] writes Lefebure. In her comparison of Sara's strong feelings with Dorothy Wordworth's recriminating remarks, Lefebure draws further attention to criticism of Sara's adherence to her private roles as an efficient mother and a dedicated wife:

> Hers [Sara's] was not a smooth or soothing personality: her spirited response to everything and everyone, her intense interest in every detail of everyday life, coupled with an energy and practicality which prompted her not only to put her finger into every pie but (conscious of her superior powers of efficiency and dispatch) to attempt to assume complete management of the said pie, ensured that anyone who became involved with her could be certain of a stimulating, not to say at moments an exasperating, time.[34]

In Sara, then, is found a more complex personality than acknowledged by Coleridge. Paradoxically, the wife he chose represents strong masculine traits of independence and intelligence that were advocated by those women reformers like Mary Wollstonecraft who were not afraid of vocalizing their feminist desires to educate women equally to men. While unable to publicize her intolerance for female submissiveness, Sara "had gusto, zest, a keen sense of humour, but she did not, certainly as a young woman, believe in the saying, 'Anything for a quiet life',"[35] explains Lefebure in her biographical sketch of Sara Fricker as a woman in bondage to love.

Earlier on in their relationship while Coleridge was still discovering the literary ability of his new wife, he included a poem entitled "The Silver Thimble" in his 1796 publication of poetry. The poem's subtitle is explained as "The Production of a Young Lady, Addressed to the Author of the Poems Alluded to in the Preceding Epistle."[36] While the 1847 text of *Biographia Literaria* notes that "Mrs. Coleridge told her daughter that she wrote but little of these verses,"[37] this suggests that she not only did compose at least some of the poem but also in collaboration with her husband. The poem is introduced with a synopsis of the story that "*She had lost her Silver Thimble, and her complaint being accidentally overheard by him, her Friend, he immediately sent her four others to take her choice of.*"[38] The poem begins, "As oft mine eye with careless glance / Has gallop'd thro' some old romance, / Of speaking Birds and Steeds with wings, / Giants and Dwarfs, and Fiends and Kings; ... Save in the dear delicious land of Faery!"[39] (lines 1–4, 12). The poem opens with the speaker describing a medieval setting of romance surrounded by mythical characters of giants and dwarfs in a land of make-believe. This is a land that mimics the idealism of the Coleridge romance at this time, a romance founded on the fantastic scheme of Pantisocratic ideals. Sara refers to an "Arch-magician" who could very well be Samuel magically perplexing her with his musical charms:

Idyllic Marriage, Motherhood, and Literary Genius 99

> My mind went to and fro, and waver'd long; / At length I've chosen (Samuel things me wrong) / *That,* around whose azure rim / Silver figures seem to swim, / Like fleece-white clouds, that on the skiey Blue, / Waked by no breeze, the self-same shapes retain; / Or ocean-Nymphs with limbs of snowy hue / Slow-floating o'er the calm cerulean plain.[40]
> (lines 19–26)

Describing the beauty and stillness of the sky, its colors and shapes, Sara unfolds her aesthetic perspective of nature's ability to produce an atmosphere of calmness and serenity.

Once the poet establishes the setting of this sublime experience, the labor of the sewing woman interrupts the calm scene with the prick of a needle, pricking her life with disappointment and strife. Needlework was very familiar to Sara and her sisters Edith and Mary who turned to sewing to support the family after their father Stephen Fricker went bankrupt. The following verse addresses the momentary pain experienced by the needlewoman:

> Just such a one, *mon cher ami,*
> (The finger shield of industry)
> Th'inventive Gods, I deem, to Pallas gave
> What time the vain Arachne, madly brave,
> Challeng'd the blue-eyed Virgin of the sky
> A duel in embroider'd work to try.[41]

The central character of Arachne as a mere mortal challenges the goddess Athena, an immortal, to a contest of weaving the best tapestry. Ovid composed this mythological tale in his book *Metamorphoses* which depicts the vanity of a mortal trying to create a needlework superior to an immortal.

> And hence the thimbled Finger of grave Pallas
> To th'erring Needle's point was more than callous.
> But ah the poor Arachne! She unarm'd
> Blundering thro' hasty eagerness, alarm'd
> With all a *Rival's* hopes, a *Mortal's* fears,
> Still miss'd the stitch, and stain'd the web with tears.[42]

The mortal must suffer the wounds of mortality, tears and blood, just like the needlewoman suffers in her livelihood of domesticity. For some young women who needed to provide financial care for family as laborers, or as dressmakers like Sara's unmarried sisters Martha and Elizabeth Fricker, the mortal experience may have been a more "callous" and loveless one.

Like the mortal woman in the poem who feared missing a stitch, the needlewoman felt the wounds of domestic strife. The mortal woman is unarmed against the immortal goddess; she can only blunder through her needlework missing a stitch, never able to achieve recognition for her own gifts and talents. Her web or "handiwork" becomes stained with tears but not for lack of trying or challenging the immortal work of the goddess.

> Unnumber'd punctures small yet sore
> Full fretfully the maiden bore,
> Till she her lily finger found
> Crimson'd with many a tiny wound;
> And to her eyes, suffus'd with watery woe,
> Her flower-embroider'd web danc'd dim, I wist,
> Like blossom'd shrubs in a quick-moving mist:
> Till vanquish'd the despairing Maid sunk low.[43]

If the "despairing Maid" were as gifted as the immortal goddess, or as a poet creating images with her poetic imagination, she would not suffer the wounds of an ordinary woman. The mortal Arachne cannot compete with the immortal goddess Athena. The tale concludes as she hangs herself in despair, but Athena grants her immortal life when she restores Arachne to immortality as a spider, not as a woman. Sara cannot compete with Samuel in the realm of the poetic imagination; her identity as a poet is overshadowed by her domestic role as a wife. She is reminded once again of her mortality and must suffer the "tiny wound" again and again which is imparted by each prick of her needle. While this poem was written early in their relationship, Sara unknowingly prophesies a married life condemned to abandonment by her socially inscribed role of a wife that for Samuel can never attain the heights of an ideal wife. Samuel's poetic concept of wife as an ideal woman is better defined by Athena than Arachne.

The third and final verse of the poem addresses the poet, "O Bard!" as one who imparts the wisdom and greatness of a prophet preaching repentance from the shores of the Jordan River to singing the immeasurable praises of "Alla." The "common Muse" cannot inspire such a lofty poet with her ordinariness as she continues to suffer each wound from the point of the needle. From the domestic act of sewing to the literary expression of sewing expressed in a poetic form, Sara tells the tale of the wife for whom sewing signifies a transformative nature in the way women choose to identify themselves in their social environments as females and as wives, sisters, and mothers.

Sewing symbolizes the limited role of women as domestic caretakers while stitching together the common and ordinary with the poetic and imaginative, thereby fitting the naturalness of language into the formality of the poetic form. The social and gender implications of the needle were expressed in an essay written by Mary Lamb in 1815 that needlework for upper and middle-class women was a form of "self-imposed slavery."[44] She published under the pseudonym Sempronia and addressed "issues of women's limited preparation for occupations, women's role in marriage, and the implicit tensions among women across social classes."[45] As Carol Shiner Wilson explains, "Lamb's essay—like the sewing icon—illuminates issues of class as it juxtaposes the distressed needleworker with the middle-class wife and mother."[46] Lamb, along with Mary Wollstonecraft, regarded needlework as the enemy of intellectual advancement. In her commentary on the domestic constraints of sewing, Wilson further elaborates on the tale of Arachne and Athena (Minerva) as the nerve center of domestic discontent:

> Warlike Minerva serves and protects the male privilege in which she participates. As the patriarchy's agent, she excludes mortal sisters from the realm of power, literary production, and recognition of genius, just as she forbids those sisters to surpass her in their needlework. Women are not deemed incapable of artistic accomplishment, but they must be careful not to reveal genius in a way that would displease the male establishment's sense of superiority.[47]

As one of the necessities of domestic life and economic survival, sewing pervaded the identity of the female from childhood through adulthood[48] and like its counterpart, teaching, had become a source of degradation for women, particularly wives, who attempted to rise above this inferior role and enter the superior place of intellectualism along with their male partners.

Women like Sara were socially limited beyond their domestic sphere of duty. Yet, Sara demonstrated to her fullest capacity within the boundaries of home, the importance of educating her children and supporting their literary interests. As part of a family community living at Greta Hall in Keswick, Sara shared the responsibilities of teaching her children and her sister Edith's children. The families had joined together to settle down in Keswick where the women could help one another in their domestic duties and the men could write and collaborate on their ideas and publications. Robert Southey writes to Charles Danvers in December 1801 of his plans to move with his wife Edith to Greta Hall:

> This vagabond life will not last very long. If at the years end Corry and I should part and I should be again afloat, I will then go to Keswick, to the same house with Mrs Coleridge and economize there—almost indifferent whether any advancement in life should remove me or not. We

should be magnificently lodged for 25 £ a year, and my annual expence if settled there, would not outrun 150 £. An odd scheme for a Secretary, you will say, and yet it is my favourite one and seems most probable.[49]

Southey had always been fond of Sara Coleridge from the time they were children, and his reference to her companionship in the letter indicates that she is a significant reason for his desire to move to a life of contentment at Greta Hall. This move would bring the two families together for a short while until Coleridge distanced himself from his wife and children.

In 1814 Sara writes to Tom Poole at the time Coleridge's play *Remorse* is performed in London, eager to hear any information regarding her husband and his theatrical accomplishments. She writes,

> Our intelligent neighbour Mr Quincey tells me, that you had been with Mr C. in London during the last year; you would naturally imagine that he would mention this circumstance to me in his letters—but unhappily for me & the dear children, & I may add, for himself, his aversion to writing of every kind seems to strengthen with every absence—we have not seen him for 2 years--& it will be 12 months in March since he wrote to Keswick—having only sent me one letter during 2 years.—

She expresses her sad disappointment at not hearing from her husband but once in two years as she further describes the circumstances in detail:

> When my brother Southey returned from London, C. promised to accompany him; we were all sadly disappointed when the Chaise arrived with only *one* person in it—S. however assured us, that he would be here shortly, having gone to Bristol to deliver a course of Lectures, after which he would set off for Keswick to meet the Boys at the *Christmas* holidays—so I kept them at home in the hope of a letter giving some direction about Hartley's studies, but none coming, I sent the poor fellows back last Monday, with their Skaits across their shoulders.[50]

Despite Sara's tone of disappointment in Samuel's lack of communication with her and the family, she is resigned to accepting an absentee husband and father. She describes rather narratively the skating activities that the boys, Hartley and Derwent, are to miss because they must return to school. Further on, her letter details Hartley's studies with an excerpt from a letter to his mother outlining the foreign languages and scholars Hartley is reading. Hartley's excerpt reiterates Sara's longing for the time when his father will return to express his satisfaction with Hartley's educational accomplishments as a reader of Homer, Virgil, and Aeschylus, and as an arithmetic student of Euclid.

Idyllic Marriage, Motherhood, and Literary Genius 103

The following Christmas at Keswick 1815 was a holiday celebration for the Coleridge and Southey families, including the young Southey children, Hartley Coleridge—now 19 years old, Derwent, and his sister Sara—almost at the age of 13. Sara writes to Poole describing the family size and togetherness:

> We have no increase of the Southey family since I wrote: 4 Girls and a dear boy is their present number—& I cannot say I am at all anxious for an addition to it—for indeed we are a house *quite* full when we are altogether—at Christmas we seemed like bees in a Hive—for now Eliza is here we are 4 women—Southey—8 children 3 servants—&.[51]

It was not until the next year of 1816 that the Coleridge family would receive a letter from their father with a new promise for financial support from his play *A Christmas Tale* to be performed at Covent Garden. Overjoyed at the news, Sara was to be disappointed once again when no further word was received from Samuel.[52] Expressing her despair over Samuel's absence, Sara reveals her intimate thoughts to her friend and Stowey neighbor Tom Poole:

> I have said but little of S.T.C. because I think it likely enough, that you have either seen him at Bristol—or heard of him from Mrs King—Southey writes to Danvers—and from him we learn that Coleridge has been very ill—but is better & intends coming soon—if he does not shortly *recollect* that he has a *wife & three children* in the *north* of England, who can *now, less than ever,* do without his pecuniary aid.[53]

With the absence of Samuel as husband and father, the Coleridge family relied on Southey as a substitute, both emotionally and financially. Greta Hall became the center of their educational activities and Sara fulfilled her role with vigor establishing an intellectually stimulating environment with regular schooling for the Southey children and her own along with her sisters Edith, Mary, and Eliza. Greta Hall was soon nicknamed Aunt Hill since there were so many aunts living there.[54] Sara apologetically writes to Poole for her "agitation of spirits" because she is writing in a room full of children:

> —for we keep regular School from ½ past nine until 4 with the exception of an hour for walking and an half hour for dressing—Mrs Lovel keeps school in a small room for English and Latin—and the writing and figures—french—italian &c are done with me in the *dining room* with the assistance of Aunt Eliza—and Southey teaches his wife and daughters to read spanish in the . . ? . . and

his son Greek—should we not all be very learned! –At Miss Barkers are displayed accomplishments of a different kind—she is proficient in drawing—plays pretty well at the Harp & Harpsichord--& is (between ourselves) a bit of a poetess—now I give you full leave to laugh at this pompous description of our occupations— &.[55]

Not only does Sara emphasize the intellectual diversity of studies, but she also makes a distinction regarding the elevated status of Miss Barker as a "poetess" noting the importance of teaching the children an aesthetic education. Sara's devotion to the educational advancement of her children surpasses a more common desire to raise well-rounded and highly cultured individuals and even further emphasizes literary identity above nurturing her daughter to become someone's wife. Her children are expected to become accomplished students as the sons and daughter of a poetic genius with the encouragement of an intuitively and intellectually aware mother. Her daughter Sara grows up to fulfill her mother's dreams as she becomes her own author and the author of her father's unpublished literary remains after his death in 1834.

Sara's expressions of motherhood and her brand of poetic genius were promulgated by her life as Samuel's wife; her feelings of despair, abandonment, and separation from her husband fostered her individuality. She writes to Poole,

You will be shocked to hear that I never hear from C. I dare not dwell upon the painful consequences of his desertion but if in the Spring he does not exert himself to pay some of my debts here—I really do not know what will be the result.[56]

Sara's concern is not only for herself but, more importantly, for the welfare and support of her children as they grow into literary adults. She continues to keep Poole informed of her financial needs, how hard Hartley is studying, and his opportunities for a position in College so he might achieve what his cousins have as fellows. Moreover, the Coleridge family takes an interest in Hartley's education so that Sara is not without her family's encouragement:

General Peachey tells me, that a *Postmastership* at Merton is the same thing as a *Scholarship* in other Colleges—with this exception, that it ceases in 4 years,—but we hope in four years he [Hartley] will be advancing towards a fellowship—his cousins John & Wm are both fellows.[57]

Hartley's Uncle G. C. [George Coleridge] further implores him to study his Latin and learn to perfect the first six books of Euclid.[58] Within this

Idyllic Marriage, Motherhood, and Literary Genius   105

circle of family and friends Sarah generates an intellectual environment stimulating scholarly learning both in the privacy of her own home and in the public setting of a higher educational institution that offer her children the kind of literary careers in keeping with her husband's literary stature. She is never forgetful of the gratitude she owes her intimate friends such as Poole to whom she writes:

> —I believe dear Sir, I have mentioned every needful particular, relative to this business which you are so good as to interest yourself in, and before I conclude I must mention the great kindness and solicitude we have experienced from Wordsworth & his family respecting an unfortunate situation, with promises of assistance &c.—and to Southey I am in every manner everlastingly bound: I pray heaven to reward you all, for yr. goodness!—[59]

Sara's efforts as a mother and her endowment of poetic ability are integral to her success in raising children of literary parents despite her lack of public achievement. Her generosity and kindness of character permeate her friendships giving her children the kind of opportunities lost to them because of their father's absence. She transmits her love and appreciation for the nature of poetic genius to her children, a love that grew within her from the time before she met Coleridge and more than likely contributed to their mutual attraction.

Notes

1 Stephen Potter, ed., *Minnow among Tritons* (Bloomsbury: Nonesuch Press, 1934), 1. Sara writes to her neighbor Thomas Poole who is in Nether Stowey. She has been in Bristol caring for her mother and ill son [11 February 1799].
2 See James Sketchley's *Bristol Directory 1775* with an introduction by Bryan Little (Bath: Kingsmead Reprints, 1971).
3 See James Sketchley's *Bristol Directory 1775*.
4 Lawrence Stone, *The Family, Sex and Marriage in England 1500–1800* (New York: Harper & Row, Publishers, 1977), 32.
5 Stone, *The Family*, 35.
6 See Rebecca Probert's discussion for various opinions on the benefits and restrictions in marriage law on English society. Probert maintains, "It has even been claimed that the Act fundamentally altered the very meaning of marriage for the participants, transforming marriage from a private and meaningful rite to a bureaucratic transaction." Rebecca Probert, *Marriage Law and Practice in the Long Eighteenth Century: A Reassessment* (Cambridge University Press, 2009), 3.
7 Kenneth Curry, ed., *New Letters of Robert Southey, Volume 1: 1792–1810* (New York: Columbia University Press, 1965), 23.

106   *The Social Imagination of the Romantic Wife in Literature*

8   Curry, ed., *New Letters*, 22–23.
9   Heather J. Jackson, ed., *Samuel Taylor Coleridge: Selected Letters* (Oxford: Clarendon Press, 1987), 8.
10 Elizabeth Sandford, *Thomas Poole and His Friends* (Over Stowey, Somerset: The Friarn Press, 1996), 78. This letter of congratulations to S. T. Coleridge is dated 10 October 1795.
11 This poem was composed on 12 September 1795 as indicated by Elizabeth Sandford in Thomas Poole and His Friends, 79. Poole expressed his high regard for Coleridge and traveled to Bristol to hear him lecture.
12 Sandford, *Thomas Poole and His Friends*, 81.
13 Sandford, *Thomas Poole and His Friends*, 115.
14 Sandford, *Thomas Poole and His Friends*, 115.
15 Sandford, *Thomas Poole and His Friends*, 116.
16 Sara Coleridge expresses her grief over her son's death to their neighbor in Nether Stowey. See Potter, ed., *Minnow*, 1.
17 Sara adheres to the Christian ethic of fortitude, an eighteenth-century trait of the virtuous wife. See Potter, ed., *Minnow*, 1.
18 The following poems are directly quoted from a 4×6 leaflet in the collection of letters written by Sara Fricker Coleridge at the Harry Ransom Center, University of Texas in Austin. One poem is written on the front page and the other on Berkeley's death is written inside. An envelope written in the hand of Sara Fricker Coleridge describes the contents quoted above.
19 See *Sara Fricker Coleridge Collection* of unpublished letters from the Harry Ransom Center at the University of Texas in Austin. The descriptions of Berkeley's illness and death appear in two letters dated 1 November 1798 and 13 December 1798 addressed to Samuel Taylor Coleridge from Sara, and two letters dated 24 January 1799 and 11 February 1799 of Sara's correspondence with Thomas Poole.
20 Molly Lefebure, *Bondage of Love: A Life of Mrs. Samuel Taylor Coleridge* (New York: Norton, 1987), 22.
21 Lefebure, *Bondage of Love*, 22.
22 Lefebure, *Bondage of Love*, 21.
23 Lefebure, *Bondage of Love*, 21–22.
24 Maurice H. Fitzgerald, ed., *Letters of Robert Southey: A Selection* (New York: AMS Press, 1977), 340.
25 Fitzgerald, ed., *Letters of Robert Southey*, 341.
26 Unpublished account of Sara Fricker Coleridge as *Mrs. Codian Remembrances of RS & STC* from the Harry Ransom Center (Austin: University of Texas), no date.
27 In his essay "The Uneducated Imagination: Romantic Representations of Labor," Kurt Heinzelman explains Southey's concern over the relationship between the working class and poetry: "Underlying Southey's essay is his personal fear that this commonality of laborer-poets might augur a political solidarity of laborers as such." Mary A. Favret and Nicola J. Watson, eds., *At the Limits of Romanticism: Essays in Cultural, Feminist, and Materialist Criticism* (Bloomington: Indiana University Press, 1994), 101.

28 Heinzelman, "The Uneducated Imagination," 101–102.
29 Heinzelman, "The Uneducated Imagination," 112.
30 Samuel Taylor Coleridge, *The Collected Works of Samuel Taylor Coleridge*, vol. 7: Biographia Literaria, or Biographical Sketches of My Literary Life and Opinions, vol. II: chapter 17, eds. James Engell and Walter Jackson Bate (Princeton: Princeton University Press, 1983), 54. Coleridge references Schiller's comment on the distinction between the modern, or sentimental poet versus the naïve poet. See editorial note on p. 54.
31 According to Whalley, Coleridge's poem Soliloquy "embodies the spontaneous, almost brotherly, gaiety of his early association with Sara and indicates the unfastidious character of Sara's original intention in making up her book." George Whalley, *Coleridge and Sara Hutchinson and the Asra Poems* (Toronto: University of Toronto Press, 1955), 29–31.
32 Lefebure, *Bondage of Love*, 25.
33 Lefebure, *Bondage of Love*, 25.
34 Lefebure, *Bondage of Love*, 26.
35 Lefebure, *Bondage of Love*, 26.
36 Ernest Hartley Coleridge, ed., *Coleridge: Poetical Works*, (Oxford: Oxford University Press, 1988), 104.
37 Coleridge, E. H., ed., *Coleridge: Poetical Works*, 104.
38 Coleridge, E. H., ed., *Coleridge: Poetical Works*, 104.
39 Coleridge, E. H., ed., *Coleridge: Poetical Works*, 104.
40 Coleridge, E. H., ed., *Coleridge: Poetical Works*, 105.
41 Coleridge, E. H., ed., *Coleridge: Poetical Works*, 105.
42 Coleridge, E. H., ed., *Coleridge: Poetical Works*, 105.
43 Coleridge, E. H., ed., *Coleridge: Poetical Works*, 105.
44 Carol Shiner Wilson, "Lost Needles, Tangled Threads: Stitchery, Domesticity, and the Artistic Enterprise in Barbauld, Edgeworth, Taylor, and Lamb." Carol Shiner Wilson and Joel Haefner, eds., *Re-Visioning Romanticism: British Women Writers, 1776–1837* (Philadelphia: University of Pennsylvania Press, 1994), 185.
45 Wilson, "Lost Needles," 185.
46 Wilson, "Lost Needles," 186.
47 Wilson, "Lost Needles," 188.
48 Carol Shiner Wilson explains,

> Needlework was integral to all girls' education, regardless of their social class, and for a girl or woman to be at her "work" meant to be at her *needle*work. Patient and silent, the little girl hunched over samplers on which she stitched mottos of obedience to God and her parents. As adults, the wealthy tended to do *fancywork*, embroidery with expensive threads and fabric, and some *plainwork*, chiefly for male members of the family or inexpensive charity clothing for the poor.
>
> (167–68)

49 Kenneth Curry, ed., *New Letters of Robert Southey, Volume One: 1792–1810* (New York: Columbia University Press, 1965), 260.

50 Potter, ed., *Minnow*, 22.
51 Potter, ed., *Minnow*, 27.
52 Lefebure, *Bondage of Love*, 218.
53 Potter, ed., *Minnow*, 28.
54 Lefebure, *Bondage of Love*, 218.
55 Potter, ed., *Minnow*, 37.
56 Potter, ed., *Minnow*, 32.
57 Potter, ed., *Minnow*, 31.
58 Potter, ed., *Minnow*, 31.
59 Potter, ed., *Minnow*, 32.

References

Coleridge, Ernest Hartley, ed. *Coleridge: Poetical Works*. Oxford: Oxford University Press, 1988.

Coleridge, Samuel Taylor. *The Collected Works of Samuel Taylor Coleridge*, vol. 7: Biographia Literaria or Biographical Sketches of My Literary Life and Opinions, eds. James Engell and Walter Jackson Bate, vol. II: 5–234. Princeton: Princeton University Press, 1983.

Coleridge, Sara Fricker. *Sara Fricker Coleridge Collection 1794–1931:* Unpublished Letters and *Mrs. Codian Remembrances of RS & STC*, undated. Harry Ransom Center. Austin: University of Texas.

Curry, Kenneth, ed. *New Letters of Robert Southey, Volume 1: 1792–1810*. New York: Columbia University Press, 1965.

Favret, Mary A., and Nicola J. Watson, eds. *At the Limits of Romanticism: Essays in Cultural, Feminist, and Materialist Criticism*. Bloomington: Indiana University Press, 1994.

Fitzgerald, Maurice H., ed. *Letters of Robert Southey: A Selection*. New York: AMS Press, 1977.

Jackson, Heather J., ed. *Samuel Taylor Coleridge: Selected Letters*. Oxford: Clarendon Press, 1987.

Lefebure, Molly. *Bondage of Love: A Life of Mrs. Samuel Taylor Coleridge*. New York: Norton, 1987.

Potter, Stephen, ed. *Minnow among Tritons*. Bloomsbury: Nonesuch Press, 1934.

Sandford, Elizabeth. *Thomas Poole and His Friends*. Over Stowey: The Friarn Press, 1996.

Sketchley, James. *Bristol Directory 1775*. Introduction by Bryan Little. Bath: Kingsmead Reprints, 1971.

Stone, Lawrence. *The Family, Sex and Marriage in England 1500–1800*. New York: Harper & Row, Publishers, 1977.

Whalley, George. *Coleridge and Sara Hutchinson and the Asra Poems*. Toronto: University of Toronto Press, 1955.

Wilson, Carol Shiner, and Joel Haefner, eds. *Re-Visioning Romanticism: British Women Writers, 1776–1837*. Philadelphia: University of Pennsylvania Press, 1994.

6 Circle of Friends and Family

> *as to those Women who find themselves born for Slavery and are so sensible of their own Meanness as to conclude it impossible to attain to any thing excellent, ... ought to be best acquainted with their own Strength and Genius.*[1]
> (Mary Astell, *Reflections Upon Marriage*)

In Jeremy Taylor's treatise *The Measures and Offices of Friendship*, published in 1662, he presents ideas on negotiating contradictory notions of friendship that were later expressed in the novels of the eighteenth century. These contradictory notions of friendship included the universality of Christian charity as kindness to all, in contrast with the exclusivity of friendship as intimacy among a few individuals. From the universal to the personal, these various expressions of friendship can be seen to affect the harmony of the marriage relationship, and in particular, the Coleridge marriage.

Eighteenth-century friendships encompassed many aspects of companionship, often blurring lines of modesty and chastity, those moral virtues that determined outward behavior. Social customs among families and households of the eighteenth century noted a familial intimacy among family members who relied on each other more routinely than seen in our culture today. Looking more closely at the Coleridge marriage, for example, one can discern how several intimate friendships with individuals outside of the marriage disrupted the equanimity of their marital relations. How does a wife accommodate the literary friendships of her husband with other women such as Dorothy Wordsworth or Sara Hutchinson? How are we to understand the emotional and moral implications for a wife who intimately befriends a close neighbor, Tom Poole, and a brother-in-law, Robert Southey, with whom she shares a household?

From among the diverse relationships that exist within a nuclear household, the bonds of parent and child as well as siblings complicate emotional attachments of husband and wife. Nevertheless, these emotional

DOI: 10.4324/9781003504238-6

bonds created between adult brothers and sisters often mimicked the husband/wife association. These intimate friendships exhibit genuine feelings of tenderness such as exist between a husband and wife while, at the same time, are devoid of the sexual attraction or physical affections that also define a marriage. Choosing a marital partner during the eighteenth century was a matter of family acceptance, economic stability, and feminine instruction on wifely manners. Unfortunately, the constraints of Christian orthodoxy and the complexities of the marriage laws would often bind young couples to an emotionally unfulfilling legal contract. The Coleridges wrestled with these restraints, each one searching for comfort and happiness in friendships peripheral to their marriage.

Beginning with their son Berkeley's death in 1799 and Coleridge's subsequent addictions, Sara learned to express the kind of fortitude that many wives could not. Perhaps her ability to cope with these inconsistencies in her marriage came from her intimate friendships. Despite her feelings of loss and suffering, she persisted in handling the business of her son's death with the help of her brother-in-law Southey. She tells Poole, "Southey has undertaken the business of my babe's interment and in a few days we shall remove to his house at Westbury which I shall be rejoiced to do for this house at present is quite hateful to me."[2] Her ability to articulate her feelings of despair to Poole with a degree of constancy illustrates Sara's adherence to a Christian morality she shared with Coleridge's own religious beliefs. She even expects to be "tranquil" when she sees Poole in the following month and is able to greet him, in Sara's words, with "the smile of resignation."[3] Sara behaved according to the evangelical beliefs of the educated female as described by Hannah More: "An early habitual restraint is peculiarly important to the future character and happiness of woman. A judicious, unrelaxing, but steady and gentle curb on their tempers and passions can alone ensure their peace and establish their principles."[4] Sara's emotional strength is directly connected to these social expectations for young married women.

Through her emotional restraint, Sara describes the last moments of Berkeley's life as she and her sisters watch him in his cradle. Her remarks elaborate on the sufferings of her infant son in "a violent convulsive fit" and magnify her hopelessness in reaching Coleridge who remains for Sara at an inaccessible distance both geographically and emotionally. Sara pours forth her intimate feelings of grief and loss to her kind friend Poole, hoping he will "allay" her sorrows and "ease" her passions, which Taylor suggests is the natural expression of friendship. The letter continues to express her financial worries while she manages to send her kind thoughts to Tom's mother and kind respects to Mr. Ward. Sara illustrates an ability to use language not only to communicate in her letters but also to pour out her heartfelt emotions with clarity of thought, precise rhetoric, and descriptive phrasing. Poole admires Sara's strength as a mother and wife in her quiet expression of emotional grief. However, his genuine sympathy for Sara and understanding of her loss contradicts his concern for his literary friend's intellectual advancement, not wishing to disturb Coleridge while he studies in Germany. He writes to Coleridge with comforting words, praising Sara for her fortitude: "Don't conjure up any scenes of distress which never happened. Mrs. Coleridge felt as a mother ... and, in an exemplary manner, did all a mother could do."[5] Coleridge remains insulated in Germany, disconnected from the emotional loss of his second child and his wife's grief over the death. Both Sara and Samuel find their comfort in others rather than with each other. These friendships become the higher priority for the married couple who seek emotional intimacy in their neighbors and others nearby.

Friendship as an eighteenth-century term encompasses a shift toward a more enlightened view of acquaintances, families, associates, neighbors, and allies. The numerous friends of the Coleridges span each of these categories; and furthermore, from a critical perspective of their friendships, we can examine the role of the Romantic wife more closely. Intimate friendships with family and neighbors reveal how the social nature of the wife and Sara's role in the marriage reshape the attributes of the Romantic wife as friend, wife, and lover. During the early years of the Coleridge marriage, their neighbor Tom Poole became an indispensable support for the young wife as friend and ally, especially when Sara was distressed over Coleridge's absence from home. Facing his own personal disappointments, Samuel writes to his wife on Tuesday morning, 22 November 1802 from St. Clears, Carmarthen:

> Be assured, my dear Love, that I shall never write otherwise than *most* kindly to you, except after great *aggressions* on your part; and not then, unless my reason convinces me that some good end will be answered by my reprehensions—My dear Love![6]

However, despite Coleridge's attempts to profess kindness toward his wife, he continued with his treatise on Love for his family and friends in defense of his own inadequacies as a father and husband. He explains to Sara,

> let me in the spirit of Love say two things. I. I owe duties, and solemn ones to you, as my wife, but some equally solemn ones to Myself, to my children, to my friends and to society. When duties are at variance dreadful as the case may be, there must be a choice. I can neither retain my happiness nor my faculties, unless I move, live and love in perfect freedom, limited only by my own purity and self-respect and by my

incapability of loving any person, man or woman, unless at the same time I honor and esteem them.[7]

Coleridge maintains that his right as a husband is to be loved in return as he loves declaring, "My nature is quick to love and retentive." As he reasons through his own nature, he also reasons how a wife's nature ought to be saying,

> It were well, if every woman wrote down before her marriage all, she thought, she had a *right* to from her husband and to examine each in this form. By what *Law* of God, of man, or of general reason, do I claim *this* right? I suspect, that this process would make a ludicrous quantity of blots and erasures in most of the first rude draughts of these Rights of Wives—infinitely however to their own advantage, and to the security of their true and genuine rights.[8]

No wonder Sara looked to her friends and family for some comfort while she struggled to make sense of Coleridge's remarks on how best to love as a wife.

In the meantime, she was about to give birth to their daughter Sara the following month in December 1802. Coleridge was becoming more and more reliant on laudanum for his physical comforts and less and less capable of supporting his family. In the same letter he tells Sara,

> I could scarcely touch my dinner and was obliged at last to take 20 drops of Laudanum which now that I have for 10 days left off all stimulus of all kinds, excepting 1/3rd of a grain of opium at night, acted upon me more powerfully than 80 or 100 drops would have done at Keswick.[9]

After Sara, their youngest child, was born in 1802, Coleridge soon after left his wife and family in Keswick in the Lake District, and in 1804 he traveled to Malta. His absenteeism continued until 1806 with infrequent communication and failure to provide economic care for his family: Hartley, Derwent, Sara, and his wife Sara.

Yearning for emotional comfort unavailable from her absentee husband, Sara found instead a caring friend in her brother-in-law Robert Southey with whom she lived and depended on for companionship as much as she did for financial support during her critical years of child-raising. In mid-April 1807 Southey writes to John Rickman,

> What you have heard of Coleridge is true, he is about to seperate [sic] from his wife, and as he chuses [sic] to do every thing in a way different

from the rest of the world, is first going with her to visit his relations where however she has long since been introduced.[10]

Southey remained a constant support to Sara throughout their lives especially after the Coleridge separation. He recognized the marital and emotional restraints under which Sara struggled to manage for herself and her household. Southey further comments to Rickman, "The seperation [sic] is a good thing—his habits are so murderous of all domestic comfort that I am only surprised [sic] Mrs C. is not rejoiced at being rid of him."[11] From Southey's remarks comes the obvious conclusion that Sara was determined to maintain her marriage to Samuel despite his faults and weaknesses as a husband. Perhaps her adherence to her Christian faith and her love of family shaped her decision to keep the marriage relationship open to future possibilities while she raised her children in a literary environment.

Occupying the same living space with a spouse's siblings often contributes to the complications of the marriage relationship. Even though some marriages appear to thrive under these circumstances, nevertheless, many scholars who have studied friendship during the eighteenth century have discovered that family relationships were entwined in a broad range of emotional, moral, and legal entanglements. In particular, Naomi Tadmor's study of the eighteenth-century family and friendships examines the nature of friendship through the language used in selected diaries and novels from this era. She explains, "In the eighteenth century, the term 'friend' had a plurality of meanings that spanned kinship ties, sentimental relationships, economic ties, occupational connections, intellectual and spiritual attachments, sociable networks, and political alliances."[12] Her study relocates the language of kinship and their ties during this period in recognition of those family relationships derived from blood and marriage as well as "those who live in the same house."[13]

Sara's family relationships with her brother-in-law and sister, and her friendships with neighbors evolved into deeper attachments because they considered what is "natural" to friendship as defined by Jeremy Taylor. In his treatise on friendship, he asserts that the nature of a friend is to comfort the human spirit in the following ways, such as in:

> the allay of our sorrows, the ease of our passions, the discharge of our oppressions, the sanctuary to our calamities, the counselor of our doubts, the clarity of our minds, the emission of our thoughts, the exercise and improvement of what we meditate.[14]

Sara was naturally attracted to those individuals who were capable of comforting "the human spirit" as seen through her letters and communications with Tom Poole and Robert Southey. Here we witness Sara's own language of sorrow and loss, as well as the intimacy of her thoughts and daily meditations. On 28 December 1807 Sara writes from Keswick to her Nether Stowey neighbor Tom Poole:

> If Coleridge has not written to you lately, I guess, from the interest you have always taken in our concerns, you will not consider a few lines, even from my feeble pen, an unpardonable intrusion.—But where shall I begin?[15]

Sara apologetically shared her intimate concerns with Poole further explaining that her distress resulted from her husband's confusing behavior. He first appeared to his wife in an improved state of health, planning to give his Lectures in Bristol after staying three or four days at home in Keswick. However, instead of heading to Bristol to carry out his work, he remained at home an additional three weeks without any explanation. Sara, who was afraid to disturb him by questioning his delay to town, wrote to Poole, "… I durst not speak lest it should *disarrange* him."[16] Sara's reluctance to interfere with Samuel's inexplicable behavior emphasizes how ingrained the expectations were at this time for wives to be subservient and as Coleridge had described Sara as "inferior" in nature. Female conduct was taught to young women like Sara to retain a passive role in their domestic duties.

Expectations of proper female conduct were broadly addressed in the literature of conduct books, letters to young ladies, and treatises on female education in preparation for marriage during the eighteenth century. Writers such as Wetenhall Wilkes in 1740, John Gregory in 1774, and Hannah More in 1799, among others,[17] emphasized the importance of chastity, modest reserve, and propriety in female manners throughout the decades leading up to the nineteenth century. In his dissertation on chastity, Wilkes warns young ladies,

> She, who forfeits her chastity, withers by degrees into scorn and contrition; but she who lives up to its rules, ever flourishes, like a rose in *June*, with all her virgin graces about her—sweet to the sense, and lovely to the eye.[18]

As Bridget Hill states,

> The eighteenth century opens and closes with a wave of evangelical enthusiasm when fears of social disorder in a period of great moral laxity and dissoluteness led to an urgent need for the middle and upper classes to set an example to those below them in the social hierarchy, to

work for the inculcation of the principles of Christian morality in the labouring class.[19]

The impact of these conduct books can be seen in the lives of women like Sara Fricker who was entrenched in a literary world even before her marriage to Samuel as well as being schooled in this social culture.

Friendship in marriage, as Taylor describes its further significance, extends beyond consolation for our sorrows and a "sanctuary" for our calamities. In its very nature, friendship in marriage enhances the improvement and clarity of our minds. One example from the Coleridge marital relationship that points to such an exchange of minds can be seen in how Samuel fondly addresses Sara. A playful use of language began early in the marriage when Coleridge affectionately dubbed Sara "Sally Pally." As Lefebure explains,

> Sara was S. T. C.'s 'dearest friend' in terms of fraternity, equality and marriage; but S. T. C. being S. T. C., with his boyhood roots firmly implanted in London's Christ Hospital and the cockney haunts of Newgate Street, he naturally hailed a friend as a pal; thus Sara, having become Sally (for democratic reasons, Sally being more a name of the people than Sara) next progressed to Pal, and from there it was a mere versifying step to Sally Pally.[20]

In this manner Coleridge exercised Wollstonecraft's desire for a wife to be considered more as a friend to her husband than a domestic partner. As Sara became acquainted with the reinvention of language, she furthered her own interests in creating names and descriptive language within the family. The lighthearted use of Sara's "Lingo Grande" among letters between the Coleridge children shows the influence of its impact on the family. Hartley Coleridge fondly refers to himself as "Snouderumpusson," his nickname for Mrs. Coleridge, in his letter of 6 November 1836 that he signs in Greek letters. In another letter of 19 February 1821 written to his brother Derwent at St. John's College in Cambridge, Hartley uses his mother's nickname for Derwent, "Snifterbreedus," with reference to James Gillman, his father's doctor, as "Doctissimus."[21] The Coleridge family associates their intimacy with an emotional attachment to language just as Coleridge associates his emotions through rhetorical expressions in his writing.

In his examination of Coleridge's use of language, Emerson R. Marks notes a similarity between Ferdinand de Saussure's linguistic system and Coleridge's system: "His [Coleridge's] own life-long interest in language went far beyond its use as an artistic medium, ranging from the most complex issues of its status as an index of human consciousness to the minutest details of grammar, syntax, and vocabulary."[22] In fact, Coleridge writes to John Murray in 1814 describing his "long habits of meditation on Language, as the symbolic medium of the connection of Thought with Thought, & of thoughts, as affected and modified by Passion & Emotion... ."[23] Coleridge's symbolic language has been closely examined in his poetics where he connects thought and emotion through natural imagery. However, as Marks recognizes, Coleridge's attention to language reaches beyond the artistic, or poetic, to the domestic in the full range of human consciousness. For Coleridge, the poetic expression of his daily life with Sara turned domestic affection from an ordinary experience into an extraordinary but unrealistic relationship. Ironically, while he desperately yearned for domestic affection from his wife, he could not sufficiently grasp the issues of married life in order to maintain his marriage or perceive Sara's individual qualities as an intellectual.

As a more complete portrait of Sara develops, we see her as a woman whose literary sympathies are sensitive to her children's poetic abilities. Her literary tastes and even criticism are evidenced in her letters when she remarks to Poole in September 1815 of two distinct opinions on William Wordsworth's "Excursion" and "The White Doe," hers and Sir George and Lady Beaumont, who "think him the finest of literary poets." She also comments on Robert Southey's poem "Roderick" which "has had a rapid sale, and is I believe pretty popular."[24] Sara's interest in Southey's printing of his second volume on the history of Brazil appears to be a genuine recognition of his achievements and is as meaningful as her comments on Coleridge's latest publishing efforts. Sara thoughtfully explains,

> Coleridge, it appears, has sent 2 vols: to the press; a republication of the former poems, with others, & a literary life of the Author, which has grown out of the preface; & is, if we may believe his son, an interesting part of the work: it is printing at Bristol but is to be, I suppose, published in London.—Heaven knows I have great reason to pray for its success, but it appears to me that Mr Morgan is too sanguine when he hopes C. will get some hundreds for this publication.[25]

Sara's attachment to the success of her children is also apparent in her desire to see her husband succeed even though she has little or no relationship with him. Without Coleridge's financial or emotional support, Sara persists in furthering her children's education. There is no weakness in her manner as she writes to Poole in January 1815,

> My brother Southey wrote a statement of our situation to Mr. G. Coleridge, who promised to try, through his nephews, to get some exhibition at one of the colleges for this 'fatherless child' (as he

affectionately termed him) and engaged to allow him £40 a year— ... which with £30 from Lady Beaumont, and your £10, make £80 per Annum—but that unless they could raise a hundred & thirty he thought he could not be supported there.[26]

Worried that Hartley will not be able to return home on vacations for lack of money, Sara expresses her dismay over the family's financial woes.

Yet, she continues to express her warmth and caring for neighbors and friends as she tells Poole of a visit by Mrs McT, who was accompanied by Miss Lee of Bristol, describing the details of their travels and sharing news of other mutual friends. Sara practices in her life what Coleridge philosophizes in his writings and lectures. The desire for domestic affection both within the family and town is of primary importance to both of them. However, for Coleridge, the capacity to work through the difficulties of human relationships is lacking in proportion to his ability to express Platonic idealism of friendship and love in his poetry. As Anthony Harding notes, Coleridge asserts that "... truth itself, the knowledge of the means toward human happiness, is discoverable only by the man who is endowed with the true philanthropy that is 'produced and nurtured' by family relationships; ... ."[27] While there is no question that Coleridge was earnest in his faithfulness to this assertion, one he cherished throughout his life, it is Sara, whose love for the family with the help of others, who nurtures the happiness of their children.

Several years later when the children are all adults, Sara writes to her son Derwent on 25 July 1825, with news of Hartley and Sara, keeping the family together on the latest of their escapades. She begins her letter with a Shakespearean reference, "All's well that ends well," and continues,

> Hartley was here when your letter arrived, much interested about you, and Sara is to transmit particulars from your next letter to us, for she left us yesterday. H. is grown stout and looks behind, just like his father in miniature: he is cheerful and healthy but will not continue so long, I fear, if he is not more prudent ... he often drinks more than he ought which is a grief to me, and to your dear, good sister.[28]

Sara's encouragement of Hartley's literary career is also included: "I do wish Hartley would write an article for it [Legends for the Quarterly], but he has only just begun the article on poetry for Mr Smedley... ."[29] Still trying to elicit Coleridge's involvement with his children, she says, "I suppose you will write to your father as soon as you are settled: *don't forget*. He has done nothing towards getting the exhibitions for you I suppose."[30] Sara knows the importance of the exhibitions to the publication of their writing. The literary success of her children is Sara's constant occupation even when her children are adults. Sara's literary sympathies and expectations illustrate a deeper appreciation for poetic language than for which she has been given credit.

Despite her lack of public recognition, as a mother and literary writer Sara expresses domestic power in her desire to educate her children in an intellectual environment. Her generosity and kindness of character permeate her friendships giving her children the kind of opportunities lost to them because of their father's absence. She transmits her love and appreciation for the nature of poetic genius to her children, a love that grew within her from before the time she met Coleridge and more than likely contributed to their mutual attraction. While her husband and his literary friends have maligned her character for apparently trivial and self-serving causes, other family members, including her son-in-law Henry Nelson Coleridge, her children, and grandchildren, have witnessed and given tribute to Sara's intelligence and compassion. In his letter to his wife Sara dated 24 September 1834, Henry Nelson Coleridge exclaims,

> All the notices about your mother are vile; & the affectation of candor is the worst of the whole. I will gently impose my poem upon the [opiumist?] [De Quincey] one of these days,—the little finger of retaliation would bruise his head.[31]

From her daughter Sara Coleridge's biographer Bradford Keyes Mudge we learn that Sara consequently defends her mother against these "vile notices" in her letter to her husband during the same month of September, following her father's death on 25 July 1834. She writes,

> My Father's errors arose from weakness of the will alone, but Dequincey's fall has been effected by an irritable vanity as well as the proneness to self indulgence... The impression which the account of my mother would leave is that she is a mean-minded unamiable woman with some respectable qualities and that my Father married her from opportunity rather than much attraction of hers. My mother's *respectability* it did not rest with him to establish: her attractions he greatly under-rates and the better points of her temper and understanding are not apparent in his partial sketch.[32]

In fact, Mudge confirms Sara's (Mrs. Samuel Taylor Coleridge's) strength of character and perseverance as a literary mother. He writes, "For although Coleridgean apologists from the Wordsworths on have painted her as a petty, selfish, small-minded woman, Mrs. Coleridge was in fact both clever and enterprising—and, unlike her husband, most capable of perseverance on behalf of her children."[33] In her letter of 20 September

1834, her daughter Sara continues her mother's defense as she writes to her husband,

> Some women, like Mrs. Wilson and Mrs. Wordsworth, see the skirts of a golden cloud—they have unmeasured faith in a sun of Glory—and a sublime region stretching out far beyond their ken—and proud and happy to think that it belongs to them, are ready to give all they have to give in return. This faith—this docility is quite alien to the Fricker temperament.... But to say broadly or to imply unreservedly that she is harsh-tempered or narrow minded (that is, of an ungenerous spirit) or more unintellectual than many women who have pleased my Father is to misrepresent the subject.[34]

Criticism of her father, the poet, was anticipated in a public forum of essay writing; however, the harsh remarks put forth by Thomas De Quincey about Sara's mother seemed an underhanded, scathing, and false representation. Another reaction from Sara Fricker's brother-in-law Robert Southey appears in his letter to Joseph Cottle in April 1836 explaining why he has not sent Cottle's book on Coleridge to De Quincey:

> I have had no opportunity of sending your book to De Quincey, who is living at Edinburgh in the precincts of Holyrood House, very disreputably, having long subsisted by any shifts that could raise him a present supply. He too has published Recollections of S. T. C. in *Tait's Magazine*, and spoken in such a manner of Mrs C. that if Hartley C. had been like any body else, he would have walked to Edinburgh to pull his nose. Yet I am sorry for De Quincey. There was good enough about him to make one regret (even without reference to his extraordinary abilities) that he should become the castaway that he is. There is a taint of insanity in his family.[35]

Ill health was a constant worry to Sara Fricker Coleridge especially concerning her husband's condition, his addiction to opium, and the well-being of their children. In an earlier letter written to Southey on the 25 August 1803, Sara describes these concerns while also remembering her kindness toward others. She writes,

> Last Monday my husband, W. Wordsworth and D. W. set off for Scotland in an Irish-Car and one horse—W—is to drive all the way, for poor Samuel is too weak to undertake the fatigue of driving—he was very unwell when he went off, ... It will be no consolation to you my dear sister to hear that my poor Sara is at this moment in a very poor way, with her teeth,—she was in a high fever, she is just

the age that Robert Lovell was, but she is not as yet I thank God! any thing like so bad as he was; and if we can stop the diarrhea she will be well again; she is 8 months old to morrow, but has no sign of Teeth:—I am frightened to death if any thing ails the children in thier [sic] father's absence... . Every thing I can do for your comfort and for the consolation of you both—and for the happiness of us all, I will do—depend on it—my husband is a good man—his prejudices—and his prepossessions sometimes give me pain, but we have all a somewhat to encounter in this life—I should be a very very happy woman if it were not for a few things—and my husband's ill health stands at the head of these evils![36]

Despite Coleridge's frailties, Sara remains hopeful and attentive to the family's needs. Her strength of character shows her determination to keep harmony within the marriage and family while naturally worried about their health.

Since her birth in December 1802, their youngest child Sara experienced ill health with a delicate and weak constitution. In her adult memoirs, Sara later recounts her physical weakness and attributes much of her psychological nervousness to the circumstances of her birth, an absentee father on the day she was born and during most of her life. Through her poetic sensibilities and, eventually, her editorial duties in the publication of her father's posthumous writings, Sara envisions herself as both the inheritor of his intellectual nature and his susceptibility to sickness, but she also embodies the female strengths of her mother. She writes to her mother on the 16 November 1836, describing the discomfort of her feminine symptoms along with the joys of wife and mother,

> My beloved Mother—I have received your kind letter—when I read that your [?] had ceased I nearly cried for joy—& you will be glad to learn that my *illness* arrived last night, quite healthily and properly. Today my sensations are quite changed—I am much weaker than any time since my last period—(soon after I arrived here) & my spirits are low—But I am not so full of horrid phantoms as I was... . I dare not think of Hampstead. The happiness of finding myself on the little bed in the little room with husband mother & children around me is more than I dare think of now.[37]

Sara comforts herself with thoughts of returning home from Ilchester to Hampstead and to the comfort of her children and husband.

In her biographical account of Sara Fricker Coleridge, Lefebure also recognizes that Sara's character has been unfairly treated and her intention is to portray a more accurate portrait of this woman. She states,

Mud-encoated, she has become a symbol of the unloved, unloving and unlovable wife; ungenerous in spirit, small in mind. Indeed, more than mud-caked, Mrs Coleridge has become silted up and lost to view. The time has come to restore her to light; to make true acquaintance with one of whom even Dorothy Wordsworth was obliged to admit (albeit in baffled tones), 'Mrs Coleridge is a most extraordinary character—'.[38]

Along with family biographers Lefebure and Mudge, and the compelling accounts of Sara's compassionate and generous nature in her over 200 letters with family and friends that have survived, I intend to represent Coleridge's wife in a true light of her image as a wife, a mother, and most importantly, an articulate and literary woman in her own right. Her grandson's essay on Sara Fricker Coleridge illustrates her legacy as the wife of the lake poet as described in Chapter 4 who rose above the turmoil of a literary circle of individuals to exercise her individual voice. Ernest Hartley Coleridge (1846–1920) writes,

> Mrs S. T. C. has received something less than justice at the hands of her husband's biographer. She united fine moral qualities with intellectual powers which were certainly above the average... . She is a fine reader of English poetry, an excellent letter-writer—where she took pains in her letters to Tom Poole remain to testify. It is a fact that she learned Italian in order to teach her daughter, ... She is a thoughtful good woman truthful intentions, loyal & generous.[39]

He continues to recognize Sara for her humorous family language of "Lingo Grande" and insists that she was not deserving of the neglect she suffered at the hands of her husband.

If we are to re-read Sara's surviving private letters to friends and family through an awareness of a modern sensibility of language, then she becomes an integral part of an elite literary community during this era. Exercising her determination to provide for her children, financially and emotionally, Sara confines herself to the domestic sphere of friends and family members. Her ability to effectively articulate her family's needs and further their literary achievements in a public setting establishes Sara within a masculine sphere that is both literary and political. It becomes apparent that Wollstonecraft's treatise on the moral and intellectual independence of women heavily influenced Sara from within the safety of her domestic life. Sara's experiences beyond the comfort of home limit her progress as a public example of female independence; however, following Wollstonecraft's feminization of experience, Sara achieves her status as an independent wife. Wollstonecraft addresses the privacy of family life in her *Letters Written During a Short Residence in Sweden, Norway, and*

Denmark in 1796, as Harriet Guest explains, "Wollstonecraft represents Scandinavia, in her *Letters,* through the doubled lens of disappointed love and disappointed enthusiasm for the revolution in France."[40] Guest further suggests that this correlation between Wollstonecraft's personal loss of affection and political loss of feeling "draws on the centrality of conceptions of the family to political debate in the 1790s, inflecting that debate with notions of sensibility which focus its articulation in the sexual and political desires, the libidinized reveries, of the individual subject."[41] The intersection of Wollstonecraft's personal and political interests as explored in the previous chapters shows how she represents the paradigm of the wife, friend, and lover who is shaped by natural virtue and friendship. Wollstonecraft's public protests of her private feelings of disappointment become politicized in her letters, giving voice to the silence of Sara and other wives who are confined to the realm of family.

The uprooting of traditional family values during this period brings Sara's personal family conflicts into the political arena in which Coleridge debates the anti-institutional principles of human happiness advocated by William Godwin in his treatise *Political Justice* (1793). The Coleridge and Godwin debate challenges traditional family loyalties as upheld by Edmund Burke and Coleridge against Godwinian theories of injustice. As Harding explains,

> Both the desire for social improvement and the knowledge of the means by which it is to be achieved originate in the family, for the first is a necessary precondition of the second; one who does not constantly and sincerely desire the happiness of mankind will have no true perception of the means by which it can be realized.[42]

Despite Coleridge's claims for the social necessity of marriage and his personal desires for domestic affection, he consistently struggles with an incompatibility in his own marriage. His disappointment in his marriage to Sara, however, feeds his poetic imagination with a Platonic conception of human relationships to his wife, his children, and his friends. For Sara, on the other hand, friendship enlarges its dimension from acquaintance to protector, provider, and admirer of her individual needs and those of her family. Her circle of friends enlarged her social embodiment of marriage and nurtured her emotional stability as a wife.

Notes

1 Bridget Hill, ed., *The First English Feminist: Reflections Upon Marriage and Other Writings by Mary Astell* (New York: St. Martin's Press, 1986), 86. Mary Astell contributed to early feminist writing through her conservative

philosophy of a woman's individual right to assert her intellectual equality with a man. Her Reflections upon marriage (1706) severely attacks the inconsistencies between husband and wife while maintaining a wife's submissive stature.
2. Potter, ed., *Minnow*, 1.
3. Potter, ed., *Minnow*, 1.
4. Hill, *Eighteenth-Century Women*, 19–20.
5. Elizabeth Sandford, *Thomas Poole and His Friends*, Over Stowey, Somerset: The Friarn Press, 1996, 157.
6. Kathleen Raine, ed., *Letters of Samuel Taylor Coleridge*, Selected & with an Introduction by Kathleen Raine (London: The Grey Walls Press Ltd., 1950), 123.
7. Raine, ed., *Letters of Samuel Taylor Coleridge*, 123.
8. Raine, ed., *Letters of Samuel Taylor Coleridge*, 123–124.
9. Raine, ed., *Letters of Samuel Taylor Coleridge*, 125.
10. Kenneth Curry, ed., *New Letters of Robert Southey Volume One: 1792-1810* (New York: Columbia University Press, 1965), 448.
11. Curry, ed., *New Letters of Robert Southey*, Vol. 1, 448.
12. Naomi Tadmor, *Family and Friends in Eighteenth-Century England: Household, Kinship, and Patronage* (Cambridge: Cambridge University Press, 200), 239.
13. Samuel Johnson, *Dictionary of the English Language* (London, 1755), s.v., family.
14. Jeremy Taylor, *Measures and Offices of Friendship* (London: Printed for R. Royston, 1662), 10–12.
15. Stephen Potter, ed., *Minnow Among Tritons: Mrs. S. T. Coleridge's Letters to Thomas Poole 1799-1834*, (Bloomsbury: Nonesuch Press, 1934), 7. In this letter of 28 December 1807, Sara Coleridge remarks on her friendship with Mr. de Quincey, as well as her neighbor Tom Poole. She refers to de Quincey's friendship as a "protecting wing" since he had proposed to accompany Sara and her children into Cumberland on a visit to Wordsworth and Southey. See pp. 7–8.
16. Potter, ed., *Minnow*, 7.
17. See Vivien Jones' *Women in the Eighteenth Century: Constructions of Femininity* (London: Routledge, 1990).
18. See Wetenhall Wilkes' excerpt from *A Letter of Genteel and Moral Advice to a Young Lady* in Vivien Jones, ed., *Women in the Eighteenth Century: Constructions of Femininity* (London: Routledge, 1990), 29.
19. Bridget Hill, *Eighteenth-Century Women: An Anthology* (London: George Allen and Unwin Ltd., 1984), 17.
20. Molly Lefebure, *Bondage of Love: A Life of Mrs. Samuel Taylor Coleridge* (New York: Norton, 1987), 80.
21. Earl Leslie Griggs, ed., *Letters of Hartley Coleridge* from the original letters at the Harry Ransom Humanities Research Center in Texas.
22. Emerson R. Marks, *Coleridge on the Language of Verse* (Princeton: Princeton University Press, 1981), 6–7.
23. Earl Leslie Griggs, ed., *Collected Letters of Samuel Taylor Coleridge 1772-1834*, Vol. III. 1807-1814 (Oxford: Clarendon Press, 1956–1971), 522.

124 *The Social Imagination of the Romantic Wife in Literature*

24 Potter, ed., *Minnow*, 37.
25 Potter, ed., *Minnow*, 36.
26 Potter, ed., *Minnow*, 29-30.
27 Anthony Harding, *Coleridge and the Idea of Love: Aspects of Relationship in Coleridge's Thought and Writing* (Cambridge: Cambridge University Press, 1974), 23–24.
28 Sara Fricker Coleridge, Autograph letter dated 25 July 1825, *Sara Fricker Coleridge Collection 1794–1931*, Harry Ransom Center (Austin: University of Texas).
29 Coleridge, S. F., Autograph letter dated 25 July 1825, *Sara Fricker Coleridge Collection 1794–1931*, Harry Ransom Center (Austin: University of Texas).
30 Coleridge, S. F., Autograph letter dated 25 July 1825, *Sara Fricker Coleridge Collection 1794–1931*, Harry Ransom Center (Austin: University of Texas).
31 Henry Nelson Coleridge, Autograph letter signed and dated 24 September 1834, *Henry Nelson Coleridge Collection 1808–1849*, Harry Ransom Center, (Austin: University of Texas).
32 Sara Coleridge Coleridge, Autograph letter dated 20 September 1834, *Sara Coleridge Coleridge Collection 1791–1951*, Harry Ransom Center (Austin: University of Texas).
33 Bradford Keyes Mudge, *Sara Coleridge, A Victorian Daughter: Her Life and Essays* (New Haven: Yale University Press, 1989), 19.
34 Coleridge, S. C., Autograph letter dated 20 September 1834, *Sara Coleridge Coleridge Collection 1791–1951*, Harry Ransom Center (Austin: University of Texas).
35 Kenneth Curry, ed., *New Letters of Robert Southey, Vol. 2: 1811-1838* (New York: Columbia University Press, 1965), 451–52.
36 Coleridge, S. F., Autograph letter signed and dated 25 August 1803, Pierpont Morgan Library Dept. of Literary and Historical Manuscripts. Partial publication in Griggs, *Collected Letters*, Vol. II, 975.
37 Coleridge, S. C., Autograph letter dated 16 November 1836, *Sara Coleridge Coleridge Collection 1791–1951*, Harry Ransom Center (Austin: University of Texas).
38 Lefebure, *Bondage of Love*, 18.
39 Ernest Hartley Coleridge, Autograph essay on Sara Fricker Coleridge, n.d., *Sara Fricker Coleridge Collection 1794–1931*, Harry Ransom Center (Austin: University of Texas).
40 Harriet Guest, *Small Change: Women, Learning, Patriotism, 1750–1810* (Chicago: University of Chicago Press, 2000), 305.
41 Guest, *Small Change*, 305.
42 Harding, *Coleridge and the Idea of Love*, 23.

References

Coleridge, Ernest Hartley. *Autograph Essay, n.d. Sara Fricker Coleridge Collection 1794–1931*. Harry Ransom Center. Austin: University of Texas.
Coleridge, Hartley. *Hartley Coleridge Collection 1796–1933*. From the original letters unpublished at the Harry Ransom Center. Austin: University of Texas.

Coleridge, Henry Nelson. *Autograph Letter. Henry Nelson Coleridge Collection 1808–1849*. Harry Ransom Center. Austin: University of Texas.

Coleridge, Sara Coleridge. *Autograph Letters. Sara Coleridge Coleridge Collection 1791–1951*. Harry Ransom Center. Austin: University of Texas.

Coleridge, Sara Fricker. *Autograph Letters. Sara Fricker Coleridge Collection 1794–1931*. Harry Ransom Center. Austin: University of Texas.

---, S. F. *Autograph Letter* dated 25 August 1803. *Pierpont Morgan Library Dept. of Literary and Historical Manuscripts*. New York: Pierpont Morgan Library. Partial publication in Griggs, *Collected Letters*, Vol. II, 975.

Curry, Kenneth, ed. *New Letters of Robert Southey, Volume 1: 1792–1810*. New York: Columbia University Press, 1965.

---. *New Letters of Robert Southey, Volume 2: 1811–1838*. New York: Columbia University Press, 1965.

Guest, Harriet. *Small Change: Women, Learning, Patriotism, 1750–1810*. Chicago: University of Chicago Press, 2000.

Griggs, Earl Leslie, ed. *Collected Letters of Samuel Taylor Coleridge 1772–1834*. Vol. III 1807–1814. Oxford: Clarendon Press, 1956–71.

Harding, Anthony. *Coleridge and the Idea of Love: Aspects of Relationship in Coleridge's Thought and Writing*. Cambridge: Cambridge University Press, 1974.

Hill, Bridget. *Eighteenth-Century Women: An Anthology*. London: George Allen and Unwin Ltd., 1984.

Hill, Bridget, ed. *The First English Feminist: Reflections Upon Marriage and Other Writings by Mary Astell*. New York: St. Martin's Press, 1986.

Johnson, Samuel. *Dictionary of the English Language*. London, 1755.

Jones, Vivien. *Women in the Eighteenth Century: Constructions of Femininity*. London: Routledge, 1990.

Lefebure, Molly. *The Bondage of Love: A Life of Mrs. Samuel Taylor Coleridge*. New York: Norton, 1987.

Marks, Emerson R. *Coleridge on the Language of Verse*. Princeton: Princeton University Press, 1981.

Mudge, Bradford Keyes. *Sara Coleridge, A Victorian Daughter: Her Life and Essays*. New Haven: Yale University Press, 1989.

Potter, Stephen, ed. *Minnow Among Tritons: Mrs. S. T. Coleridge's Letters to Thomas Poole 1799–1834*. Bloomsbury: Nonesuch Press, 1934.

Raine, Kathleen, ed. *Letters of Samuel Taylor Coleridge*. Selected & with an Introduction by Kathleen Raine. London: The Grey Walls Press, 1950.

Sandford, Elizabeth. *Thomas Poole and His Friends*. Over Stowey, Somerset: The Friarn Press, 1996.

Tadmor, Naomi. *Family and Friends in Eighteenth-Century England: Household, Kinship, and Patronage*. Cambridge: Cambridge University Press, 2001.

Taylor, Jeremy. *Measures of Offices and Friendship*. London: Printed for R. Royston, 1662.

7 National and Domestic Identities

Cries of horrour and indignation resounded throughout the kingdom; and the nation, with one voice, demanded justice—Alas! justice had never been known in France. Retaliation and vengeance had been it's fatal substitutes.[1]

(Mary Wollstonecraft)

Inflammatory rhetoric jeopardized the safety and security of both the aristocratic and the mercantile classes conjuring up words like liberty, virtue, and equality at the center of a debate[2] between the natural and artificial interpretations of their symbolic meaning. Within a few short years after the revolutionary explosion in France on 6 October 1789, Mary Wollstonecraft wrote her 1794 treatise on *An Historical and Moral View of the French Revolution*. During that same year, Samuel Taylor Coleridge and Robert Southey collaborated on a dramatic text entitled *The Fall of Robespierre*. The language that emerged during this tumultuous period from both dramatic and political rhetoric transformed the roles of women and nations from the comfort and protection of domestic and traditional customs to independent habits of thought that liberated women and the common population. From an exploration within the domestic sphere, the role of patriotic women suggests a defining influence on the progress of civilized society.

One question at the heart of this debate is whether women considered themselves patriotic citizens whose voices carried beyond the domestic sphere. Karen O'Brien acknowledges the rise of domesticity in a public sphere despite the apparent lack of acceptance for women in positions of patriarchal authority. In her study of British women in the Enlightenment, O'Brien explains, "The static, or even deteriorating, legal and political situation of women, and the dichotomised, gendered language of much political and economic public debate did not, however, correspond to a diminishing sphere of social operation for women in this period."[3] Harriet

DOI: 10.4324/9781003504238-7

Guest offers a more encouraging view that marks a definite shift in feminist thinking beyond the social to the political sphere, from private to public influence. She states,

> By the early nineteenth century, the conditions (of consciousness or imagination at least) necessary to nineteenth-century feminist debate were emerging; some women of liberal education could assume that it was their right and duty to have opinions about what happened in the world; they did not see their exclusion from participation in the public life of the nation as natural; indeed, in some senses they did not think of themselves as excluded at all.[4]

Wollstonecraft is clearly one of those women who saw her domestic role as a natural intrusion on the political sphere. Wollstonecraft's detailed account of the French Revolution and her analysis of the deterioration of moral character provide evidence to support this rise of feminist rhetoric that serves to stabilize a society in social and political upheaval.

In addition, Karen O'Brien recognizes other women scholars and their contributions to this debate. For instance, Eve Tavor Bannet argues for the direct correlation of the married woman's role within the family and, as O'Brien writes, "a repositioning of the family, and of women within it, at the heart of the nation, ..."[5] that further identifies the importance of the wife in civilizing society. Yet, in O'Brien's estimation, women writers of the Enlightenment remained confined to the domestic sphere, whereas Guest suggests a more progressive role for women in the civilizing process of society, one that I argue is accomplished largely through Wollstonecraft's use of the Romantic imagination in her political rhetoric. Moreover, O'Brien acknowledges that Wollstonecraft's religious and moral sentiments bridge the gap between the religious factions of the Anglicans and Dissenters "despite the increasingly adversarial relationship between those two religious tendencies in this period."[6] She writes, "None of this is to downplay the power and originality of Wollstonecraft's intervention in the Enlightenment debate about women," but rather, as O'Brien asserts, " to bring to the fore her remarkable intellectual fertility and eclecticism in deploying the vocabularies of that debate to radical and feminist ends."[7] Many studies that examine the rise of feminist rhetoric have also considered the language of prominent women from the English and Scottish Enlightenments such as Catherine Macaulay, Lady Mary Wortley Montagu, Elizabeth Carter, Mary Astell, Mary Hays, and Anna Laetitia Barbauld, among others.[8] While these studies provide an historical foundation to my discussion of Wollstonecraft's liberal ideas, the focus here is to examine Wollstonecraft's political rhetoric among Romantic writers like

Coleridge, Southey, and Godwin, whose literary friendships and political ideologies emphasize the shift between conservative and radical thinking following the rationalism of the Enlightenment.

On 6 October 1789 the French ushered their king and queen from Versailles to Paris, permanently changing King Louis XVI's role from king of France, the nation, to king of the French, the people. This linguistic shift from property to person marked an historic moment in the revolutionary language of the period and the identity of each individual. Marie-Antoinette who had been welcoming the market women with their loyal and affectionate tokens of floral bouquets in Versailles would no longer entertain the common speeches of the women known as fishwives and their uncultivated language called *poissard*,[9] a language offensive to the educated aristocrats. Symbolically, the women dressed in white and appeared "cleansed of the smells of the marketplace."[10] Simon Schama describes the important shift from loyal to revolutionary sentiments as the use of *poissard* changed from comic to abusive language when the market women sang songs in a revolutionary spirit. He states, "The Duc of Orléans regularly performed *poissard* plays in his private theater, and in 1777 the Queen summoned a group of fishwives and market women to the Trianon to teach her amateur troupe how to pronounce *poissard* correctly."[11] However, by 1789, market women threatened the authority of the Queen as the lines of an early revolutionary song, "Motion of the Herring Women of La Halle," indicate:

> If the High-ups still make trouble
> Then the Devil confound them
> And since they love Gold so much
> May it melt in their traps
> That's the sincere wish
> Of the Women Who Sell Fish[12]

Just as the market women appear as a threatening symbol to the monarchy in France, the rising threat of feminist rhetoric accompanies revolutionary acts toward freedom. The rhetorical lines dividing classes were blurred by revolutionary principles of liberty, virtue, and equality. As Lynn Hunt suggests in her analysis of the French Revolution and its rhetorical influence, "The political culture of revolution thus had both symbolic and social sources of coherence."[13] With the reinvention of political boundaries in France, a new class of citizens defined their social behavior by new representatives of family and its members. Hunt notes, "Ironically, therefore, the lack of social definition of the new political class made the experience of revolution all the more dramatic in its challenge to custom and tradition."[14] For Wollstonecraft, the passions ignited by the French

National and Domestic Identities 129

Revolution and the reason needed to direct the French people toward sound judgment were the same passions that governed her domestic and political affections.

Not only were radical ideologies emerging among the political thinkers and writers of the revolutionary period of the 1790s, but also a new language was forged through the efforts of these radicals to establish principles of liberty that redefined the infrastructure of governing bodies, constitutional and aristocratic institutions. From an examination of Mary Wollstonecraft's writing on liberty and virtue and Samuel Taylor Coleridge's poetic and dramatic interpretation of these dominant issues emerges an organic relationship between language and action that establishes the linguistics of revolutionary speech on a moral foundation, one critical to the heart of their revolutionary ideologies. Both writers approach the changing sociopolitical forces through a changing language from philosophies that rise out of a natural and organic perspective of the world. Both Wollstonecraft and Coleridge share a commitment to an underlying morality conceived from spiritual values that transcend outward forms of political institutions. In order to be effective, liberty must be based on a morality that is inherent to human nature as Wollstonecraft and Coleridge identify in their writings. As Angela Esterhammer notes, "The notion that language is not merely descriptive of reality, but that it affects, shapes, alters, or even creates reality, underlies several interrelated currents of theory and practice from the 1780s onward."[15] Building on Esterhammer's point of view, the formation of revolutionary language in the writings of Wollstonecraft and Coleridge determined a new political reality in England and France.

A love of liberty, a desire for happiness, and an adherence to moral principle characterize the fundamental compatibility between Wollstonecraft and Coleridge. As John Whale has noted in his study of the revolutionary period and its sensibility to language reform, the imagination, as he defines it, is the "crucial link" between these two writers. In his examination of I. A. Richards' 1934 study of Coleridge's imagination, Whale asserts,

> Coleridge's exploration of imagination provides Richards with precisely the example he needs in order to further his dream of a scientific criticism. It gives him the crucial link between language and psychology and in particular an understanding of language which is at once abstract and specific, linguistic and experiential, philosophical and poetic.[16]

This crucial link of how the imagination operates linguistically for both writers identifies their need for reforming a society that restricts and enslaves the weaker members, women, children, and the poor. As these social roles became re-identified through a rhetorical interpretation, the ordinary wife among a common population achieved greater status.

Both Wollstonecraft and Coleridge rely on the imagination to create a vision of an ideal society; for Coleridge it was creating a community of families working and living together, and for Wollstonecraft it was envisioning the ideal family or cottage life on a farm. While both utopian schemes embraced a poetic idealism unrestrained by patriarchal authority, the reality of an ideal domestic space remained unattainable in the experiences of the writers. Whale also recognizes how the imagination supports moral progress in Wollstonecraft's desire for social change while providing her with the hope for a better future. He explains,

> Imagination, for Wollstonecraft, functions as an agent of moral improvement. It supports the present moment of revolutionary critique with the reassuring speculative capacity of seeing into the future, of sustaining an act of faith that the project to reform the present really is part of a larger moral, even metaphysical, narrative of improvement.... It sustains her optimism in the narrative of the moral and civilising progress of history and it acts as a bolster to individuals like herself, who are engaged in a dominantly self-abnegating process of social change.[17]

During this volatile period in history when change was overriding the stability of family and the nation, Wollstonecraft became the voice of optimism for wives like Sara Coleridge who could not publicly voice their desire for independent thought and action outside the home. Ironically, Coleridge provides a voice for virtue through his natural language of poetry that he does not encourage in the speech of his own wife. Wollstonecraft details the immoral characteristics of the French yet struggles for social approval for her own behavior. The moral contradictions that exist between experience and imagination complicate the unity of the domestic with the national female identity. In the excerpts that follow in this chapter on the dramatic moments of the French Revolution as told by Wollstonecraft and Coleridge in their writing, the nature of feminist rhetoric emerges as a dominant theme through the natural language of poetry and the stark language of prose, voicing freedom and virtue.

Along with the German influence on Coleridge's concept of language was his search for critical principles found in the natural language of poetry. Uncommitted to any one particular philosophic system, religious or poetic, Coleridge explains his understanding of how art and metaphysics relate through the senses. He insists that the Scriptures provide

> the living *educts* of the Imagination; of that reconciling and mediatory power, which incorporating the Reason in Images of the Sense, and

organizing (as it were) the flux of the Senses by the permanence and self-circling energies of the Reason, gives birth to a system of symbols, harmonious in themselves, and consubstantial with the truths, of which they are the *conductors*.[18]

In his later autobiographical work Coleridge remarks how his earlier writing received laudatory reviews for their potential but criticism for their "elaborate diction":

The critics of that day, the most flattering, equally with the severest, concurred in objecting to them [his writings], obscurity, a general turgidness of diction, and a profusion of new coined double epithets.[19]

Most importantly, Coleridge learned "... that Poetry, even that of the loftiest, and, seemingly, that of the wildest odes, had a logic of its own, as severe as that of science; ...," and he also acknowledged that "[i]n the truly great poets, he [Rev. James Bowyer, Christ Hospital head master] would say, there is a reason assignable, not only for every word, but for the position of every word; ... ."[20] Therefore, from classical examples of the Greek poets and a strict teacher of language, Coleridge developed his style for the "natural and real"[21] which he applied to his dramatic account of *The Fall of Robespierre* in 1794. Coleridge's use of feminized revolutionary rhetoric by the male characters in his drama significantly addresses a sensibility for the natural to form a changing national identity, one uniting with the domestic or more feminized expression of language.

The opening scene of the play occurs at the Tuileries, palace of the former kings of France, located between the Louvre and the Tuileries gardens, the meeting place for the National Assembly in 1794. Fictional and non-fictional characters combine to create the political tensions apparent in the debate over revolutionary loyalties. Barrere's opening speech centers on the imagery of a gathering tempest as he ponders where to seek shelter for his safety, a metaphor for the paradox of loyalty and patriotism that fuels the debate. Uncertain as to which side would secure not only his patriotism but also his moral duty, Barrere contemplates the soul of the tyrant, afraid of the control he holds over him. He states, "... I fear the Tyrant's *soul*-- / Sudden in action, fertile in resource, / And rising awful 'mid impending ruins;" (I.3–5). His speech further contrasts images of the impenetrability of a meteor with the vulnerability Barrere feels in the face, or the eye, of this tyrant. He continues, "In splendor gloomy, as the midnight meteor, / That fearless thwarts the elemental war. / When last in secret conference we met, / He scowl'd upon me with suspicious rage, / Making his eye the inmate of my bosom" (I.6–10). The contradictions of patriot and tyrant, loyalist and revolutionary, are embedded in symbols of nature's unpredictable acts of violence, the tempest, the meteor, and later in the dialogue, the thunder cloud, and impenetrable polar ice. Yet, the intimacy and penetration of the tyrant's eye finds itself within the "bosom" or heart of its enemy in an unnatural and intimidating brotherly closeness.

As Barrere and Robespierre argue over the tyrannous acts of the loyalists, Robespierre scolds Barrere for his cowardly fear. Barrere's apprehension of the treacherous members of parliament comes in response to Couthon's decree, a law prohibiting open parliamentary debate that gave rise to the period of the Great Terror. Barrere states, "Yet much they talk—and plausible their speech" (I.141). Seeing through the treachery while also acknowledging its opacity, Robespierre exclaims, "Transparent mask! / They wish to clog the wheels of government, / Forcing the hand that guides the vast machine / To bribe them to their duty—*English* patriots!" (I.144–47). Then Robespierre mounts the Tribune at the convention to speak, and in this speech he extends the metaphor of the mask as he strips away "... a labyrinth of words" and "Perplex'd, in silence seem'd to yield assent" (II.17–18). Words uttered in this debate reflect the power of speech to overwhelm, to silence, to confuse, and to coerce thinking. He honors the spirit of his revolutionary friend Marat while appealing to the cause of justice to reveal the sincerity of his words and faithfulness to France. His silence mimics the domestic silence of women confined to a social space where they cannot utter opposition, only assent to the male authority.

The rippling effect of Robespierre's execution from France to England found its voice in the British drama of Coleridge and Southey where both men express a complexity of emotions, blending their voices as one in the character of St. Just: "I am of no one faction. I contend / Against all factions" (II.212–13). Representing the voice of the people, Robespierre sacrifices his life with hope for a better society, leaving his words to echo in the consciousness of his persecutors. Coleridge's reaction to the death of Robespierre resulted in his collaborative drama with Southey. In addition, as Nicholas Roe notes, "... he continued to explore Robespierre's character and motives in his political lectures of 1795."[22] Coleridge pursued his interest in Robespierre that he shared with John Thelwall, a leading British reformist, "and both agreed that the British prime minister Pitt lacked Robespierre's political skill."[23] Roe further points out that Coleridge's political determination overlaps with his idea of the imagination when on 16 June 1795 he gave his opening remarks in his *Lecture on the Slave Trade*. Coleridge states,

> To develop the power of the Creator is our proper employment—and to imitate Creativeness by combination our most exalted and self-satisfying Delight…. Our Almighty Parent hath therefore given to us Imagination that stimulates to the attainment of *real* excellence by the

contemplation of splendid Possibilities that still revivifies the dying motive within us....[24]

Coleridge built his defense for liberty on the power of the imagination as primary to employing the power of the Creator.

Tom Furniss also describes the controversial reaction among London Dissenters and radicals to applaud or to mourn the death of Robespierre and a dying revolution. He remarks, "The 'Revolution Controversy' of 1789–95 was as much about the implications of the Revolution for Britain as it was about the Revolution itself,"[25] stirring further political rhetoric and debate. In Book II Chapter IV of *An Historical and Moral View*, Wollstonecraft contributes her perspective of the British sentiment following the events at Versailles. Her view shows how her political ambition for justice supports Coleridge's political inference in his drama and lecture. She remarks,

> The effect produced by the duplicity of the courts must be very great, when the vicissitudes, which had happened at Versailles, could not teach every person of common sense, that the moment was arrived, when subterfuge and treachery could no longer escape detection and punishment; and that the only possibility of obtaining the durable confidence of the people was by that strict attention to justice, which produces a dignified sincerity of action.[26]

Wollstonecraft insists on justice in an environment of "duplicity of the courts" to weed out erroneous effects of treachery. Like Coleridge, Wollstonecraft embraced a more universal solution to gain the "confidence of the people."

Wollstonecraft supported the radical intellectualism in London as part of the Dissenting movement and as a member of the radical publisher, Joseph Johnson's circle. Influenced by the Dissenting preacher, Dr. Richard Price, Wollstonecraft found herself at the center of this revolutionary controversy. When Price published his sermon *A Discourse on the Love of Our Country* in November 1789, British conservatives reacted with fear that British support for the Revolution would spark similar discontent in England. Price advocated a revolutionary approach to Britain's constitutional history that had begun with a fight for liberty in England at the time of the Glorious Revolution in 1688. Wollstonecraft built her political ideology firmly on beliefs she attained through her close relationship to Price and his Dissenting views. Politically, Wollstonecraft and Coleridge voiced their controversial ideas among the many disparate voices and factions through their ability to turn to the imagination for hope in the future.

When Edmund Burke, Whig politician and political philosopher, read Price's *Discourse*, he reacted vehemently in his *Reflections on the Revolution in France* published one year later on 1 November 1790. Burke emphasized his concern for the destruction of social and cultural values in Europe based on the aristocracy, monarchy, and church.[27] As Furniss notes, "Burke's attack on Price's sermon and character was thus an attempt to repress the symptoms of revolutionary enthusiasm at work in Britain."[28] Price's influence was felt among the Dissenting movement, reaching writers such as Wollstonecraft whose earlier ideas were formed by British radical writers on democratic principles, natural rights, and moral sensibility. Reshaping ideas of virtue and liberty became the focus of her writings, a departure from the rhetoric of masculinized chivalry, as she emphasized Jean-Jacques Rousseau's new masculine sensibility and also relied on John Locke's political theories of civil and religious liberty in a government concerned with the equality of the masses and not the traditional history of the few as Burke sought to protect.

Wollstonecraft's first response to Burke appeared in her *Vindication of the Rights of Men* in November 1790. Continuing her title with a direct address to Burke, *in a Letter to the Right Honourable Edmund Burke: Occasioned by his Reflections on the Revolution in France*, Wollstonecraft writes, "to shew you to yourself, stripped of the gorgeous drapery in which you have enwrapped your tyranic principles."[29] Whether enveloped in the drapery of luxury, as Wollstonecraft suggests the conservatives are, or pursued by the threat of a tyrannical government, the citizens of France struggled to attain a society founded on principles of liberty and equality that were natural to each individual and in each home. As Chris Jones explains, "There is no contradiction for her [Wollstonecraft] in holding the domestic affections sacred while applying to the relations of husband and wife or parents and children the Lockean doctrine of a contract with reciprocal duties."[30] For Wollstonecraft, the national character of the people should reflect the same virtues as the domestic environment. Jones recognizes her influence on the political thought of the Romantic writers who like Coleridge "regarded her as a genius." As Jones notes, "Her development of republican and democratic principles in domestic and affective terms provided a powerful critique of Burke's use of domestic feelings to support the conservative model of community."[31]

In her treatise *An Historical and Moral View of the French Revolution*, Wollstonecraft reveals her Romantic imagination through five books that address the social, political, and literary complexities of a society fraught with conflict between ancient traditions of chivalry, virtues defined by masculinity, and modern ideologies of liberty and equality in a climate of

National and Domestic Identities   135

changing principles and reform. She grounds her argument on her rejection of the belief that "human nature is intrinsically degenerate" suggesting that "the frivolity of the french character" has arisen from habits of thought, dress, and education that pervade their daily lives.[32] She addresses the progress of society, the end of government, and the rise of a political consciousness with an adept social awareness that demands a distinct change in virtue and liberty as the natural inheritance of the people. Through her *Vindications* Wollstonecraft ardently attacked the feminine weaknesses in the social order of family and marriage; however, in this volume of historical and social criticism, she arrives at the root of society that forms the domestic nature of both women and men through their national identities. In her analysis of the French Revolution she notes,

> When we contemplate the infancy of man, his gradual advance towards maturity, his miserable weakness as a solitary being, and the crudeness of his first notions respecting the nature of civil society, it will not appear extraordinary, that the acquirement of political knowledge has been so extremely slow; / or that public happiness has not been more rapidly and generally diffused.[33]

Wollstonecraft criticizes the lack of progress in the moral development of the human experience, accounting for the weakness in civil society to attain public happiness.

Her recognition of Locke's political view on the opposition of the divine right of kings from his *Two Treatises of Government* (1690) provided Wollstonecraft with the basis for a vocabulary about freedom for every individual from the despotism of the mind and heart as much as from the tyranny of injustice. Wollstonecraft states,

> Locke, following the track of these bold thinkers, recommended in a more methodical manner religious toleration, and analyzed the principles of civil liberty: for in his definition of liberty we find the elements of *The Declaration of the Rights of Man*, which, in spite of the fatal errours of ignorance, and the perverse obstinacy of selfishness, is now converting sublime theories into practical truths.[34]

Instead, her criticism focuses on an intolerance of the masculine virtues that subjugate and degrade women and the common people through class, rank, and social distinctions. Her hopes for an improved society rest on her vision that natural virtues will form the character of each individual. Expecting the destruction of despotism and tyranny through an embrace of natural virtue, Wollstonecraft writes,

> But these evils are passing away; a new spirit has gone forth, to organise the body-politic; and where is the criterion to be found, to estimate the means, by which the influence of the spirit can be confined, now enthroned in the hearts of half the inhabitants of the globe? Reason has, at last, shown her captivating face, beaming with benevolence; and it will be impossible for the dark hand of despotism again to obscure it's [sic] radiance, or the lurking dagger of subordinate tyrants to reach her bosom.[35]

Wollstonecraft represents reason in the image of woman with her unselfish character and benevolent face that will overpower the darkness of tyranny. With her reliance on God she serves to unite her hope with civil progress while sheltered by another emblematic image of woman, liberty. She states, "The image of God implanted in our nature is now more rapidly expanding; and, as it opens, liberty with maternal wing seems to be soaring to regions far above vulgar annoyance, promising to shelter all mankind."[36] Along with woman's identity as a national figure of liberty, she symbolizes the hope for all mankind, the happiness of society (family), and the progress of civilization.

Moreover, Wollstonecraft displays a deeper understanding of the social ills pervading the discontented French and English societies, recognizing that the national character of the French is suffering from degeneracy, a loss of natural virtue:

> What has hitherto been the political perfection of the world? In the two most celebrated nations it has only been a polish of manners, an extension of that family love, which is rather the effect of sympathy and selfish passions, than reasonable humanity. And in what has ended their so much extolled / patriotism? In vain glory and barbarity – every page of history proclaims. And why has the enthusiasm for virtue thus passed away like the dew of the morning, dazzling the eyes of it's [sic] admirers? Why – because it was factitious virtue.[37]

She explains that every attempt to glorify the appearance of refined culture and its superficial manners in France and to imitate these same vanities in Britain sacrifices the reasonable actions of humanity and promotes artificial virtues. As Tom Furniss points out, "It was a commonplace in eighteenth-century Britain to claim that the old order of France exhibited a fatal combination of political tyranny and luxury."[38] The structure of the *ancien régime* with its feudal system reinforced "the spiritual and intellectual slavery produced by the superstitions of Roman Catholicism."[39] Pointing to an excess in courtly manners often described by French writers such as Racine, Wollstonecraft identifies theatricality as the pervasive and destructive force of the French society:

> Their national character is, perhaps, more formed by their theatrical amusements, than is generally imagined: they are in reality the schools of vanity. And, after this kind of education, is it surprising, that almost every thing is said and done for stage effect?[40]

Education in these courtly manners distorts an individual's proper tastes, asserts Wollstonecraft, who would rather the French people be educated by writers such as Molière who insisted on the magnitude of the human passions.

Society was changing and the revolutionary principles that undermined the traditional order of the *ancien régime* created a new reality. Along with this new order of reality came a new language. Esterhammer explains,

> When the revolutionaries undertook to create a new social order in 1790s France, they did so by giving new names to its citizens, places, dates, weights, measures, and institutions. By decree of the National Assembly, the titles of the nobility were abolished in 1790 and even *monsieur* was replaced by the universal *citoyen*; ... in the Republican calendar, the months and years received new names.[41]

While eliminating politically sensitive words from the French language and introducing a more neutral term like citizen elicited the kind of equality revolutionaries sought to achieve, Wollstonecraft emphasized a more gradual change in character through the moral education of society. Even the legal and contractual aspects of daily life were swept into this cleansing of the pernicious and insidious activities of the people. Esterhammer has taken notice of these kinds of utterances as well:

> New procedures governed the most important of officially sanctioned performative utterances: marriage ceremonies and divorce proceedings, wills and bequests, courtroom oaths. More aggressively, the revolutionaries engaged in a project of unifying the country by standardizing the French language, which involved suppressing dialects and local vernacular languages. Their campaign, virtually a form of linguistic terrorism, included proposals that it be made a punishable crime to utter words that threatened to cause controversy among the revolutionary forces—including "Jacobins," "moderates," or "alarmists," but also "Mountain," "Plain," or "Marsh," since these words had come to be associated with political factions.[42]

The natural and real utterances of language embraced by both Coleridge and Wollstonecraft stripped away the factitious virtues of society and re-established the origin of man on organic principles. As revolutionary change slowly, and often painfully, subsided into a natural order of reality, Wollstonecraft expressed her confidence in the essential good of the people. She comments, "Anarchy is a fearful state, and all men of sense and benevolence have been anxiously attentive, to observe what use frenchmen would make of their liberty, when the confusion incident to the acquisition should subside: ...," and she acknowledges, "... it is perhaps, difficult to bring ourselves to believe, that out of this chaotic mass a fairer government is rising than has ever shed the sweets of social life on the world."[43] Wollstonecraft warns the age against anarchy in their attainment of liberty and insists on natural virtue to establish an orderly society. Locating man's natural birthright on organic principles, she describes an individual unencumbered by the drapery of artificial and static limitations in her direct response to Burke:

> The birthright of man, to give you, Sir, a short definition of this disputed right, is such a degree of liberty, civil and religious, as is compatible with the liberty of every other individual with whom he is united in a social compact, and the continued existence of that compact.[44]

Melding all voices into one social compact, Wollstonecraft assures Burke that each individual expresses an equal right to civil and religious liberty.

From the powerful rhetoric of this revolutionary controversy came social and political change, some as small change as Harriet Guest characterized in a moment-by-moment experience, and some as dramatic change as in the wrenching political shift from monarchy to republicanism. However, critical change in the domestic sphere came about more subtly, and even quietly, through the noisier presence of political upheaval. With a change in the marriage laws came a cultural shift in the perception of a socially constructed role of wife. From this intimate relationship where a man and a woman vow to love, honor, and cherish each other through a deeply sentimental commitment, to a legal bond that ties two individuals together unless a court severs these ties, there exists a gap that demands some further exploration. Rooted in the medieval concept of a religious union, marriage has remained a relationship built on antiquity, a Roman model celebrating the sexual union of a man and a woman. The pairing of individuals often secured fortunes and legacies with little concern for compatibility of feelings. In the eighteenth century, however, with the rise of industrialism and a middle class, the age of Enlightenment sparked the affections and desires of couples with increasing autonomy over their intimate relationships. Companionate marriages grew in number and the marriage laws were under pressure to legally redefine this relationship to suit a new culture of individualism.

Notes

1. Janet Todd and Marilyn Butler, eds., *The Works of Mary Wollstonecraft: An Historical and Moral View of the French Revolution*, vol. 6: 1–236 (New York: New York University Press, 1989), 40.
2. Language became an important instrument for implementing radical changes of political position and power during the French Revolution. As Tom Furniss remarks, "The French Revolution was a drawn-out process rather than a single event. But the dramatic events of the Revolution's early phase provoked one of the most important political debates in British history." It was the sermon delivered by Richard Price on 4 November 1789 that initiated the argument for Britain to follow the example of the French revolutionaries in England. "Mary Wollstonecraft's French Revolution," *The Cambridge Companion to Mary Wollstonecraft* (Cambridge: Cambridge University Press, 2002), 59–81.
3. Karen O'Brien, *Women and Enlightenment in Eighteenth-Century Britain* (Cambridge: Cambridge University Press, 2009), 10.
4. Harriet Guest, *Small Change: Women, Learning, Patriotism, 1750-1810* (Chicago: University of Chicago Press, 2000), 14.
5. O'Brien, *Women and Enlightenment*, 10.
6. O'Brien, *Women and Enlightenment*, 174.
7. O'Brien, *Women and Enlightenment*, 174.
8. For a thorough background on the political history of feminist rhetoric, see Karen O'Brien's *Women and Enlightenment in Eighteenth-Century Britain* (Cambridge: Cambridge University Press, 2009); Barbara Taylor's *Mary Wollstonecraft and the Feminist Imagination* (Cambridge: Cambridge University Press, 2003); Anne K. Mellor, *Mothers of the Nation: Women's Political Writing in England, 1780-1830* (Bloomington: Indiana Press University, 2000); Eve Tavor Bannet, *The Domestic Revolution: Enlightenment Feminism and the Novel* (Baltimore: Johns Hopkins University Press, 2000).
9. The true speech of the marketplace, *poissard*, was considered comic and abusive language. As Simon Schama notes, "Its name deriving from the French word for 'pitch' (*poix*), the *genre poissard* was not so much a true patois as what its historian Alexander Parks Moore has characterized as a systematic assault on grammar." *Citizens: A Chronicle of the French Revolution* (New York: Alfred A. Knopf, 1989), 456.
10. Simon Schama, *Citizens: A Chronicle of the French Revolution* (New York: Alfred A. Knopf, 1989), 456.
11. Schama, *Citizens: A Chronicle of the French Revolution*, 457.
12. Schama, *Citizens: A Chronicle of the French Revolution*, 457.
13. Lynn Avery Hunt, *Politics, Culture, and Class in the French Revolution* (Berkeley: University of California Press, 1984), 215.

140   *The Social Imagination of the Romantic Wife in Literature*

14 Hunt, *Politics*, 215.
15 Angela Esterhammer, *The Romantic Performative: Language and Action in British and German Romanticism* (Stanford: Stanford University Press, 2000), 23.
16 John Whale, *Imagination under Pressure 1789-1832: Aesthetics, Politics and Utility* (Cambridge: Cambridge University Press, 2000), 187.
17 Whale, *Imagination under Pressure*, 70.
18 Samuel Taylor Coleridge, *The Statesman's Manual*, ed. R. J. White (Princeton: Princeton University Press, 1972), 29. See Samuel Taylor Coleridge's *The Collected Works of Samuel Taylor Coleridge*, vol. 6: Lay Sermons (London: Routledge; Princeton: Princeton University Press, 1972).
19 Samuel Taylor Coleridge, *The Collected Works of Samuel Taylor Coleridge*, vol. 7: Biographia Literaria or Biographical Sketches of My Literary Life and Opinions, eds. James Engell and Walter Jackson Bate, vol. I (Princeton: Princeton University Press, 1983), 6.
20 Samuel Taylor Coleridge, *The Collected Works of Samuel Taylor Coleridge*, vol. 7: Biographia Literaria or Biographical Sketches of My Literary Life and Opinions, eds. James Engell and Walter Jackson Bate, vol. I, 9.
21 Samuel Taylor Coleridge, *The Collected Works of Samuel Taylor Coleridge*, vol. 7: Biographia Literaria or Biographical Sketches of My Literary Life and Opinions, eds. James Engell and Walter Jackson Bate, vol. I, 17.
22 Nicholas Roe, "Imagining Robespierre," *Coleridge's Imagination*, eds. Richard Gravil, Lucy Newlyn and Nicholas Roe (Cambridge: Cambridge University Press, 1985), 161.
23 Roe, "Imagining Robespierre," 161.
24 Samuel Taylor Coleridge, *The Collected Works of Samuel Taylor Coleridge*, vol. 1: Lectures 1795 on Politics and Religion, eds. L. Patton and P. Mann (London: Routledge & Kegan Paul, 1971), 235.
25 Tom Furniss, "Mary Wollstonecraft's French Revolution," *The Cambridge Companion to Mary Wollstonecraft*, ed. Claudia L. Johnson (Cambridge: Cambridge University Press, 2002), 59.
26 Janet Todd and Marilyn Butler, eds., *The Works of Mary Wollstonecraft*: An Historical and Moral View of the French Revolution, vol. 6: 1–236 (New York: New York University Press, 1989), 107.
27 Furniss, "Mary Wollstonecraft's French Revolution," 60.
28 Furniss, "Mary Wollstonecraft's French Revolution," 60.
29 Mary Wollstonecraft, *A Vindication of the Rights of Men*, eds. D. L. Macdonald and Kathleen Scherf (Ontario: Broadview Press, 1997), 37.
30 Chris Jones, "Mary Wollstonecraft's *Vindications* and Their Political Tradition," *The Cambridge Companion to Mary Wollstonecraft*, ed. Claudia L. Johnson (Cambridge: Cambridge University Press, 2002), 46.
31 Jones, "Mary Wollstonecraft's *Vindications*," 57.
32 Furniss, "Mary Wollstonecraft's French Revolution," 70.
33 Todd and Butler, eds., *The Works of Mary Wollstonecraft*: An Historical and Moral View of the French Revolution, vol. 6: 1–236, 15.

34 Todd and Butler, eds., *The Works of Mary Wollstonecraft:* An Historical and Moral View of the French Revolution, vol. 6: 1–236, 16.
35 Todd and Butler, eds., *The Works of Mary Wollstonecraft:* An Historical and Moral View of the French Revolution, vol. 6: 1–236, 22.
36 Todd and Butler, eds., *The Works of Mary Wollstonecraft:* An Historical and Moral View of the French Revolution, vol. 6: 1–236, 22.
37 Todd and Butler, eds., *The Works of Mary Wollstonecraft:* An Historical and Moral View of the French Revolution, vol. 6: 1–236, 21.
38 Furniss, "Mary Wollstonecraft's French Revolution," 71.
39 Furniss, "Mary Wollstonecraft's French Revolution," 70.
40 Todd and Butler, eds., *The Works of Mary Wollstonecraft:* An Historical and Moral View of the French Revolution, vol. 6: 1–236, 25.
41 Angela Esterhammer, *The Romantic Performative: Language and Action in British and German Romanticism* (Stanford: Stanford University Press, 2000), 24.
42 Esterhammer, *The Romantic Performative: Language and Action in British and German Romanticism*, 24.
43 Todd and Butler, eds., *The Works of Mary Wollstonecraft:* An Historical and Moral View of the French Revolution, vol. 6: 1–236, 47.
44 Wollstonecraft, *A Vindication of the Rights of Men*, 37.

References

Coleridge, Samuel Taylor. *The Collected Works of Samuel Taylor Coleridge*, vol. 1: Lectures 1795 on Politics and Religion, eds., Lewis Patton and Paul Mann. London: Routledge & Kegan Paul, 1971.
---. *The Collected Works of Samuel Taylor Coleridge*, vol. 6: Lay Sermons, ed. R. J. White. London: Routledge; Princeton: Princeton University Press, 1972.
---. *The Collected Works of Samuel Taylor Coleridge*, vol. 7: Biographia Literaria or Biographical Sketches of My Literary Life and Opinions, eds. James Engell and Walter Jackson Bate, vol. I: 5–295. Princeton: Princeton University Press, 1983.
Esterhammer, Angela. *The Romantic Performative: Language and Action in British and German Romanticism*. Stanford: Stanford University Press, 2000.
Furniss, Tom. "Mary Wollstonecraft's French Revolution." *The Cambridge Companion to Mary Wollstonecraft*, ed. Claudia L. Johnson, 59–81. Cambridge: Cambridge University Press, 2002.
Guest, Harriet. *Small Change: Women, Learning, Patriotism, 1750–1810*. Chicago: University of Chicago Press, 2000.
Hunt, Lynn Avery. *Politics, Culture, and Class in the French Revolution*. Berkeley: University of California Press, 1984.
Jones, Chris. "Mary Wollstonecraft's *Vindications* and Their Political Tradition." *The Cambridge Companion to Mary Wollstonecraft*, ed. Claudia L. Johnson. Cambridge: Cambridge University Press, 2002, 42–58.
O'Brien, Karen. *Women and Enlightenment in Eighteenth-Century Britain*. Cambridge: Cambridge University Press, 2009.

Roe, Nicholas, Richard Gravil, and Lucy Newlyn, eds. *Coleridge's Imagination*. Cambridge: Cambridge University Press, 1985.
Schama, Simon. *Citizens: A Chronicle of the French Revolution*. New York: Alfred A. Knopf, 1989.
Todd, Janet, and Marilyn Butler, eds., *The Works of Mary Wollstonecraft: An Historical and Moral View of the French Revolution*, vol. 6: 1–236. New York: New York University Press, 1989.
Whale, John. *Imagination under Pressure 1789–1832: Aesthetics, Politics and Utility*. Cambridge: Cambridge University Press, 2000.
Wollstonecraft, Mary. *The Vindications: The Rights of Men and the Rights of Woman*, eds. D. L. Macdonald and Kathleen Scherf. Ontario: Broadview Press, 1997.

8 Marriage Law and the Rights of Woman
Sacred to Secular

> *Let the honest heart shew itself, and* reason *teach passion to submit to necessity; or, let the dignified pursuit of virtue and knowledge raise the mind above those emotions which rather imbitter than sweeten the cup of life, when they are not restrained within due bounds.*[1]
>
> (Mary Wollstonecraft)

If Sara Fricker had been friends with Mary Wollstonecraft in 1794—she was certainly aware of her book on the rights of woman—she would have described her attraction to Coleridge in much the same manner as Wollstonecraft describes: "Let the honest heart show itself…," a relationship based on the passions. On 18 September 1794, Samuel Taylor Coleridge wrote to Robert Southey in a most enthusiastic and star-struck tone:

> My God! how tumultuous are the movements of my Heart—Since I quitted this room what and how important Events have been evolved! America! Southey! Miss Fricker!—Yes—Southey—you are right—Even Love is the creature of strong Motive—I certainly love her. I think of her incessantly & with unspeakable tenderness—with that inward melting away of Soul that symptomatizes it.[2]

The argument of the heart and the imagination of the soul overpower the ability to reason in both these relationships and temper the political reason and religious thinking of William Godwin and Samuel Taylor Coleridge. The coincidence of their diametrically opposed views, morally and politically, eventually finds a strong meeting place through the influence of their domestic relationships. Both marriages were inspired by love but fraught with the weaknesses of an institution that restricted female independence.

Resistance to the institution of marriage in the eighteenth century was accompanied by an individual desire to control this intimate relationship

DOI: 10.4324/9781003504238-8

without the interference of legal restraints. Male authority in the household and lack of property rights left women with little recourse in abusive or unhappy marriages. Through her own experiences growing up in an abusive household, Mary Wollstonecraft chose to ignore the propriety of a legal marriage and to advocate for freedom from social constraints that degraded women, intellectually and emotionally. While she adhered to a moral value that promoted Christian benevolence, she found even the religious institutions suspect of denying women their equal rights.

Looking at the historical narrative of marriage provides further insight into the cultural bands that defined the role of the Romantic wife and its inherent difficulties in equalizing the roles of husband and wife in the domestic sphere. As Henry Prater explains,

> During the Middle Ages the law of marriage throughout the states of Europe consisted for the most part of the rules of the Canonists, engrafted upon those of the Civil Law. At an early period in the history of the Church the maxim was established 'that matrimony is an holy thing in which the secular power hath no authority'.[3]

The medieval basis for the marriage law prohibited the advancement of women beyond their domestic responsibilities and limited their independence. The issues for female independence revolved around property ownership, rationalistic thinking, and financial freedom that constitute the national identity of women. The historian Catherine Macaulay addresses these issues in her writing on education where she discusses the importance of identifying oneself as a republican. As Karen O'Brien explains, "Macaulay's histories are directly and indirectly engaged with this republican notion of qualification, and she ponders the virtues of independence, rational self-control and financial autonomy which might qualify some individuals as potential British citizens."[4] This recognition of female education brings together the political importance for women during the 1790s, a critical turning point in the social consciousness of the institution of marriage, to implement female engagement in national concerns.

The adherence to ceremonial law for marriage remained an obstacle to equal rights not only for women within their domestic sphere, but it also prohibited their rise as national citizens. The restrictions of the law to determine the present and the future conditions of the marriage relationship encouraged rationalist thinkers like Wollstonecraft to resist institutional authority and act independently of the law. Prater clarifies the two positions of the law, ecclesiastical and civil, that complicate the progress of women as British citizens, whose restrictive roles as wives inhibited the possibilities for a wife to acknowledge herself or be acknowledged by others as a citizen. He explains, "Among the Romans marriage was usually preceded by a ceremony which was called espousals (*sponsalia*), and which consisted of a solemn betrothment (*sponsio*) of the female (*sponsa*) to the male (*sponsus*) by their respective parents (*sponsores*)."[5] The separation of roles—parental, husband, and wife—delineates parental control and male dominance where the holiness of the marriage as a sacred contract underlies the laws of eighteenth-century marital relationships. As a result, dependence on ecclesiastical authority for marriage was the main source of legal conflict between England and Scotland whose marriage laws were based on the canonical law in England and on the civil law in Scotland.

According to Scottish marriage law, there was no longer any requirement for parental consent or an ecclesiastical ceremony. An individual's right to choose one's partner based on feelings rather than property or wealth undermined the authority of parents and the clergy. The marriage law in Scotland took a civil perspective, as Prater explains,

> Far different have been the changes in Scotland, where the marriage law appears to have been more strict before than after the Reformation. In order to be legally complete (*legitimum*) it was indispensable at one time, even in Scotland, that marriage should be solemnized *in facie ecclesia*. (d) But the temporal courts of that country departed further from the tenets of the ancient religion than those of England, and the abolition of episcopacy was followed by the decline of those doctrines which had been the support of Catholicism. Instead of being regarded as a sacrament, marriage was viewed merely as a civil contract.[6]

Since marriage was legalized under civil law in Scotland, ecclesiastical ties were severed along with medieval virtues of chastity. For Wollstonecraft and other virtuous women who honored passion as the expression of virtue, these changes to the marriage laws liberated women from the restraint of medieval values of female obedience and submission. However, the freedom to choose one's marriage partner did not include an acceptance of sexual freedom. Young women continued to embrace the importance of their social identity as wives; the alternatives left women vulnerable, dependent, and often alone. Through her treatise on the education of women, Wollstonecraft recognizes the fallibility of retaining doctrinal restraints. She writes, "What does history disclose but marks of inferiority, and how few women have emancipated themselves from the galling yoke of sovereign man?"[7] Wollstonecraft was unafraid to face social opposition directly when she chose Gilbert Imlay as her spiritual partner; she risked denigrating herself in public opinion to elevate virtue as a state of natural goodness from the degradation of moral righteousness.

In addition, as Suzanne Desan explains in her analysis of marriage and citizenship, "The interconnection between citizenship and marriage did not emerge seamlessly in the 1790s, nor did it have the same ramifications for men and women."[8] Desan points out that husbands and wives were not treated equally as citizens, but more importantly, she emphasizes how social and political forums determined citizenship and created visions for conjugal reform. She states, "The very act of building a secular state and creating the legal individual called the gendered practices of intimacy into question."[9] Moving from a sacred to a secular role of marriage, husbands and wives gained the freedom to re-examine their most intimate roles within the larger context of the laws of the nation.

The discrepancies in the marriage laws between England and Scotland caused further confusion and encouraged deception among those opportunists who took advantage of them. As Prater shows, the Consistorial Court of Edinburgh describes these irregular marriages, those that were contracted out of the church, as complicated:

I. That the law of Scotland relative to irregular marriages is often the cause of seduction under a promise of marriage.
II. That it opens a door to attempts by women of bad character to inveigle young men into disreputable marriages with them, and *vice versa*.
III. That it occasions controversies between women respecting the *status* of wife to the same man, and between different men respecting the *status* of husband to the same woman; and
IV. That it holds out to persons entrusted with the property or education of infants, an opportunity of committing breaches of trust with comparative facility.[10]

One case cited by Prater is the situation of a woman who believed that the promise of matrimony followed seduction. In the following case of Linning v. Hamilton, the courts ruled that seduction had occurred; however, there was no legal enforcement of the marriage contract:

The woman who claimed she was seduced believed herself to have contracted marriage and went 'to the nuptial bed with as much purity of mind and of person, with as little violation of delicacy, and with as little loss of reputation, as if her marriage had been graced with all the sanctities of religion.[11]

Under English law, marriage could not be mistaken as seduction; however, under Scottish law, a woman was easily deceived that a promise of marriage followed by consummation meant that the marriage contract would follow. The rise of individualism that defined the Romantic Era fundamentally addressed the social weaknesses in the marriage laws just as rapidly as dissenting views toward political governance questioned civil laws.

When Wollstonecraft decided to consummate her relationship with Imlay, she anticipated the promise of matrimony even in a spiritual relationship, if not a legal one. She yearned for the promise of a home, a family, and a husband that would fulfill her desires. In her analysis of Wollstonecraft's philosophy of the family, Eileen Hunt explains Wollstonecraft's vision of the ideal family that appeared in her response to Edmund Burke's *Reflections on the Revolution in France*:[12]

> It is an idyllic family farm, set far from the vices of cities, where the children can grow strong in body, mind and character, in touch with their natural selves. 'Domestic comfort' and 'civilizing relations' with one's family would soften labor and make life contented. No longer torn apart and corrupted by conflicts over hereditary property, families would be haven of comfort, civility, and contentment. Natural affection between parent and child, brother and sister, husband and wife would no longer be perverted and stunted by unnatural hierarchies.[13]

Wollstonecraft exercised her intellectual genius in her response to Burke's *Reflections* attacking class, rank, and tradition. Her desire to equalize the social aberrations between husband and wife strengthened her resolve in a public expression of liberty. She never hesitated in her criticism of Burke's conservative views especially with regard to women. In her *Vindication of the Rights of Men*, Wollstonecraft challenges Burke's reference to vile women in his description of the events at Versailles:

> A sentiment of this kind glanced across my mind when I read the following exclamation. 'Whilst the royal captives, who followed in the train, were slowly moved along, amidst the horrid yells, and shrilling screams, and frantic dances, and infamous contumelies, and all the unutterable abominations of the furies of hell, in the abused shape of the vilest of women'. Probably you mean women who gained a livelihood by selling vegetables or fish, who never had had any advantages of education; or their vices might have lost part of their abominable deformity, by losing part of their grossness.[14]

Wollstonecraft's retort to Burke may appear harsh, but her defense of the fishwives and their innocence, lack of education and even their vices, is a powerful example of rhetoric that reflects the disturbing atmosphere of these revolutionary times. Her public advocacy serves to identify her national self while her private struggle with passion shapes her domestic identity as a wife. Her speech and writing motivate the silent women to form a new language and identity carved out of equality and liberty. As wives, both the silent Sara Fricker Coleridge and the outspoken Mary Wollstonecraft Godwin influence their husbands to bring opposing ideas together, joining religious, political, and social interests into viable avenues for the progress of civilization.

As their dissenting views and liberal sentiments had drawn Wollstonecraft and Godwin together, Coleridge and Sara Fricker were attracted through their sensibilities of intellect and moral values. Yet both couples suffered from confrontations regarding their views as their lives became intertwined in mutual efforts to elevate natural virtue over medieval religious and restrictive political laws. Meeting Godwin among her radical circle of friends in November 1791, Wollstonecraft auspiciously began a new direction in her life which later challenged both writers' adherence to their anti-establishment conventions. They regarded marriage as property and property as the source of inequality between classes and genders, in contrast with Coleridge's more elitist views on property ownership. However, Godwin's philosophical ideas on benevolence and a rational intellect formulated the core principle of Coleridge's Bristol lectures in 1795 and provided both Coleridge and Godwin with a utopian idealism that directly linked their political and personal relationships. Their divisive moral–political outlooks moved the two married couples, the Coleridges and the Godwins, into an intellectual discourse that fostered change to their distinctive theories, marking a permanent shift in moral sentiments.

The engagement of Coleridge and Godwin in a debate on the moral principles of government illustrates a sympathetic understanding of the development of gender influences that changed their friendship from an adversarial one to a collaborative union. Finally, with the publication of Wollstonecraft's writings on vindicating women from customary domestic roles and her tempering of Godwin's extreme views on political justice and marriage, the role of the Romantic wife was redefined as an intellectual partner, friend, and lover. The political influence on marriage shifted toward the feminine intellect not just in theory but in practice. As Nicola Trott suggests, "*Political Justice* [Godwin's fundamental treatise] gave new impetus to the debate between private affections and general benevolence."[15] The coincidence of their ideologies on a system of "disinterested benevolence" further secularized the Calvinist doctrine, while at the same time, established a more permanent foundation for domestic affections arising from a spiritual source. The Presbyterian minister William Enfield sympathized with Coleridge's view of the universality of divine love in his essay that appeared in the *Monthly Magazine* where he asks,

"'Is Private Affection inconsistent with Universal Benevolence?'"[16] Moreover, as the debate between private affection and religious doctrine became central to Coleridge and Godwin's discourse, the two philosophers found mutual understanding among their varying beliefs. Although Godwin's atheistic ideology was tempered by his views on a benevolent society, his dissenting views continued to rankle Coleridge's religious adherence to a higher authority.

Godwin, who was raised a Calvinist and later declared himself an Atheist, attacked institutional influences on public and private lifestyles that contradicted the moral beliefs advocated by Coleridge. Godwin's moral and social theories on human nature were primarily driven by a philosophy of determinism, referred to as the doctrine of necessity. His reliance on environmental causes for human actions precludes his belief in a mystical cause as Coleridge would claim. Yet even though both men derive their theories based on the writings of Joseph Priestley and David Hume, each one's approach counteracts the other. Arguing against the theory of free will, Godwin turns to a more scientific explanation of law than Coleridge.[17] In his moral philosophy and political theory Godwin adheres to several basic propositions about human nature that encompass self-interest, good and evil, equality, human perfectibility and individuality which are also the substance of Coleridge's inquiries.[18] The intellectual pursuits of both Coleridge and Godwin unite the men as literary sparring partners but also serve to unite their domestic relations as well. By the time Godwin's intimate relationship with Mary Wollstonecraft was established in 1796 and Coleridge had already married Sara Fricker in 1795, their contradictory views on marriage and politics were felt even more personally.

In his letter to Benjamin Flower[19] on 11 December 1796, Coleridge set forth a vehement "Answer" to William Godwin's doctrine of moral necessity, a defense of Atheism and treatise on human happiness.[20] Classifying Godwin as an Infidel, Coleridge assigns Godwin's doctrine to a timeless argument against all moral systems that have ever contradicted the Gospel. Coleridge intends passionately, as he states,

> to shew not only the absurdities and wickedness of *his* System, but to detect what appear to me the defects of all the systems of morality before & since Christ, & to shew that where they have been right, they have exactly coincided with the Gospel.... My last chapter will attack the credulity, superstition, calumnies, and hypocrisy of the present race of Infidels.[21]

Coleridge focused his opposition not only on Godwin's religious infidelity but also on what appeared to him to be Godwin's indifference to the importance of domestic feelings as a foundation for social development in family, church, and country. Despite his hard-lined view of Christian theology as the basis for the abolition of private property in favor of communal ownership, Coleridge met Godwin's atheistic views as somewhat of an outsider of reform during the 1790s.[22] Coleridge's rigid theological beliefs shifted when he adopted the doctrinal reform of Unitarianism from the strict theology of the Trinitarians. In the spring of 1795, he challenged the traditional theological beliefs of the Anglican Church with his more liberal views as a Unitarian in his *Lectures on Revealed Religion*. His association with Godwin grew from opposing radical views to moral sentiments highly debated in the rhetoric of religion and politics. This ongoing debate on morality and theology encompassed a deeper philosophical inquiry into human nature. As a result, the debate over the religious ideologies of both these intellectuals, Coleridge and Godwin, provides insights into human nature as it was defined in eighteenth-century English culture.

Another critic of Coleridge's lectures on revealed religion, the radical speaker and atheist John Thelwall, vehemently disputed "questions of love, marriage and religion."[23] Accusations of abusive rhetoric by John Thelwall unsettled Coleridge who responded in his own defense against Godwin's system of moral and political principles. Coleridge wrote in a letter to Thelwall on 13 May 1796:

> You deem, that I have treated 'systems & opinions with the furious prejudices of the conventicle, & the illiberal dogmatism of the Cynic—' '—that I have layed 'about me on this side & on that with the sledge-hammer of abuse.' I have, you think, imitated the 'old sect in politics & morals' in their 'outrageous violence,' and have 'sunk into the clownish fier[c]eness of intolerant prejudice.'—I have 'branded' the presumptuous children of Scepticism 'with vile epithets & hunted them down with abuse.'—'*These be hard words, Citizen! & I will be bold to say, they are not to be justified*' by the unfortunate page which has occasioned them.[24]

Deeply offended by Thelwall's criticism that Coleridge upheld the old dogma, he refutes his scathing rebuke. Coleridge felt the personal affront of this attack on his reputation while he became further frustrated by an unsuccessful run of *The Watchman*, a journal that left his funds depleted after 14 weeks of publication. His personal expenses compounded his frustrations over his professional failure as well. With additional concerns for his family's financial needs, he complains to his friend Tom Poole that Mrs. Coleridge asked for baby linen and the funeral expenses for her mother.[25]

However, Coleridge continues to challenge the immorality of Godwin's liberalism when he asks Thelwall in a sarcastic tone, "Why should you not have intercourse with *the Wife* of your friend?—From the principles in your *heart*—Verily, Thelwall! I believe you—on your *heart* I should rest for my safety!"[26] Coleridge trusts in the goodness of Thelwall's heart rather than in the didacticism of moral principles. He then establishes the certainty of his own moral and religious beliefs as a follower of Godwin's Necessarian views and as a Christian when he explains,

> What more do we mean by *Marriage* than that state in which it would be criminal *at one moment*, criminal always: in other words, *Marriage is indissoluble*. For surely, if it would be wrong in *you* to solicit my *Wife*, it must be wrong in my *Wife* to solicit *you*—and if neither make advances, Marriage will be preserved indissoluble—You do not suppose, I attribute any magic to ceremonies—or think that the *Priest* married me—Great indeed are the moral uses of Marriage—.[27]

Here Coleridge affirms virtuous behavior on the moral principles of benevolence and optimism that arise from his faith in Christian values rather than falsely adhering to religious doctrine.

In his notes Godwin attributes a change of heart, probably occurring around 1799–1800, to the influence of Coleridge's ideas on his religious thinking:

> In my forty-fourth year I ceased to regard the name of Atheist with the same complacency I had done for several preceding years, at the same time retaining the utmost repugnance of understanding for the idea of an intelligent Creator and Governor of the universe, which strikes my mind as the most irrational and ridiculous anthropomorphism. My theism, if such I may be permitted to call it, consists in a reverent and soothing contemplation of all that is beautiful, grand, or mysterious in the system of the universe, and in a certain conscious intercourse and correspondence with the principles of these attributes, without attempting the idle task of developing and defining it—into this train of thinking I was first led by the conversations of S. T. Coleridge.[28]

The significant shift in Godwin's theistic beliefs, as he attributes the change to Coleridge, accounts for the manner in which both philosophers define happiness in marriage. While Coleridge acknowledges the indissolubility of the marriage law, he confirms that affections in the marital relationship are attributable to principles of the heart, not legislated by canonical law.

As Coleridge developed his lectures on revealed religion from the works of Joseph Priestley, David Hartley, and others, he grounded his principles on the imagination, on methods, and on scientific theories. His lectures evidence Priestley's ideas of optimism with the view of improving the human race through the progress and advancement of the human mind and spirit. In Priestley's *Essay on the First Principles of Government* of 1768, Coleridge found an intellectual source for a more conservative view of optimism. As Lewis Patton and Peter Mann, the editors of *Lectures 1795 On Politics and Religion*, suggest,

> The system of optimism in Hartley and Priestley seems actually to imply a quietist and conservative view of the world rather than a reformist one, and Coleridge's Lectures on Revealed Religion reflect in a more acute form the difficulty of holding simultaneously the theological view that all evil is ultimately an obscure good and the view that social and moral evils are dependent upon circumstances and are consequently remediable.[29]

The editors remark that at times Coleridge shifts his viewpoints between lectures sometimes defending Christianity against the Atheists and at other times attacking the political system for creating human circumstances of misery by the inequality of property ownership and laws.[30] However, his firm reliance on Priestley has been noted to be less indebted to his moral and religious principles and more possibly to his fundamental rejection of Godwinism as a philosophy.[31] Turning to Unitarianism furthered his uncertainty with Priestley's and Hartley's system of optimism, but his wife's experience with a painful pregnancy and the subsequent death of his son Berkeley by 1799 forced Coleridge to forsake his previous association as a Necessitarian, as he declared to Thelwall in 1796.[32] His relationship with Godwin grew from their mutual concern for the social progress and creative potential of man, while Coleridge continued to confirm man's existence and happiness from a position of morality and his Christian faith. Along with Coleridge's influence on Godwin's skepticism of a universal creator came another significant reformer of Godwin's atheistic beliefs, his future wife Mary Wollstonecraft.

When Wollstonecraft retaliated against the eighteenth-century paradigm of womanhood in her *Vindication of the Rights of Woman* (1792), she was criticized for her masculinity of language and rhetorical frankness against Burke, Rousseau, Gregory, and Fordyce who advocated for feminine passivity and modesty of intellect in females. She advanced female rights for equality of education and dispelled myths of feminine sensibility in partnerships with men. Sexual passions were to be tempered by reason, and yet when she renewed her friendship with Godwin in 1796, she found herself attracted to a man who pursued Wollstonecraft for her female manners rather than her intellect.[33] Undeterred by his masculine desires for her feminine delicacy, Wollstonecraft found the friendship a welcome intimacy. Their romance melted Godwin's stern resistance to the institution of marriage since he was unwilling to make her a social outcast. He explains,

> I had for many years regarded marriage with so well-grounded an apprehension, that, notwithstanding the partiality for Mary that had taken possession of my soul, I should have felt it very difficult, at least in the present stage of our intercourse, to have resolved on such a measure.[34]

Wollstonecraft's pregnant condition in April 1797 gave Godwin sufficient reason to fulfill the ceremonial part of their marriage. Despite Godwin's criticism of Wollstonecraft as a less accomplished essayist, she quietly acknowledges his lack of understanding on the subject of the imagination.[35] "Godwin says I am weakest when I try to write a work of reason rather than of imagination,"[36] writes Wollstonecraft who recognizes Godwin's masculine authority over her supposed feminine weakness.

Despite the social implications of marriage as a sign of masculine authority, Godwin recognized how damaging it would be to Wollstonecraft's reputation and destructive to her desires to advocate for female independence. Sadly, the marriage was brief when Mary suffered from puerperal fever at childbirth, dying only days after her daughter was born. Yet, shortly after her unfortunate death on 10 September 1797, Coleridge and his wife and family kept up their correspondence and visits to Godwin's home in London. In May 1800 Coleridge writes to Godwin expressing his affections for him and his children, Mary and her half-sister Fanny:

> My dear Godwin! I remember you with so much pleasure & our conversations so distinctly, that, I doubt not, we have been mutually benefited—but as to your poetic & physiopathic feelings, I more than suspect, that dear little Fanny & Mary have had more to do in that business than I. Hartley sends his Love to Mary. 'What? & not to Fanny?' Yes—& to Fanny—but I'll *have* Mary.—He often talks about them.[37]

The affectionate remarks from Coleridge to Godwin confirm a relationship that went beyond their political and religious interests, a relationship situated in domestic feelings secured by their principles of natural virtue. Godwin's biographer Ford K. Brown comments further on the close friendship noting that "... the Coleridges had Christmas dinner with Godwin in 1799," and in Coleridge's letter to Southey on 24 December 1799, he illustrates the familiarity of the two families. He tells Southey that his son Hartley called Godwin: Mister Gobwin, and that he "gave the philosopher such a rap on the shins with a ninepin that Gobwin in huge pain *lectured* Sara on his boisterousness."[38] As the two families exchange domestic intimacies, they also illustrate an adherence to those principles of natural virtue that incorporated the sacred elements of marriage in a secular environment.

While the evolution of marriage laws may define historical progress with the long-awaited Marriage Act of 1754, the intellectual and philosophical views of Coleridge and Godwin epitomize political and moral changes, in an era of social awareness that elevates feminine authority. The relinquishment of religious authority over marital relations to allow for the rise of individual affections occurs because of increasing domestic desires for women to attain intellectual equality as Wollstonecraft advocated. Without these ongoing debates and controversial views of government, religion, and education, the English society would have remained in the Middle Ages. The growth of female acceptance within the social and legal institutions gave a literary identity to all women, married and unmarried alike. As the social imagination of the Romantic wife developed through these discursive exchanges among male writers who were previously disciplined by the ecclesiastical and canonical laws, the secular lives of the ordinary wife established women's authority among masculine traditions.

From their intellectual pursuits and contentions with marriage, Godwin and Wollstonecraft each influenced English society and its domestic concerns, privileges, and conventions, whereas Coleridge and his wife upheld the social standards that adhered to the traditional roles of husband and wife through their more religious orthodoxy. Godwin and Wollstonecraft, on the other hand, attracted the friendships of liberal political and religious thinkers. Earlier in her experience in 1784, an independent and unmarried Wollstonecraft developed close relationships with Richard Price, Dissenting minister, and Joseph Priestley, Dissenter and scientist, when as a young woman at the age of 25 she founded her boarding school for young women in Newington Green. Within this circle of Dissenters, Wollstonecraft found friendship and encouragement for her educational writings that were later published under the title of *Thoughts on the Education of Daughters; with Reflections on Female Conduct, in the More Important Duties of Life* (1786).

From traditional to liberal beliefs in the eighteenth century, societal values continuously evolved in social, political, and economic manners, changing the form and substance of ordinary life as more relaxed religious groups sprang up, challenging rigidly held beliefs on family, God, and politics. The dissenting views and liberal sentiments arising from the pursuit of intellectual and religious freedoms questioned the established relationship between church and state. How these views and emotions affected individuals have been examined in the collaborative relationship between the two prominent literary writers and political activists of the late eighteenth century, Coleridge and Godwin, and who, ironically, maintained opposing religious positions. Despite their contradictory religious beliefs, these men collaborated on literary and political ideas as each one embraced and popularized their original views on marriage, individual rights, and justice.

Moreover, Wollstonecraft and Coleridge shared an intellectual pursuit that marks the revolutionary period as a transition for marriage and citizenship from sacred to secular in a progressive society of thinkers. Both the Coleridge and Godwin marriages demonstrate a dynamic shift in authority between masculine and feminine concerns domestically and nationally. As Desan explains, "The new politics required fraternal bonds and stoic valor, but also a kind of moral acuity and sensitivity that could only come from intimate relationships and companionship with women."[39] Certainly, the rise of feminist intellectualism radicalized doctrinal beliefs during the eighteenth century, an age enlightened by many intellectual thinkers who through their adherence to dissenting views led a middle class from ignorance and obedience to a rational self-interest and, to use Lawrence Stone's term, an "affective individualism"[40] by advancing "the enquiring spirit." As the concluding chapter will show, the younger generation of Coleridge and Godwin children, Sara Coleridge Coleridge and Mary Godwin Shelley, inherit their mothers' independent spirits and further illustrate the literary identity of the Romantic wife forged from the intellectual and emotional exchanges in a domestic setting.

Notes

1 Mary Wollstonecraft, *The Vindications: The Rights of Men and the Rights of Woman*, eds. D. L. Macdonald and Kathleen Scherf (Ontario: Broadview Press, 2001), 141. See Wollstonecraft's admiration for historian Catherine Macaulay who wrote,

> In order to take from public sentiment a reproach which leaves a deep stain on human character, and to correct many irregularities, and even enormities, which arise from incorrect systems of ethics, it ought to be the first care of education to teach virtue on immutable principles.
> (*The Vindications*, 400; Wollstonecraft remarks, "The very word respect brings Mrs. Macaulay to my remembrance." *The Vindications*, 231)

2 Griggs, ed., *Collected Letters, Vol. I. 1785-1800*, 103.
3 Henry Prater, *Cases Illustrative of the Conflict Between the Laws of England and Scotland with Regard to Marriage, Divorce and Legitimacy as a Supplement to an Essay Upon the Law Respecting Husband and Wife* (London: Saunders & Benning, 1835), 3.

156 *The Social Imagination of the Romantic Wife in Literature*

4 Karen O'Brien, *Women and Enlightenment in Eighteenth-Century Britain* (Cambridge: Cambridge University Press, 2009), 170. See also Vivien Jones' *Women in the Eighteenth Century: Constructions of Femininity* where Catherine Macaulay further explains in her 1790 *Letters on Education, Part One*, Letter IV, "The social duties in the interesting characters of daughter, wife, and mother, will be but ill performed by ignorance and levity; and in the domestic converse of husband and wife, the alternative of an enlightened, or an unenlightened companion, cannot be indifferent to any man of taste and true knowledge" (London: Routledge, 1990), 113.
5 Prater, *Cases Illustrative of the Conflict Between the Laws of England and Scotland*, 4.
6 Prater, *Cases Illustrative of the Conflict Between the Laws of England and Scotland*, 9.
7 Wollstonecraft, *The Vindications*, 145.
8 Suzanne Desan, "The Politics of Intimacy: Marriage and Citizenship in the French Revolution," *Women, Gender and Enlightenment*, eds. Sarah Knott and Barbara Taylor (New York: Palgrave Macmillan, 2005), 631.
9 Desan, "The Politics of Intimacy," 631.
10 Prater, *Cases Illustrative of the Conflict Between the Laws of England and Scotland*, 11–12.
11 Prater, *Cases Illustrative of the Conflict Between the Laws of England and Scotland*, 16.
12 Wollstonecraft, *The Rights of Men*, 93.
13 Eileen M. Hunt, "The Family as Cave, Platoon and Prison: The Three Stages of Wollstonecraft's Philosophy of Family," *The Review of Politics*, vol. 64, no. 1 (Winter 2002), 106–107.
14 Wollstonecraft, *The Rights of Men*, 62.
15 Nicola Trott, "The Coleridge Circle and the 'Answer to Godwin'," *The Review of English Studies*, New Series, vol. 41, no. 162 (May 1990), 215.
16 Trott, "The Coleridge Circle," 216.
17 According to John P. Clark,

> Godwin believes that the evidence for the existence of necessity in nature is compelling. He notes that as scientific investigation into the workings of nature has progressed, a continually increasing proportion of natural phenomena has been explained by scientifically formulated law.
> (*The Philosophical Anarchism of William Godwin* (Princeton: Princeton University Press, 1977), 41)

18 Clark, *The Philosophical Anarchism*, 60.
19 Benjamin Flower was editor of the *Cambridge Intelligencer* in 1796 at the time Coleridge and Godwin debated their opposing philosophies on religious and political issues.
20 William Godwin defines his doctrine of moral necessity as "a body of events in systematical arrangement." He explains,

> In the life of every human being there is a chain of events, generated in the lapse of ages which preceded his birth, and going on in regular procession

Marriage Law and the Rights of Woman 157

> through the whole period of his existence, in consequence of which it was impossible for him to act in any instance otherwise than he has acted.
> (*Enquiry Concerning Political Justice and its Influence on Morals and Happiness*, vol. 1, ed. F. E. L. Priestley (London: Printed for G. G. and J. Robinson, Paternoster-Row, 1798; Toronto: University of Toronto Press, 1946), 384)

21 E. L. Griggs, ed., *The Collected Letters of Samuel Taylor Coleridge, Vol. I. 1785-1800* (Oxford: Oxford University Press, 1956), 267–68.
22 According to Michael R. Watts, the Church of England may have contributed largely to the rise in non-conforming religious groups, so Coleridge's adherence to basic tenets of the Church and his subsequent shift of religious beliefs indicates that a broader movement of fluctuating beliefs was ongoing. Watts states,

> It was Anglican efforts to revive the religious life of England and Wales that had prepared the way for the Evangelical revival in the eighteenth century, ... But the Anglican church at the turn of the eighteenth and nineteenth centuries, with its formal worship, cold sermons, and absence of lay participation, lacked the excitement, the emotional fervor, and the opportunities for involvement provided by Methodist chapels and Non-conformist meeting-houses.
> (*The Dissenters: Volume II The Expansion of Evangelical Nonconformity* (Oxford: Oxford University Press, 1995), 113)

23 John Cornwell, *Coleridge: Poet and Revolutionary 1772–1804 A Critical Biography* (London: Penguin Books, 1973), 136.
24 Griggs, ed., *Collected Letters, Vol. I. 1785–1800*, 212–13.
25 Griggs, ed., *Collected Letters, Vol. I. 1785–1800*, 208.
26 Griggs, ed., *Collected Letters, Vol. I. 1785–1800*, 213.
27 Griggs, ed., *Collected Letters, Vol. I. 1785–1800*, 213.
28 C. Kegan Paul, *William Godwin: His Friends and Contemporaries*, Vol. I (New York: AMS Press, 1970), 357–58.
29 Lewis Patton and Peter Mann, eds., See the editors' introduction in *The Collected Works of Samuel Taylor Coleridge*, vol. 1: Lectures 1795 On Politics and Religion (Princeton: Princeton University Press, 1971), lxiii.
30 Patton and Mann, eds., *Collected Works*, lxiii.
31 Patton and Mann, eds., *Collected Works*, lxiii.
32 Patton and Mann, eds., *Collected Works*, lxvi.
33 Godwin and Wollstonecraft first met on 13 November 1791 at Joseph Johnson's house in a less than cordial manner. According to Godwin's biographer Peter H. Marshall, Godwin disliked Wollstonecraft's writing style and gloomy manner. He explains, "Thus when he [Godwin] lauded Horne Tooke, Dr. Johnson, and Voltaire, she declared prescription, prejudice, and the British Constitution." They met only three times during the following year and not again until 1796. *William Godwin* (New Haven: Yale University Press, 1984), 84–85.

34 William Godwin, *Memoirs of Mary Wollstonecraft*, ed. W. Clark Durant (New York: Haskell House Publishers, 1969), 103.
35 Jean Detre, *A Most Extraordinary Pair: Mary Wollstonecraft and William Godwin* (New York: Doubleday, 1975), 20.
36 Detre, *A Most Extraordinary Pair*, 21.
37 Griggs, ed., *Collected Letters*, Vol. I. 1785–1800, 588.
38 Ford K. Brown, *The Life of William Godwin* (London: J. J. Dent & Sons, 1926), 179.
39 Desan, "The Politics of Intimacy," 644.
40 Lawrence Stone investigates the concept of individual freedom as it arose in eighteenth-century England among all classes of society. He explains,

> Individualism is a very slippery concept to handle. Here what is meant is two rather distinct things: firstly, a growing introspection and interest in the individual personality; and secondly, a demand for personal autonomy and a corresponding respect for the individual's right to privacy, to self-expression, and to the free exercise of his will within limits set by the need for social cohesion: a recognition that it is morally wrong to make exaggerated demands for obedience, or to manipulate or coerce the individual beyond a certain point in order to achieve social or political ends.

He identifies this shift in personal freedom as a change from the sacred to the secular when he acknowledges, "But it was the post-1660 cultural supremacy of the anti-Puritan character type which built on this foundation decisively to change attitudes towards authority, affection and sex within the middle and upper ranks of society." *The Family, Sex and Marriage in England 1500–1800* (New York: Harper & Row, 1979), 223–25.

References

Brown, Ford K. *The Life of William Godwin*. London: J. J. Dent & Sons, 1926.
Clark, John P. *The Philosophical Anarchism of William Godwin*. Princeton: Princeton University Press, 1977.
Coleridge, Samuel Taylor, *The Collected Works of Samuel Taylor Coleridge*, vol. 1: Lectures 1795 On Politics and Religion, eds. Lewis Patton and Peter Mann. Princeton: Princeton University Press, 1971.
Cornwell, John. *Coleridge: Poet and Revolutionary 1772–1804 A Critical Biography*. London: Penguin Books, 1973.
Desan, Suzanne. "The Politics of Intimacy: Marriage and Citizenship in the French Revolution." *Women, Gender and Enlightenment*, eds. Sarah Knott and Barbara Taylor. New York: Palgrave Macmillan, 2005, 630–48.
Detre, Jean. *A Most Extraordinary Pair: Mary Wollstonecraft and William Godwin*. New York: Doubleday, 1975.
Godwin, William. *Enquiry Concerning Political Justice and its Influence on Morals and Happiness*. vol. 1, ed. F. E. L. Priestley. London: Printed for G. G. and J. Robinson, Paternoster-Row, 1798; Toronto: University of Toronto Press, 1946.

---. *Memoirs of Mary Wollstonecraft*, ed. W. Clark Durant. New York: Haskell House Publishers, 1969.
Griggs, E. L., ed. *The Collected Letters of Samuel Taylor Coleridge, Vol. I. 1785–1800*. Oxford: Oxford University Press, 1956.
Hunt, Eileen H. "The Family as Cave, Platoon and Prison: The Three Stages of Wollstonecraft's Philosophy of Family." *The Review of Politics*, vol. 64, no. 1, Winter 2002.
Marshall, Peter H. *William Godwin*. New Haven: Yale University Press, 1984.
O'Brien, Karen. *Women and Enlightenment in Eighteenth-Century Britain*. Cambridge: Cambridge University Press, 2009.
Paul, C. Kegan. *William Godwin: His Friends and Contemporaries*. Vol. I. New York: AMS Press, 1970.
Prater, Henry. *Cases Illustrative of the Conflict Between the Laws of England and Scotland with Regard to Marriage, Divorce and Legitimacy as a Supplement to an Essay Upon the Law Respecting Husband and Wife*. London: Saunders & Benning, 1835.
Stone, Lawrence. *The Family, Sex and Marriage in England 1500–1800*. New York: Harper & Row, 1979.
Trott, Nicola. "The Coleridge Circle and the 'Answer to Godwin'." *The Review of English Studies*. New Series, vol. 41, no. 162, May 1990.
Watts, Michael R. *The Dissenters: Volume II The Expansion of Evangelical Nonconformity*. Oxford: Oxford University Press, 1995.
Wollstonecraft, Mary. *The Vindications: The Rights of Men and the Rights of Woman*, eds. D. L. Macdonald and Kathleen Scherf. Ontario: Broadview Press, 2001.

Conclusion
"*Love in Fairy-land*"—Sara Coleridge Coleridge and Mary Godwin Shelley[1]

> *Coarse-minded thing! she can't endure Fairy-land, where the lovers are as fine as mists, and the ladies evanescent as rainbows.*[2]
>
> Sara Coleridge Coleridge

The language of the heart is a wellspring from which emanates the progress of civilization. The feminine spirit of inquiry examines social and political conditions from a source of tenderness and grace even when the rhetoric bespeaks a masculine attitude. From observations of the daughters of both Mary Wollstonecraft and Sara Fricker Coleridge, the feminine spirit is recognized and its afterlife of impressions continues to endorse virtues of natural goodness. As the daughters of women who marked the rise of the intellectual wife, Mary Shelley and Sara Coleridge embraced feminine virtues of liberty, justice, and intellect, escaping the orthodox restraints of female delicacy and sublimation. Both of these young women grew up in literary environments and were nurtured by the political and social ideologies of the Romantic writers. As a result, Mary Shelley and Sara Coleridge became recognized publicly as professional writers, each contributing to the legacies of their literary parents. The intersection of domestic identity with a literary life is recognized by authors such as Elizabeth Shand, Robin Schofield, and Jeffrey W. Barbeau in their analyses of Sara Coleridge and her writing. Shand explains, "At the same time that Sara worked to reconcile her gender and work as editor of her father's writings, she returned to her novel and wrote interchangeably as author, critic, editor, mother, romantic admirer, and widow."[3]

From her infancy, William Godwin raised his daughter, Mary Godwin, later Shelley, and his adopted daughter Fanny, Mary's half-sister, after his wife, Mary Wollstonecraft Godwin, died from puerperal fever several days following her daughter's birth. Throughout her youth, Sara Coleridge spent her time with her mother who educated Sara in her uncle Robert Southey's household. She was estranged from her father, Samuel Taylor

Coleridge, for most of her childhood while he battled with his opium addiction. After her birth in 1802, her father spent less than two years with his family in Keswick until he left in 1812. For the next 11 years, neither Sara nor her mother would see Coleridge again until January 1823. Through the kindness of Mrs. Gillman, the wife of Dr. Gillman who cared for Samuel during his addiction, Sara Coleridge received the admiration and sympathy of her father's caregivers. Mrs. Gillman writes to young Sara on the death of her father in 1834 describing her own personal loss:

> My dearest Sara,
> "A light is indeed gone out of the World"—He truly has shone in the Darkness, & the Darkness knew him not—I do feel for you my dear Sara—& for you all—and I bless God & have long done so, for the Blessing he has been to me & mine— ... His forgiving nature, his heavenly mindedness, his care not to give offence unless a duty called on him to tell some truth—his sweet & cheerful temper—and so many moral qualities of more or less value & all adorned by his Christian principles.[4]

However, despite death and desertion, these young women discovered an absent parent through literary remains from which they established their relationships. The powerful influences of the writings of Mary Wollstonecraft on Mary Shelley and Samuel Taylor Coleridge on young Sara Coleridge created an intellectual foundation that distinguishes these young women in the literary culture of the nineteenth century.

For Mary Shelley, reading her mother's treatise on *A Vindication of the Rights of Woman* strengthened her resolve to attain intellectual equality with men. Through these powerful writings on the social importance of women, especially young wives, Mary Wollstonecraft inspired her daughter Mary with the faith she placed in divine benevolence to guide human goodness. As Jane Rendall reminds us,

> It must be remembered, of course, that underlying the *Vindication* is Mary Wollstonecraft's profound religious belief in the work of the Creator, that Divine Providence who has through the gift of reason enabled men to pursue and to achieve virtue.[5]

Her persistence in the reformation of those moral virtues based on doctrinal beliefs and supported by popular opinion changed the concept of femininity from a masculine-driven need to a feminine-derived standard. Rendall further explains, "Such qualities as courage should not be seen as primarily masculine, counterposed to the insipidity of gentleness in women."[6] Wollstonecraft attacked beliefs that repressed female independence of thought as she continued to rely on principles of natural virtue. In her *Thoughts on the Education of Daughters: With Reflections on Female Conduct, in the More Important Duties of Life*, she writes, "There cannot be any thing more dangerous to a mind, not accustomed to think, than doubts delivered in a ridiculing way."[7] Wollstonecraft attacks those who ridicule the uneducated female warning of the damage to the naïve female thought. Wollstonecraft explains that young women might not commit vices because they fear the world's rebuke; however, since their thoughts are unrestrained by instructive principles, their behavior should follow their hearts: "'For out of them are the issues of life'."[8] Citing a verse from Proverbs, Wollstonecraft reminds young women of the Scriptural soundness of natural virtue but, at the same time, she emphasizes the importance of intellectual thinking to discern good behavior.

In a similar manner, these virtues can be seen in Sara Coleridge's[9] advice in correctly caring for their children when she writes to her husband, Henry Nelson Coleridge in October 1835, on the need to displace severity with a higher aim of parental discipline. Her sincere goal is the intelligent care of her children, a lesson she learned from her mother's devotion to her and her education in her father's absence. She says,

> for the improvement of our children's moral nature I put my trust in no methods of discipline: these may answer well for a warring prince or general who has a particular external object to gain, and cares not for his instruments, except *as* instruments. I, too, have a particular object to gain—that our children should acquire a certain portion of book-learning; but my *whole* aim is their general welfare—as it must be that of every truly parental heart—the growth of their souls in goodness and holiness;
>
> .... Indeed, I do not strictly *put my faith* in any thing but the power of grace in the heart.[10]

Her depth of spiritual assurance in higher influences illustrates Sara's commitment to the moral instruction of the Scriptures while she remains an independent thinker. Her benevolent approach to child-raising shows her spiritual awareness, as does her humble attitude in editing her father's writing. In Bradford Keyes Mudge's biographical account of Sara, he takes notice of her humility as a literary writer. When she assumes her role as editor of her father's literary remains, she establishes her female authorship but within the boundaries of feminine propriety. Mudge challenges her self-ascribed humility when he states,

Her "humble tasks", her numerous scholarly editions and her long, densely written introductions and appendixes, are, however, humble only in two related senses: first, in that they assume female authorship to be a transgression of the well-established codes of propriety that celebrated and enforced women's intellectual, emotional, and economic selflessness; second, in that they position themselves by choice in the margins of precedent literary, philosophical, and theological texts.[11]

Mudge further argues for Sara's literary accomplishments even as a non-published nineteenth-century female writer, a lack of recognition complicated by cultural values, then and now, that circumscribed the value of the domestic role of an intellectual wife. He writes,

In other words, Sara Coleridge's humble tasks should be considered anything but humble; they were, at the time, complicated strategies by which an extremely intelligent woman uninterested in writing fiction and partial to theology and philosophy both exercised her mind and attempted to influence her contemporaries.[12]

Mudge's perspective on Sara Coleridge lifts her role as mother, wife, and literary agent to a similar view re-imagined in this book for her mother, that to acknowledge these women as intellectual wives fulfills an important gap in literary scholarship. While her mother's unpublished literary works pale in proportion to her daughter Sara's, Sara Fricker Coleridge has lacked recognition as an intellectual and literary figure in her own right while wrongly condemned by critics and friends as an ill-tempered and insensible wife.

Like her mother, Sara Coleridge was drawn to her father's poetic genius. Her conservative nature and weak constitution softened her spontaneity and creative spirit while she pursued her writing in poetry, letters, and essays. As Mudge explains,

. . . her sense of female propriety forbade the forceful assertion of the Romantic "genius" so quintessentially represented in her father, and neither a propitious political climate (as in the case of Wollstonecraft) nor financial need (as in the case of Shelley and Austen) forced Sara to violate cultural prohibitions.[13]

However, when Thomas De Quincey published his scathing criticism of her mother in *Tait's Edinburgh Magazine* in 1834 along with his attack on Coleridge's reputation as a poet and philosopher, Sara rebounded with her intellectual abilities to preserve an accurate memory of both parents. In defense of her mother, she writes to her husband Henry,

> The impression which the account of my mother would leave is that she is a mean-minded unamiable woman with some respectable qualities and that my Father married her from opportunity rather than much attraction of hers. My mother's *respectability* it did not rest with him to establish... .[14]

Henry and Sara Coleridge properly measured these unfavorable views of her mother and father and were determined to direct their literary efforts to finish the publication of Coleridge's writings. As Mudge describes, "Sara was headstrong but not precipitant. Rather than lower herself and her husband to the level of undignified journalistic bickering, she decided to begin a long-term editorial campaign."[15] Sara became engaged in her literary works along with her duties as a mother and shared an editorial role with her husband as his intellectual equal.

Some of Sara Coleridge's accomplishments as a poet have recently reached fruition in a 2007 collection of her poems edited by Peter Swaab.[16] Her own poetic works took a backseat to the publication of her father's writing. Sara was content to keep her writing an intimate effort until others recognized her literary identity through her achievements as a poet years after her death. As Swaab emphasizes,

> Despite the admiration of Blunden and a handful of others, Sara Coleridge's poetry has had to wait more than 150 years to be published as a collection, and she is meagerly represented, when at all, in several recent anthologies of nineteenth-century women's poetry, including some which have gone well off the beaten track to publish writers forgotten since their own day.[17]

However, she was not forgotten nor neglected as a writer by her brother Derwent Coleridge. After she died of breast cancer in May 1852, her brother Derwent completed the publication of *Coleridge's Poetical Works*, an edition that he edited with his sister Sara. He writes in the opening advertisement of the edition,

> This volume was prepared for the press by my lamented sister, Mrs. H. N. Coleridge, and will have an additional interest to many readers as the last monument of her highly-gifted mind. At her earnest request, my name appears with hers on the title-page, but the assistance rendered by me has been, in fact, little more than mechanical. The preface, and the greater part of the notes, are her composition:—the selection and arrangement have been determined almost exclusively by her critical judgment, or from records in her possession. A few slight corrections

and unimportant additions are all that have been found necessary, the first and last sheets not having had the benefit of her own revision.

(Derwent Coleridge
St. Mark's College, Chelsea
May, 1852)[18]

Sara's literary life and her death were interwoven within her identity as a wife and mother. She honored these female roles with her poetic genius as a product of an intellectually astute mother and a poetically intuitive father.[19]

In his biography of her life, Bradford Keyes Mudge compares Sara to Mary Wollstonecraft, at first contrasting their gender values and then situating them both as religious philosophers. He states,

> Unlike Mary Wollstonecraft, however, Sara Coleridge spoke out stridently for the paternalistic virtues as manifested in the writings of her father; she was, moreover, singularly responsible for packaging and dispensing Coleridge as the patriarchal remedy needed to cure the social ills of the 1830s and 1840s.[20]

While Wollstonecraft advocated for women to establish their virtues separate and apart from masculine desires, Sara praised the patriarchal order for its stability as her father did in his writing. Sara's self-denunciation of her own writing in order to publicize her father's literary remains illustrates a self-deprecation of the female that her mother had not embraced in her own life. Even as a conservative thinker and moralist, Sarah Fricker Coleridge, Sara's mother, would not have approved of a self-effacing wife. As Mudge points out, "Thus, like Mary Shelley, who evidenced a sense of propriety stronger than that felt by her mother, Sara harbored deep misgivings about the status of female authorship."[21] Mudge recognizes that Sara's "reactionary writings" (empowering traditional values) fit the propriety of her time, as she naturally relied on a paternal order conducive to the social and political context of nineteenth-century society. The shifting values of female virtues bring the literary and domestic roles of the wife closer in the mid-1800s.

As the daughter of an unorthodox and radical thinker such as Mary Wollstonecraft, Mary Shelley, like Sara Fricker Coleridge's daughter Sara Coleridge, relied more on traditional values of patriarchal authority than her mother did. However, also like Sara Coleridge, Mary Shelley embraced a religious affinity that their mothers shared as well. From William Godwin's *Memoirs*, we read of how her son-in-law, Percy Bysshe Shelley poetically praises Mary Wollstonecraft. In the Dedication to his wife in

Revolt of Islam (1817), Shelley writes about Mary Shelley's filial relationship with her mother and father:

> They say that thou were lovely from thy birth,
> Of glorious parents, thou aspiring child;
> I wonder not—for one then left this earth
> Whose life was like a setting planet mild,
> Which clothed thee in the radiance undefiled
> Of its departing glory; still her fame
> Shines on thee, through the tempests dark and wild
> Which shake these latter days; and thou canst claim
> The shelter, from thy Sire, of an immortal name.[22]

Her mother's life is described as a "setting planet mild / Which clothed thee in the radiance undefiled / Of its departing glory." Wollstonecraft gently endowed her daughter Mary with her faith in divine benevolence. In her daughter's words, Mary Shelley describes her mother as:

> One of those beings who appear … to gild humanity with a ray which no difference of opinion nor chance of circumstances can cloud. Her genius was undeniable… . Her sound understanding, her intrepidity, her sensibility and eager sympathy, stamped all her writings with force and truth, and endowed them with a tender charm which enchants while it enlightens.[23]

Mary Shelley exalts her mother's genius and empowers her language with the "force and truth" of "sound understanding" to enchant and enlighten her readers. With a fixed foundation in religious and philosophical principles, Wollstonecraft changed the social outlook, in general, on the role of the wife, and in particular, on her daughter's role as a wife, through her powerful writings.

As a young adolescent, Mary Shelley read her mother's social treatise on vindicating women's rights and her novels alongside her father's political treatise on justice. In her biography of Mary Shelley, Emily Sunstein explains how at 15 years old, Mary is educated through her mother's work. She writes,

> Though Godwin doubtless worried about the effect, he could no longer prevent her from reading his *Memoirs* of her mother, Wollstonecraft's *Vindication of the Rights of Woman*, her letters to Imlay, and her last novel, *The Wrongs of Woman: or, Maria*.[24]

Sunstein insists that Mary idolized her mother as a "rational intellectual and romantic heroine who had defied injustice, custom, and prudence."[25]

Conclusion 167

It is no surprise that a few years later, she falls in love with the radical poet Shelley and they quickly make plans to elope, hoping that Shelley's wife Harriet would grant him a legal separation. On her visit to St. Pancras graveyard with Shelley, a ritual Mary performed to bring herself closer to her mother, she embraced her destiny as his future wife.

In a journal she kept with her husband that was begun on the day of their elopement to Paris on 28 July 1814, Mary and Percy exchange their daily habit of reading and walking together. On Thursday, 22 September 1814, Mary writes, "Walk out & buy prints. Mary reads Political Justice—Shelley writes Greek...," and a few days later, "PBS read[s] Diogenes Laertius I read Political Justice—walk out with Shelley... ."[26] Mary continues to record this pattern of reading and adds their preparations to pack their things, secure lodgings in Somerstown, and return to England. Each day Mary's entries record the reading of her parents' writings with her husband. As she continues to describe their reading and walking activities, Mary includes Jane Clairmont, her step-sister, in their company: "Read Political Justice. We walk out—when we return Shelley talks with Jane and I read Wrongs of woman—in the evening we talk & read."[27] Her entries are casual and informative while several entries by Shelley are more critically described: "Jane for some reason refuses to walk—we traverse the fields towards Hampstead. Under an expansive oak lies a dead calf . . . the cow lean from grief is watching it."[28] At just 17 years of age, Mary Shelley, then Godwin, elopes with a married man and jeopardizes her reputation as a virtuous young woman. Her relationship with Shelley begins as a spiritual marriage much like her mother's relationship did with Gilbert Imlay. Unlike her mother's first love affair, Mary's affair with Shelley is legalized several weeks after his wife Harriet commits suicide. Absorbed in her mother's writings, Mary identifies with her mother's radical view on feminine virtue. Although contrary to her mother's dissenting views, Mary conforms to the role of a wife who reclaims the Puritan values of an obedient wife.

Others admired Wollstonecraft's sincere contributions to the reformation of virtue. Her passion to elevate women to an equal social and intellectual status to men shaped her actions, and as a result, she steadfastly corrected injustices in the marriage relationship and to the law. One of Wollstonecraft's sincere friends, Mary Hays, identified herself along with Wollstonecraft as "an apostle of Enlightenment." Hays emulated the fortitude of her friend's beliefs and printed a notice in *The Monthly Magazine* following Wollstonecraft's death. Hays writes, "This extraordinary woman ... [a] wife, a mother, surrounded by tender, admiring, intelligent friends, her heart expanded, her powers acquired new vigour, life brightened, and futurity opened a prospect beaming with hope and promise."[29] Wollstonecraft's promise for the future of all women, wives, mothers, and companions, is recognized in the attainment of the ideal wife as the three-fold nature of friend, lover, and wife. While women were still excluded from academic institutional life, Gina Luria Walker notes, "But within enlightened circles, individual men made space for particular women to participate in an exchange of ideas."[30]

Samuel Taylor Coleridge and Robert Southey were among those men who

> treated aspiring women seriously; they shared their texts and libraries with them; read, commented on, and edited their manuscripts; discussed and recommended specific books and publishers; and, singly or in clusters, pointed the way for women who desired to become public intellectuals.[31]

In his notes of 1796 Coleridge writes, "Epistle to Mrs Wolstoncraft urging her Religion. Read her Travels."[32] Kathleen Coburn, editor of the Coleridge notebooks, remarks, "*Letters written during a short Residence in Sweden, Norway and Denmark* by Mary Wollstonecraft (1796) was reviewed in the *British Critic* June 1796 (VII 602-10)." As Coburn indicates, the reviewer was most likely Coleridge who suggests to the writer of *Letters* to rely strongly on the religious messages of Christianity. He states, "The more accurately Mrs Wollstonecraft understands Christianity, the more she will find it to be by far the most benevolent, the most useful, and the most comfortable system ever proposed to man."[33] The religious significance of their writings for both Coleridge and Wollstonecraft reveals a moral foundation on which their imaginations and genius built their literary and personal principles. In their daily lives, Wollstonecraft and Coleridge met only occasionally; however, Wollstonecraft's influence on Coleridge can be seen in their debate on the usefulness of religious principles on moral behavior and passions. In her close analysis of Wollstonecraft's brand of feminism as a religious thinker, Barbara Taylor emphasizes Wollstonecraft's vision for the progress of society and women with its religious underpinnings. Taylor explains,

> . . . unlike Rational Dissenters, Wollstonecraft regards "eros" as "the core of the religious experience" (p. 108), for "amatory identification with God" enhances and indeed revolutionizes female subjectivity and its yearnings, whereas, in the present state of society, relations between the sexes seem doomed to failure and degradation.[34]

Experiencing personal failure in their desire for a love relationship, both Wollstonecraft and Coleridge searched for domestic happiness in their religious experience, and thereby revolutionized the feminine identity in society.

Through an understanding of the lives and writings of Mary Wollstonecraft and Sara Fricker Coleridge, two distinct portraits emerge. The literary portrait of an intellectual wife defines Wollstonecraft's desires and efforts to reform the role of the wife while the domestic portrait of an independent and spirited wife shows Sara Fricker Coleridge's determination and intelligent management of a literary family. Their development as intellectual partners for the men in their households creates a common bond that elevates the role of the wife above moral restraints, orthodox views, and in general, strengthens the weaker portraits of women as wives. In his biographical account of the lives of these literary families—the Wordsworths, Coleridges, and Hutchinsons—John Worthen insightfully explains the nature of writing biography from the various perspectives of several lives instead of centering on one life:

> A detailed biography of the Wordsworths, the Coleridges and the Hutchinsons, covering a brief period, is therefore a good way of describing the lives led by people who wrote such poetry, recited it to each other, sent it to each other, copied it for each other, and who lived in such an extraordinarily intimate way.[35]

Following his model, in my retelling of the lives of two women from within the ordinary role of the wife, an honest portrait emerges from their relationships and correspondence with their children, husbands, and friends. These women then help us to envision what the role of the wife was like and how it was changing during the late eighteenth century from the perspective of public literary figures, like Godwin and Coleridge, and from their private intimacies as husband and wife. As Worthen remarks,

> Modern biography at times seems to have learned almost nothing from history, sociology, or even psychology, all of which constantly stress the impossibility of telling any kind of truth about individuals divorced from the impinging lives and histories of other individuals.[36]

The ordinary desires, hopes, and failures of these two wives, Mary Wollstonecraft and Sara Fricker Coleridge, may have had extraordinary circumstances; however, within their circle of family and friends, a more truthful story is told not to idealize the wife as poetry does, but to realize the powerful nature of the wife on all those lives she embraces.

Feminist passion, revolutionary fervor, and social activism define Wollstonecraft as an individual, and because her writing is a public realm of expression, a close examination of these writings illuminates her political and social contributions to the age. Unlike her private counterpart in this study, Sara Fricker Coleridge, Wollstonecraft forged a firmer foundation for the Romantic wife in her writing. Yet, while Sara Fricker Coleridge may remain in the shadow of Wollstonecraft's literary genius, she marks an essential change in the role of the ordinary wife, raising her brand of feminism through her loyalty as a wife to a literary genius and her devotion as a mother to the literary development of her children. The domestic atmosphere of her roles softens her fierce determination but it cannot diminish its reverberations in the lives of her family and friends.

Paradoxically, poetic genius resists domestic affection while domestic affection nurtures poetic genius. In the lives and writings of Mary Wollstonecraft and Sara Fricker Coleridge, it may be this paradox of the poetic imagination that feeds the conflicts both women experience in their private lives. Wollstonecraft suffers emotional anguish in her relationship with her lover Imlay but finds a few months of domestic happiness with her husband Godwin before her death in September 1797. Coleridge suffers emotional abandonment in her relationship with her husband but finds domestic contentment in the household of her brother-in-law Southey while educating her children to pursue literary professions. The daughters of these women, Mary Shelley and Sara Coleridge, experience their own form of disruption to domestic happiness in their romantic relationships whose stories would require a sequel to the lives of their mothers. Considering the tale of Victor Frankenstein and his family in Mary Shelley's *Frankenstein, or the Modern Prometheus*, the writing of these wives can be seen as a language of protest, righting the wrongs committed in the name of affection, home, and marriage. As the critic Kate Ellis observes about the destructive forces in *Frankenstein*, she considers "the violence in the novel to constitute a language of protest, the effect of which is to expose the 'wrongs' done to women and children, friends and fiancées, in the name of domestic affection."[37] Intending to right the wrongs published about these two wives, Wollstonecraft and Coleridge, these pages elucidate and refine the minutia of their private lives and establish a bond between their domestic virtue and intellectual lives.

Throughout their correspondence and other literary sites, these two wives and mothers, Wollstonecraft and Coleridge, provide their daughters with representations of the intellectual wife that has become so familiar to us today. These wives struggled from within their domestic roles to exercise independence from restraining moral and social traditions, sometimes because of their romantic relationships, but at times, in spite of their romantic choices. Their daughters illustrate a new generation of young women and wives whose writing develops in collaborative spaces with their husbands. The confluence of masculine and feminine literary spheres shapes the poetic imagination and culture of the Romantic wife as an intellectual companion, friend, and lover. Perhaps their powerful emotional attachments to their mothers' lives led this new generation of female intellects to create their literary works within the bonds of marriage. Young Sara Coleridge writes to Mrs. Gillman in February 1843 just one month after her husband Henry Nelson Coleridge dies,

> My dearest Mrs. Gillman, you have ere now, I trust, received an announcement of my loss, of which I can not now speak. My sorrow is not greater than I can bear, for God has mercifully fitted it to my strength... . It was at Highgate, at your house, that I first saw my beloved Henry. Since then, now twenty years ago, no two beings could be more intimately united in heart and thoughts than we have been, or could have been more intermingled with each other in daily and hourly life. He concerned himself in all my feminine domestic occupations, and admitted me into close intercourse with him in all his higher spiritual and intellectual life.[38]

Her tone is sorrowful but understanding of her loss. She reminisces about her first meeting with Henry and his devotion to her domestic affection and intellectual life. Just two and a half years later on the death of her mother, Sara's tone appears less resigned to the loss. She writes on 26 September 1845 to her first cousin John, the Hon. Mr. Justice Coleridge,

> The death-silence is awful. I had to think of her every minute of the day, to be always on my guard against noise; and she was one that made herself *felt*, dear creature, every hour in the day. *I* shall never be *so* missed by any one, my life is so much stiller, and more to myself... . I always looked forward to nursing her through a long last illness. I know not how it was, I could never help looking forward to it with a sort of satisfaction. I day-dreamed about it—according to the usual way of my mind—and cut it out in fancy all in my own way. She was to waste away gradually, without much suffering, and to become more and more placid in spirit, and filled with the anticipation of heavenly things.[39]

Instead of experiencing a long illness, Sara was shocked by the sudden death of her mother, with no time to prepare herself for the change or to nurse her mother during her final hours.

Unlike Sara Coleridge, Mary Shelley never knew her mother in life, only in her writings. Her frequent visits to the graveyard at St. Pancras church where Wollstonecraft was buried offered Mary a place where she could revere her literary mother. Unsure how to fill the empty void for his motherless child, Godwin took Mary as a child to Wollstonecraft's gravestone where he taught his daughter how to "read and spell her name by having her trace her mother's inscription on the stone."[40] As Sunstein describes the vivid scene,

Godwin then took the children [Mary and Fanny] for a walk. Often they crossed the meadows to nearby ancient, stubby St. Pancras church and its quiet graveyard, and stood at her mother's pedestal-like tombstone between a pair of weeping willows Godwin had planted.[41]

It is no wonder that she continued to visit her mother's gravestone with Percy, and there, feeling overcome with romantic passion for him, she made the decision to elope. Mary's association of her mother's presence, even in death, with her lover's tenderness surpasses the natural bond between mother and child. Instead, Mary and Percy idealize Wollstonecraft as "a setting planet" whose "radiance" departs in glory just as the setting sun departs at the end of the day. Wollstonecraft has become their literary idol and representation of an exalted domestic figure.

Mary Shelley, born in 1797, and Sara Coleridge, born in 1802 just five years later, led parallel lives and died within one year of each other, the former in 1851 and the latter in 1852. Sara's married life with her husband Henry lasted nearly 13 years; Mary's life with Percy, from their elopement in 1814 to his death in 1822, covered a much shorter period of eight years. While both describe their feelings about the loss of their mothers, these women also share in their fathers' literary friendship. Godwin and Coleridge exchanged their writing and literary criticism while corresponding about their families. Coleridge must have felt deeply sympathetic to Godwin as Sunstein explains. She writes, "Coleridge, a younger father who enjoyed his own little boys' rumbustiousness, first dined at The Polygon when Mary was two years and three months old, and was distressed by the 'cadaverous silence' of Wollstonecraft's children."[42] On one visit to the Godwins, Coleridge read his poem "The Rime of the Ancient Mariner" while Mary Shelley intently absorbed the gothic richness of the verses.[43] In another of Coleridge's mystical poems, "Christabel," he portrays the central figure of Christabel as a young woman raised by her father Sir Leoline after her mother died in childbirth. Written in 1797, the same year of Wollstonecraft's death and Mary Shelley's birth, Christabel's likeness to the young Mary and Sir Leoline's similarity to Godwin illustrate Coleridge's sensibility to Wollstonecraft, whom he admired in her literary life and honored in her death.

Godwin's literary relationship with Coleridge is interwoven with the roles of father and husband. Both men experienced the loss of a wife, Godwin through Wollstonecraft's death and Coleridge through his abandonment of his wife. Furthermore, Coleridge's absence from his own daughter Sara fosters her strong dependence on her mother as seen in her desire to nurture her mother, and in later years, in her deep sorrow over her death. For instance, as a young adult, Sara assumes a nurturing role with her mother who, anxious about her daughter's illness, displays her own anxiety. On 24 October 1836, Sara writes to her mother with the guidance of a parent,

> Dear Mother, I entreat you to pray for cheerfulness and fortitude to the Giver of all good. Be sure that the effort to pray will be useful, however distracted your poor thoughts may be. Let us recollect that were we enjoying all that our worldly hearts desire, how rapidly does time move on; how soon shall we arrive at the end of our earthly course—then what will worldly good things avail us?[44]

Sara's spiritual wisdom is intended to comfort her mother and also foreshadows the deaths of loving family members as well as her own. Both Sara Coleridge and Mary Shelley aspire to a heavenly place where they may reunite with their mothers and husbands. Each dreams of a fantasy life where she will find domestic happiness. As Sunstein illustrates,

> Whenever the weather permitted, Mary walked in the afternoons to the gardens of the Temple, or those of Charterhouse School, or farther out to St. Pancras graveyard. She did not see herself as religious; religion was coming to mean superstition, empty ritual, … . But the quiet country graveyard was in effect church for her intertwined faith in the immortal human spirit, her communion with nature, romantic inspiration, and her fantasizing… . And here Mary was free to "obey Fantasia", daydream, and imagine the shining future promised by her star: "my dreams my darling sun bright dreams!" she wrote in her journal years after.[45]

Mary's dreams and aspirations, like Sara Coleridge's fairy-land, reveal the interconnectedness of their poetic imagination with their domestic happiness. In Sara's letter to Aubrey De Vere, she explains her thoughts on the composition of her drama *Phantasmion* that closely resembles Mary Shelley's fantasy. She writes,

> Before writing "Phantasmion", I thought that for the account of Fairyland Nature I need invoke no other muse than Memory; my native vale, seen through a sunny mist of dreamers, would supply all the materials I should want, and all the inspiration; but for the love part, and the descriptions of personal beauty, I invoked Venus to aid me.[46]

Sara Coleridge embodies the qualities of tenderness and grace with the intellectual curiosity of a literary genius. While she is herself recuperating from an illness, her time is consumed with reading her father's work "Literary Remains" and several devotional works by the Evangelical writer Abbott. In her letter of 25 October 1836, she remarks to her husband,

> Chemists say that the elementary principles of a diamond and of charcoal are the same; it is the action of the sun or some other power upon each that makes it what it is. Analogous to this are the products of the poet's mind; he does not *create* out of nothing, but his mind so acts on the things of the universe, material and immaterial, that each composition is in effect a new creation.[47]

Extending the metaphor of the diamond and charcoal to Mary Wollstonecraft and Sara Fricker Coleridge, the poetic mind and the domestic wife are like two substances that when illuminated by the action of another source (and possibly by each other), create a new composition, the Romantic wife.

Notes

1 This chapter was partially published as an essay titled "'Love in Fairyland': Literary Wives and Daughters" in *The Coleridge Bulletin*, New Series 52 (Winter 2018).
2 Edith Coleridge, ed., *Memoir and Letters of Sara Coleridge* (New York: Harper & Brothers, 1874), 261.
3 Elizabeth Shand, "Sara Coleridge's Annotated *Phantasmion*," *The Coleridge Bulletin* New Series 59 (NS) Summer 2022, 15. See also Robin Schofield, *The Vocation of Sara Coleridge: Authorship and Religion* (London: Palgrave Macmillan, 2018); see also Jeffrey W. Barbeau, *Sara Coleridge: Her Life and Thought* (New York: Palgrave Macmillan, 2014).
4 Mrs. Anne Gillman's letters to Mrs. H. N. Coleridge on the death of STC 1834, (S. T. Coleridge Collection, Victoria University Library, Toronto).
5 Jane Rendall, *The Origins of Modern Feminism: Women in Britain, France and the United States, 1780-1860* (New York: Schocken Books, 1984), 60.
6 Rendall, *The Origins*, 60.
7 Janet Todd and Marilyn Butler, eds., *The Works of Mary Wollstonecraft*: Thoughts on the Education of Daughters, vol. 4: 4–160 (New York: New York University Press, 1989), 42.
8 Todd and Butler, eds., *The Works of Mary Wollstonecraft*: Thoughts on the Education of Daughters, vol. 4: 4–160, 42.
9 Sara Coleridge Coleridge will be identified as Sara Coleridge throughout this chapter, noting the absence of the "h" in her name. Her mother will be identified as Sara Fricker Coleridge to distinguish between the mother and daughter.
10 Coleridge, E., ed., *Memoir and Letters of Sara Coleridge*, 117.
11 Bradford Keyes Mudge, *Sara Coleridge, A Victorian Daughter: Her Life and Essays* (New Haven: Yale University Press, 1989), ix.

12 Mudge, *Sara Coleridge*, ix.
13 Mudge, *Sara Coleridge*, 13.
14 Sara Coleridge Coleridge to Henry Nelson Coleridge, Autograph letter dated 20 September 1834. *Sara Coleridge Coleridge Collection*, Harry Ransom Center (Austin: University of Texas).
15 Mudge, *Sara Coleridge*, 76.
16 See Peter Swaab, ed., *Sara Coleridge: Collected Poems* (Manchester: Carcanet Press Ltd., 2007).
17 Swaab, ed., Introduction to *Sara Coleridge*, 2.
18 Derwent and Sara Coleridge, eds., *Coleridge's Poetical Works* (London: Edward Moxon, Dover Street, 1852), Advertisement.
19 In her account of Sara Coleridge's inherited genius from her father, Alison Hickey argues, "Sara's labors on behalf of Coleridgean genius are inseparable from the vexed issue of her relation to her father: as she herself acknowledges, her editing is 'a filial phenomenon'." Majorie Stone and Judith Thompson, eds., *Literary Couplings: Writing Couples, Collaborators, and the Construction of Authorship* (Madison: University of Wisconsin Press, 2006), 125. However, Stone's argument dismisses the importance of Sara's mother's literary influence and source of feminine genius as I clarify in my writing. See "'The Body of My Father's Writings': Sara Coleridge's Genial Labor."
20 Mudge, *Sara Coleridge*, 12.
21 Mudge, *Sara Coleridge*, 12.
22 William Godwin, *Memoirs of Mary Wollstonecraft*, ed. W. Clark Durant (New York: Haskell House Publishers, 1969), xxxiv–xxxv.
23 Godwin, *Memoirs*, xxxv.
24 Emily Sunstein, *Mary Shelley: Romance and Reality* (Boston: Little & Brown, 1989), 53.
25 Sunstein, *Mary Shelley*, 53.
26 Paula R. Feldman and Diana Scott-Kilvert, eds., *The Journals of Mary Shelley 1814-1844*, vol. I (Oxford: Clarendon Press, 1987), 28–29.
27 Feldman and Scott-Kilvert, eds., *The Journals of Mary Shelley*, vol. I, 33.
28 Feldman and Scott-Kilvert, eds., *The Journals of Mary Shelley*, vol. I, 32.
29 Godwin, *Memoirs*, xxviii.
30 Gina Luria Walker, "Mary Hays (1759-1843): An Enlightened Quest," *Women, Gender and Enlightenment*, eds. Sarah Knott and Barbara Taylor (New York: Palgrave Macmillan, 2005), 495.
31 Walker, "Mary Hays," 495.
32 Kathleen Coburn, ed., *The Notebooks of Samuel Taylor Coleridge, Vol. 1. 1794-1804* (New York: Pantheon Books, Bollingen Foundation, 1957), 259.
33 Coburn's explanation and direct quote from the *British Critic* can be found in her notes to the *Notebooks*. See 261 G. 258.
34 Claudia L. Johnson, "Book Review: *Mary Wollstonecraft and the Feminist Imagination*," *Albion: A Quarterly Journal Concerned with British Studies* 36, no. 2 (2004), 316.
35 John Worthen, *The Gang: Coleridge, the Hutchinsons, and the Wordsworths in 1802* (New Haven: Yale University Press, 2001), 5.

36 Worthen, *The Gang*, 6.
37 Kate Ellis, "Monsters in the Garden; Mary Shelley and the Bourgeois Family," *The Endurance of "Frankenstein": Essays on Mary Shelley's Novel*. eds. George Levine and U. C. Knoepflmacher (Berkeley: University of California Press, 1979), 126.
38 Coleridge, E., ed., *Memoir and Letters of Sara Coleridge*, 191–92.
39 Coleridge, E., ed., *Memoir and Letters of Sara Coleridge*, 240.
40 Sunstein, *Mary Shelley*, 26.
41 Sunstein, *Mary Shelley*, 26.
42 Sunstein, *Mary Shelley*, 25.
43 Sunstein, *Mary Shelley*, 40.
44 Coleridge, E., ed., *Memoir and Letters*, 128.
45 Sunstein, *Mary Shelley*, 50.
46 Coleridge, E., ed., *Memoir and Letters*, 261.
47 Coleridge, E., ed., *Memoir and Letters*, 129.

References

Coburn, Kathleen, ed. *The Notebooks of Samuel Taylor Coleridge, Vol. 1. 1794–1804*. New York: Pantheon Books, Bollingen Foundation, 1957.

Coleridge, Derwent, and Sara Coleridge, eds. *Coleridge's Poetical Works*. London: Edward Moxon, Dover Street, 1852.

Coleridge, Edith, ed. *Memoir and Letters of Sara Coleridge*. New York: Harper & Brothers, 1874.

Coleridge, Sara Coleridge. *Autograph Letters. Sara Coleridge Coleridge Collection, 1791–1951*. Harry Ransom Center. Austin: University of Texas.

Ellis, Kate. "Monsters in the Garden; Mary Shelley and the Bourgeois Family." *The Endurance of "Frankenstein": Essays on Mary Shelley's Novel*. Eds. George Levine and U. C. Knoepflmacher. Berkeley: University of California Press, 1979.

Feldman, Paula R., and Diana Scott-Kilvert, eds. *The Journals of Mary Shelley 1814–1844*. Vol. I. Oxford: Clarendon Press, 1987.

Gillman, Mrs. Anne. Letters to Mrs. H. N. Coleridge on the death of STC 1834. S. T. Coleridge Collection, Victoria University Library (Toronto).

Godwin, William. *Memoirs of Mary Wollstonecraft*. Ed. W. Clark Durant. New York: Haskell House Publishers, 1969.

Johnson, Claudia L. "Book Review: *Mary Wollstonecraft and the Feminist Imagination*." *Albion: A Quarterly Journal Concerned with British Studies* 36, no. 2 (2004): 316–17.

Mudge, Bradford Keyes. *Sara Coleridge, A Victorian Daughter: Her Life and Essays*. New Haven: Yale University Press, 1989.

Rendall, Jane. *The Origins of Modern Feminism: Women in Britain, France and the United States, 1780–1860*. New York: Schocken Books, 1984.

Shand, Elizabeth. "Sara Coleridge's Annotated *Phantasmion*." *The Coleridge Bulletin*. New Series 59 (NS) Summer 2022.

Stone, Marjorie, and Judith Thompson, eds. *Literary Couplings: Writing Couples, Collaborators, and the Construction of Authorship*. Madison: The University of

Wisconsin Press, 2006. https://hdl-handle-net.ezproxy.hofstra.edu/2027/heb08759.0001.001

Sunstein, Emily. *Mary Shelley: Romance and Reality*. Boston: Little & Brown, 1989.

Swaab, Peter, ed. *Sara Coleridge: Collected Poems*. Manchester: Carcanet Press Ltd., 2007.

Todd, Janet, and Marilyn Butler, eds. *The Works of Mary Wollstonecraft:* Thoughts on the Education of Daughters, vol. 4: 4–160. New York: New York University Press, 1989.

Walker, Gina Luria. "Mary Hays (1759–1843): An Enlightened Quest." *Women, Gender and Enlightenment*, 493–518. Eds. Sarah Knott and Barbara Taylor. New York: Palgrave Macmillan, 2005.

Worthen, John. *The Gang: Coleridge, the Hutchinsons, and the Wordsworths in 1802*. New Haven: Yale University Press, 2001.

Index

Note: Endnotes are indicated by the page number followed by 'n' and the endnote number e.g., 20n1 refers to endnote 1 on page 20.

Adventures of Caleb Williams, or Things As They Are (1794) 15, 60
anarchism 60, 156n17, 156n18; anarchy 138
authority 3–4, 11–17, 27, 30–2, 43, 57, 126, 128, 130, 132, 144–5, 149, 153–5, 165; patriarchal 32, 126, 130, 165

Bath (England) 47, 69–70
Bedford, G. C. 94–5
benevolence 3, 62, 72, 136, 138, 144, 148–9, 151, 161, 166
Bluestockings 22, 26–30; circle 26–7, 59
Bristol (England) 58, 69–71, 73, 86–8, 91, 102–3, 114, 116–17, 148
Burke, E. 4, 31, 43, 51, 55–6, 122, 134, 147

canonical law 145, 151, 154
Chapone, H. 25, 28–30
church 3, 11–13, 16–17, 33, 48, 56, 60, 69, 87–8, 134, 144, 146, 150, 154, 171–3; Anglican Church 11, 33, 87, 150, 157n22; Church of England 11–12, 17
civil law 87, 144–45, 147
Clarissa (1747-48) 41
Coleridge, Ernest H. 121
Coleridge, Samuel T. 43, 55–6, 66–7, 73–4, 76, 86, 88, 95, 118, 126, 129, 143, 161, 168
Coleridge, Sara C. 66, 81, 103, 112, 155, 160, 164–5; daughter (Edith Coleridge) 66; husband (Henry Nelson Coleridge) 118, 162, 171
Coleridge, Sara F. 44, 62, 66–8, 86, 89, 119–21, 148, 160, 163, 165, 169–70, 174; children (Berkeley) 18, 80–1, 91–3, 110, 152; Derwent 80–1, 102–3, 112, 115, 117, 164–5; father (Stephen Fricker) 69, 86–7, 99; Hartley 76, 80, 102–4, 112, 115, 117, 119, 153; mother (Martha Rowles) 68–9; Sara 66, 81, 103, 112, 155, 160, 164–5; sister (Edith Fricker) 68–70, 72, 87, 88, 94, 97, 99, 101, 103; sister (Mary Fricker) 68–9, 99, 103
companionship 6, 9, 76, 87, 97, 102, 109, 112, 155
Cottle, J. 70, 73, 77, 119
Corinne, or Italy (1807) 41

Darwin, Erasmus 78
De Quincey, T. 118–19, 163
de Staël, G. 1–2, 25, 41, 61
De Vere, A. 66, 173
Discourse on the Love of Our Country (1789) 133
dissenters 2, 13, 17, 22, 33, 57–8, 70, 127, 133, 154, 168; dissenting 11–12, 22, 33–4, 48, 57, 59–60, 133–4, 147–9, 154–5, 167
domesticity 26–8, 30, 33, 49, 56, 99, 126; domestic duties 101, 114; domestic role 100, 127, 163; domestic roles 25, 60, 148, 165, 170

education: female 22, 25, 27, 30, 69, 71, 78, 83n23, 114, 144; moral 22–3, 137; social 23
Emile, or On Education (1762) 22, 25, 50
Enquiry Concerning Political Justice 13
enthusiasm 1, 25, 32–6, 55, 59, 62, 72, 89–90, 114, 122, 134, 136
Evangelicals 31, 57
Evans, M. 67

Fall of Robespierre, The (1794) 126, 131
Faraday, M. 33–4
Father's Legacy to His Daughters, A 78
femininity 26–7, 46, 49, 59, 161
Frankenstein; or, The Modern Prometheus (1818) 14, 60, 170
French Revolution 6, 10, 49, 87, 126–8, 134–5
friendship 2, 5–6, 8–9, 22, 25, 27, 29–30, 33, 42–3, 45–6, 48, 76, 78–9, 90–1, 105, 109–11, 113, 115, 117–18, 122, 128, 148, 152–4, 172; friendships 6, 8, 22, 27, 33, 43, 76, 105, 109–11, 113, 118
Fuseli, H. 4–5, 51, 54

genius 25, 28, 66–7, 71, 76, 90, 95, 101, 104–5, 109, 118, 134, 147, 163, 165–6, 168, 170, 173; literary genius 66, 170, 173; poetic genius 66–7, 71, 76, 90, 104–5, 118, 163, 165, 170
Germany 5, 72, 75–6, 81, 91–2, 94, 111
Gillman, Dr. James, and Mrs. A. 115, 161, 171
Godwin, W. 6, 33, 36, 44, 51, 60–1, 122, 143, 160
Gregory, Dr. John 36, 78

happiness 2, 5–6, 8, 10–12, 16–17, 29–30, 44, 49, 53, 55, 58, 60, 71, 73, 75, 79–80, 90, 110–11, 117, 120, 122, 129, 135–6, 149, 151–2; domestic happiness 32, 46, 51, 56, 67, 168, 170, 173; *see also* domesticity
Hartley, D. 151–2

Hays, M. 1–3, 22, 24, 74, 127, 167
Historical and Moral View of the French Revolution, An 10, 126, 134
Hutchinson, M. 79
Hutchinson, S. 67, 71, 79–80, 97, 109

imagination: poetic 91, 96, 100, 122, 170, 173; social 154
Imlay, G. 4, 6–7, 44, 49, 51–4, 59, 145, 147, 166–7, 170
independence 17, 24, 32, 44, 48–9, 57, 98, 121, 144, 170; female 14, 44, 47, 70, 121, 143–4, 153, 162
individualism 11, 19n42, 55, 57–8, 139, 147, 155, 158n40
intellectuality 22–3, 96

Julie ou la Nouvelle Héloïse (1757) 41
justice 10–11, 13, 15–16, 29, 60, 71, 121–2, 126, 132–3, 148, 155, 160, 166–7; injustice 4, 14–16, 32, 122, 135, 166–7

Keswick (England) 94, 97, 101–3, 112, 114, 161

Lectures on Revealed Religion 150–2
Letters on Education 24, 72
Letters on the Improvement of the Mind (1773) 28–9
Letters Written During a Short Residence in Sweden, Norway and Denmark (1796) 54, 121, 168
liberty 3, 6, 10, 17, 22, 28, 31–2, 34, 43, 48, 72, 90, 126, 128–9, 133–6, 138, 147–8, 160
Lingo Grande 71, 94, 115, 121
Locke, J. 23, 48, 134–5
Lovell, R. 88, 120

Macaulay, C. 22, 24, 72, 127, 144
Malta (Italy) 112
marriage: contract 3, 11–13, 44, 87, 89, 146; law 4, 8, 11, 16–17, 52, 72, 87, 110, 138–9, 143, 145–7, 151, 153–4; relationship 6, 11–12, 14, 17, 29, 71, 109, 113, 144, 167; Scottish marriage law 11, 16, 145
Mary, a Fiction (1788) 8, 25, 41, 61

Index

Measures and Offices of Friendship, The 109
Milton, J. 49
morality 12–13, 25–7, 29, 33, 35–6, 43–4, 48, 69, 129, 149–50, 152; Christian 110, 115; moral excellence 2, 24–5; moral nature 27, 162
More, H. 24–5, 28, 43, 51, 58, 69, 110, 114
motherhood 24, 86, 104; literary mother 118, 171; mother 7, 9, 14, 23, 25, 33, 36, 41, 43–8, 50, 53, 57, 61, 66–7, 69, 71–2, 81, 88, 91–3, 98, 100–2, 104–5, 110–11, 115, 118–21, 150, 155, 160–7, 170–3

nation 32, 56, 126–8, 130, 146; national 6, 56, 130, 131, 134–7, 144, 148; nations 126, 136
Nether Stowey (England) 75, 89, 91, 114

"On the Influence of the Passions" (1813) 1, 25
optimism 130, 151–2
Original Stories (1788) 22–4, 34, 41

Pantisocracy 69, 86, 88–9
Paradise Lost 14, 49, 53–4
Plan for the Conduct of Female Education 78
Poole, T. 71, 75, 76, 89, 91, 94, 102–3, 109, 111, 114, 121, 150
Price, R. 12, 33, 44, 48, 57, 133, 154
Priestley, J. 33, 44, 57, 149, 151–2, 154

reason 3–4, 12, 16, 26, 31, 34–5, 48–50, 53–5, 60, 76, 80, 87, 102, 111–12, 115–16, 129–31, 136, 143, 152–3, 161, 167
Reflections on the Revolution in France (1790) 31, 56, 134, 147
Richardson, S. 30, 41
Robespierre, M. 131–3
Rousseau, J. -J. 3, 41, 43, 50, 134

sacrament 9, 11–12, 17, 145
sensibility 1, 3, 5–8, 10, 25, 31, 36, 42, 49–51, 53–4, 59, 71, 77, 95, 121–2, 129, 131, 134, 152, 166, 172

sentimentality 6, 8, 41, 54; sentiment 1, 3, 7, 9, 36, 61, 133, 147; sentimental 1–3, 8, 31, 35–6, 41, 46, 53, 60–1, 79, 113, 138
Shaftesbury, Earl of 3, 35
Shelley, M. G. 9, 160, 161, 165–7, 170–3
Shelley, P. B. 165, 167, 172
social change 50, 130; social roles 43, 130
Southey, R. 68, 72–3, 86, 88, 94–5, 101, 109, 112, 114, 119, 126, 143, 168

Taylor, J. 109, 113
Thelwall, J. 132, 150–2
Thoughts on the Education of Daughters (1786) 24, 48, 154, 162
tradition 4, 26, 30, 33, 35, 43, 61–2, 67, 128, 147; traditional 6, 25–6, 32, 34, 49, 51, 57, 75, 78, 89, 92, 122, 126, 134, 137, 150, 154, 165; traditions 4, 10, 16, 33, 44, 58, 134, 154, 170
Trinitarians 150
Two Treatises of Government (1690) 135

Unitarian 57; Unitarians 150; Unitarianism 150, 152

Vindications: The Rights of Men and The Rights of Woman (1792) 60, 135
virtues 1, 13, 15, 23, 26, 28, 35–6, 49–50, 54, 58–9, 78, 80, 82, 92, 109, 134–6, 138, 144–5, 160–2, 165; natural virtue 3–4, 6, 34, 36, 43, 122, 134, 136, 138, 148, 153–4, 162; natural virtues 59, 135

Watchman, The 71–2, 150
wife: ideal 81, 100; wives 11, 16, 25–6, 36, 44, 46, 49, 56, 61–2, 71, 91, 92, 97, 100–1, 110, 112, 114, 122, 130, 144–6, 148, 161, 163, 169–70
Wollstonecraft, M. 1, 22, 27, 34, 42–3, 46, 50, 60, 70, 74, 78, 98, 101, 126, 143–4, 148–9, 152, 160–1, 165, 168–70, 174; childhood friend (Fanny Blood)

9, 46–8, 53, 57; father (Edward J. Wollstonecraft) 57; mother (Elizabeth Wollstonecraft) 47; sisters (Eliza and Everina) 45–8, 57, 103

women: women's rights 17, 52, 166

Wordsworth, D. 67, 71, 77–9, 97, 109, 121

Wordsworth, W. 71, 75–6, 78–9, 80, 96–7, 105, 116, 118–19, 169

Wrongs of Woman: or, Maria, The (1798) 6, 13, 41, 49, 52, 61, 166